AVID

READER

PRESS

HOW TO
WIN
AT
TRAVEL

BRIAN KELLY

AVID READER PRESS

New York Amsterdam/Antwerp London Toronto Sydney New Delhi

Avid Reader Press
An Imprint of Simon & Schuster, LLC
1230 Avenue of the Americas
New York, NY 10020

First Avid Reader Press hardcover edition February 2025

AVID READER PRESS and colophon are trademarks of Simon & Schuster, LLC

For information about special discounts for bulk purchases, please contact Simon
& Schuster Special Sales at 1-866-506-1949 or business@simonandschuster.com.

The Simon & Schuster Speakers Bureau can bring authors to your live event.
For more information or to book an event contact the Simon & Schuster Speakers
Bureau at 1-866-248-3049 or visit our website at www.simonspeakers.com.

Interior design by Silverglass

Manufactured in the United States of America

1 3 5 7 9 10 8 6 4 2

Library of Congress Control Number: 2024949019

ISBN 978-1-6680-6865-6
ISBN 978-1-6680-6867-0 (ebook)

To Dean,

Being your dad has been the most epic journey of my life, and I am so lucky to get to experience the world again through your eyes.

Contents

Acknowledgments

I wouldn't be writing this book today if it weren't for my parents, Brian and Suzanne, who allowed me to book my first trip on points and miles at the tender age of twelve. That simple act of freedom planted a seed in my head that I could do whatever I put my mind to and also showed me the pure joy travel can bring, especially when it brings family closer together.

Tactically, I couldn't have written this book without the help of Lori Zaino, who I met on a US Airways flight from Philadelphia to Madrid in May 2005, eager for my study abroad summer program in Spain. Lori reclined her seat into my knees and I politely asked her to move up a little bit, which she kindly obliged. A week later she spotted me at a club in Madrid and we quickly became fast friends. She was one of the first freelance writers I hired when I started *The Points Guy* and she's gone on to become a top travel writer and editor.

Lori was a key collaborator on this book, helping me chart my vision and bring my story and tips to life. It was a full circle moment writing the etiquette chapter with her when the topic of how to deal with scat reclining came up!

I'd also like to thank Jason Steele who helped me research the points and miles content for this book, and Alyssa Haak, who fact-checked this book in its entirety.

Finally, I want to thank the loyalty programs (airline, hotel, and credit card) that have essentially funded my global travels for the last twenty years. I am extremely fortunate to have visited so many fascinating places leveraging my rewards and I am confident you will be able to as well after reading this book!

Brian

Author's Note

If there's one thing I love about writing about the travel industry, it's that it's constantly changing. While that is great for job security, it presents challenges in writing a book, because inevitably, information will become outdated. However, I wrote this book to teach you how to get the most value from the travel ecosystem *knowing* that the system will change. While I stand by the content and had a third party fact-check the book for accuracy at the time of publishing, policies and loyalty programs do change.

My core lesson remains the same: Everyone needs to create a personal travel strategy that works for them and continue to evolve it as the industry evolves. In my experience, having redeemed airline miles since 1995, change often brings opportunity, specifically with new credit card launches happening frequently and competition for consumers by the banks at an all-time high.

Speaking of credit cards, I can't stress enough that while credit cards can open up a world of travel, you need to play the game carefully and not get into credit card debt because the amount you pay in interest will far outweigh the amount you earn in points. As with all financial products, do your research and look at your personal situation to make the right decision for you.

And on a final note regarding transparency, this is a book by Brian Kelly, not *The Points Guy*, which is a company that I founded that is now owned by Red Ventures. The opinions in this book are my own, and any content here is intended for informational purposes only and shouldn't be construed as professional advice or the official stance of *The Points Guy* LLC, Red Ventures, or any of their affiliated organizations.

I discuss a lot of products and companies, but none of them have paid me to be featured in the book. I do want to be clear that over the years I have invested in certain startups that I think are changing the consumer travel and finance worlds in meaningful ways. I mention some of them here because I firmly believe they can be hugely beneficial to travelers. They include: Bilt Rewards, Point.me, Timeshifter, Roame.travel. *The Points Guy* also has financial relationships with most major credit card companies and banks.

Now that the disclosures are out of the way, enjoy the book! And I hope to see you in a first-class lounge in the near future.

BK

Chapter 1

Welcome to the Platinum Age of Travel

Frequent flyer miles and credit card points aren't a fad:
They're the future of travel.
—BRIAN KELLY

People always reminisce about the Golden Age of Travel as if it were this utopia of elegance and civilized behavior while flying—"They even served meals on fine china in economy!" But what if I told you that much of what you've been told about that age is distorted and possibly even false? Travel back then was an expensive affair reserved for the rich, and those images you probably have seared in your mind are not representative of travel during the time, which was time-consuming and downright dangerous.

Whether it fits the current media narrative or not, we're living in the greatest period of travel that humanity has ever experienced. This is especially true if you know how to leverage the lucrative ecosystem of loyalty programs and credit cards, *especially* in the US. In this new age of travel, the haves and have-nots aren't defined by those with or without money. The more important currency is knowledge: how to maximize the ecosystem and leverage it to your advantage. I call this new era the Platinum Age of Travel, which I firmly believe is better than the Golden Age in the areas that matter most to travelers, like safety, efficiency, and, yes, even comfort. Still don't believe me? Let's look at the data.

We can all agree that getting to our destination safely is the most important aspect of travel. While all modes of travel are safer than 50 years ago thanks to advances in technology and engineering, aviation safety has improved dramatically.

. . . .

The year 2023 was one of the busiest for air travel on record, with more than 37 million flights, and it also happened to be the safest, with no fatal commercial jet crashes and only one propeller jet crash in Nepal killing 72.[1] The chances of you dying on a commercial airplane are roughly 1 in 13.7 million, whereas your chances of dying on the road are 1 in 5,000.[2] You would need to fly every single day for 103,239 years to experience a fatal accident, yet I know so many people who drive like maniacs (or ride in the backseat of cars without seat belts) but get anxiety the minute they step on a plane. Make it make sense!

Commercial air travel today is indisputably safe, but what about that fabled Golden Age of Travel? Let's look at 1970, the year the 747 started service, which ushered in an even more luxurious era of widebody travel. In just 9.5 million flights, there were 78 fatal crashes and 1,475 deaths, or 1 in 122,000—still better than driving today. Not to mention that year there were *78 hijackings* and seven related deaths from those incidents.[3] Yes, hijackings were common in those days, yet you don't hear people reminiscing fondly about them when waxing poetic about the Golden Age of Travel.

Next up is comfort, as there's a misguided notion that the in-flight experience was so much more enjoyable in the Golden Age. While it is easy to be jealous seeing images of well-dressed flyers walking up stairs into opulent jets decked out with pianos and impeccably dressed stewardesses, it wasn't all glamour and those planes were not on every route. That would be like saying that flying the Emirates A380 in first class, with unlimited Dom Pérignon and in-flight showers for all, would be the standard of flying today. We all know that is far from the truth, so you cannot let a few iconic images speak for an era. For much of the Golden Age, people flew on propeller jets that needed to make multiple stops, and it could take days in loud cabins to get to their final destination.

And people fail to mention that those fancy cabins were also death traps because they weren't designed using modern computing technology with rigorous testing protocols to simulate in-flight situations. Often, cabins would become chaotic and dangerous scenes during turbulence, where glass walls would break because plane designers couldn't simulate events such as turbulence.

For most of us, time is our most valuable asset, and travel is much more streamlined. Modern-day jets can crisscross the globe much more efficiently. Today, the longest nonstop flight in the world is Singapore to New York (JFK) at an astounding 9,537 miles on a specially configured and quiet Airbus A350-900ULR. When Singapore Airlines first started flying to the US in 1977, you had to fly via Hong Kong, Guam, and Honolulu before reaching San Francisco and on to New York City. I don't care how nice the china is on board, time is money, and those awkward routings on more dangerous planes were much worse than your options are today.

Not only are planes more efficient and safe today but they actually provide much better passenger experiences than in the "old days." Planes nowadays are much quieter (which in itself is healthier, as there are many studies that point to excessive noise as a health risk factor). Most intercontinental jets now have lie-flat beds, and some can fly more than 19 hours nonstop.

Modern-day business and first-class suites blow away their recliner-style, Golden Age predecessors. Now, first-class travelers often have privacy doors, fast Wi-Fi, and countless hours of movies, and some modern jets have onboard bars and even showers—and you don't have to worry about sitting in a cloud of cigarette smoke from your fellow passengers while flying.

I admit the economy class experience today is less glamorous than it was in the past, but you can't compare economy class in 1970 to today because economy was priced like first class is now. Modern-day economy seating at dirt-cheap pricing is a different product that didn't exist during much of the Golden Age, and travel nowadays is cheaper and more accessible than ever before.

Pricing is currently the biggest driver of consumer travel choices. In the Golden Age, on average, it cost 5% of the average annual salary to book a round-trip domestic flight, whereas now that number is one-half of 1%. (The 2023 average domestic US flight was $381.53 according to the Bureau of Labor Statistics.[4] The average yearly salary is $63,705, and airfare prices mean that most people can afford to fly these days.)

Today 90% of Americans have flown; in 1971, it was just 49%. Not only is it more affordable when paying in cash, but air travel has become even more accessible with the proliferation of frequent flyer miles. Even if you don't have miles, though, the cost of US domestic airfare in 2024 is down 28.3% since 2000, when adjusted for inflation.

I define the Platinum Age of Travel as 2010 to the present: an unprecedented time when the proliferation of loyalty programs and credit cards made loyalty programs one of the most valuable currencies in the world and a critical revenue stream for the travel industry.

This era created a new generation of winners for those who knew how to maximize the system. Savvy consumers can leverage their good credit to travel the world for a fraction of the cost. Enterprising college students can fly first class to study abroad for less cash spent than their classmates in the last row of economy. The points economy has made it even more egalitarian, with not the richest people traveling in first class but often the savviest. Not only did opportunities to redeem miles and points skyrocket, but airfares plummeted, so unlike during the Golden Age of Travel, when only the rich could participate, the Platinum Era of Travel is more inclusive than ever, bringing the joy of travel to those who never thought they could afford it.

Beyond affordability, the perks that come along with being on the inside track of the Platinum Age of Travel (expedited airport screening, comfortable airport lounges, and travel-interruption protections) make the entire travel process more seamless and in many cases, more enjoyable. But most important, we entered aviation's safest and most efficient era, connecting the world like never before.

· · · ·

Winning at travel today depends on how you understand the current system and evolve with it as the industry adapts to record-setting traveler demand that shows no sign of abating.

As optimistic as I am about the current state of travel, I would be lying if I said that things are perfect, because they clearly aren't—and it doesn't take long at any airport to see the conflict and drama for yourself.

I'm a firm believer that there's no greater ongoing sociological experiment than the modern-day airport. As a professional people watcher, I am thankful that my career allows me to spend so much time in airports, as they are bustling petri dishes of people from nearly all societal classes, all comingling and dealing with the same challenges, such as long lines and flight cancellations.

Travel disruptions can test the patience and virtue of even the calmest, most even-keeled people, and I've witnessed the monster it can make out of an otherwise "normal" person. I've seen everything from grown men sobbing and "cool moms" becoming petulant Karens at the first hint of a flight delay—and taking their aggression out on the poor frontline employees who have absolutely no control over the current situation.

On the flipside, I've seen amazing situations, like an entire airport terminal cheering for a wish kid (a child part of the Make-A-Wish program) as they boarded their flight and airline ground staff paying tribute to the body of a fallen soldier.

While we often focus on the bad, a lot of good comes out of travel. People would be better, more understanding travelers if they knew how travel worked, gaining insight into the reason behind delays and seemingly arcane rules and how to navigate them, especially during adverse travel situations.

I believe that travel is a sport (my favorite one) and it takes training and the right equipment to excel at it. Would you enjoy learning how to play a new sport if you started your first day practicing with the top professional team? While a novelty at first, you'd quickly feel embarrassed and want to give up since you're not trained to perform at their level.

I see the same happening in airports. Some understand the system and leverage it to their advantage. Meanwhile, newbies get jostled around and don't know their rights or the tricks to get themselves out of bad situations. We're all playing the same sport, on the same field, but the odds are stacked in favor of the team that's not necessarily been playing the longest but has the most knowledge. The goal of this book is to give you the knowledge to perform better at the sport of travel, a game of acquiring knowledge in understanding how the system operates. You can't win at a sport if you don't know the rules of engagement.

Like sports, some people have natural abilities and some have the grit and determination to win, even if they don't have superior physical traits. In travel, winning is far more a mental game, though at times travel can also test your physical fortitude.

So how does someone get the right training? We don't learn how to travel at school or how to save for a school trip or a study abroad program. Those trips are more about cultural immersion than practical travel skills during the act of travel. Unless you grew up in a family that traveled, no one ever taught you how to travel and it's up to you to figure it out as you go. If, like most Americans, you only have a couple weeks of vacation a year, chances are you're traveling infrequently and you're constantly in a novice state, especially as travel policies and technology change. You're never really getting ahead.

So why do some people have a deep desire to travel and others not so much? My hunch was that the urge to travel is a genetic trait, so I began to research if there was a test to see if someone was predisposed to travel. And I quickly went down a rabbit hole on the dopamine D4 receptor (aka DRD4-7R), or the "wanderlust" gene.

This is a genetic marker that dates back 40,000 years, linked to nomadic populations. This genetic trait is far more popular in North America, where most of the population migrated to, than it is in Asia, for example, where there was far less mass migration of nomadic people coming from Europe.

I found an at-home lab company, Dynamic DNA, that tests for the DRD4 variant that has 48 letters in its sequence, linked to those who are more curious and adventurous. And after $49 and a quick dose of saliva later, I had the results.

I'm negative. I don't have the gene for traveling, but I'm still an expert traveler.

This further motivated me to write this book, because travel *is* a skill you can learn, even if you aren't genetically predisposed to be good at it or love it. While the internet and social media are helpful resources, we've gotten to a point where there's just too much information (and rampant misinformation), making it difficult to figure out how to win at travel.

If you're hoping to build a solid foundation for travel and learn how to travel better, more affordably, and savvier, this book is for you. I hope after reading this book you'll at least begin to pick up the skills necessary to travel smarter, safer, and better.

This book is for everyone, from newbies to experts. Even if you don't plan to travel frequently, winning at travel means you can save money on travel and use that money for the things that matter the most to you. This book will teach you how to analyze an ecosystem you might not be familiar with and learn how to get the most value from it for yourself. The fundamentals that I've learned in travel, points, and miles, I've used in other areas of my life, like getting the best mortgage rate or getting the best price on a new car. It's not just about winning at travel; these strategies can help you win at life.

Why I Wrote This Book (and What You'll Learn from It)

The main goal of this book is to save you money and time. To get your share of the system, you need to know how it operates. Companies make money at every step of the travel booking process, but you can cut out the unnecessary middlemen and put some of that money back in your pocket and, in many cases, also get better treatment.

Credit cards are a key part of the travel ecosystem, but you need to understand credit and have a good credit score to play the game. Understanding how credit works doesn't just open up a world of nearly free points and miles; it also helps you improve your credit score, which opens up a lifetime of lower interest rates. If you employ the tips I share, not only should you see your points balances rise but also your credit score.

Travel should be fun, enjoyable, and memorable. You may think travel is horrible across the board, but it's amazing when the system works for you. When I travel, I rarely wait in lines. I don't pay for food and drinks in airports. You can do the same, and I'll show you how.

You need to know how to troubleshoot and stand up for yourself when things go wrong. Unfortunately, most people start screaming at the employees they need to get on their side.

When travel disruptions occur, I don't whine and let it ruin my trip;

I turn it into an opportunity and often get points or vouchers that help pay for the next trip. When flights are canceled I don't wait around and beg for the next flight—I'm often automatically rebooked. I usually know when a flight is canceled before the gate agents do, and I've already snatched the last seat on the next flight before you could even ask for it. This book will help you learn how to do the same.

I also want to help you get to know me better through the tips and personal stories and anecdotes, and, of course, iconic points redemption advice I provide. I always laugh when people find out there's an *actual* Points Guy, and though I love travel, I'm much more than that. So while the book will mainly focus on practical information to make your life better, you'll get to know me, and if that's not enough, you'll have to follow me on Instagram: @briankelly.

I hope to give you a level of travel fluency so you can speak eloquently about it and even become the travel expert in your group of friends or family. Just beware, once people know you're an expert, they won't stop coming to you for tips. But hey, you might be able to turn it into a career (or serious side hustle) just like I did.

But let me start at the beginning. How does one become The Points Guy?

Chapter 2

Becoming The Points Guy

I've always been a travel aficionado no matter the mode of transport. My poor mother found this out the hard way on March 7, 1983.

It was a chilly March afternoon on Long Island, New York, and I was a week away from my due date. My mom had her weekly OB-GYN checkup to make sure everything was looking good. I was her third baby, so she had childbirth down by this point.

But something happened on this routine visit—her water broke. She looked at her doctor and said, "What do I do?" And in typical 1983 fashion, he said, "Well, get to the hospital. You'll be fine to drive yourself. North Shore Hospital is only 15 minutes away."

Anyone familiar with the Long Island Expressway knows that nothing is ever guaranteed, especially at 3:45 p.m. on a Monday. My poor mother hurriedly hobbled into her 1973 Gran Torino and sped off to the hospital.

As she entered the LIE and hit the gas, intense and all too familiar pains started pulsing throughout her abdomen. I can only surmise that I felt the excitement of the moment and wanted to be a part of the fun. Luckily for both of us, there was no gridlock traffic that afternoon. When she pulled up to the ER, she left the car running and announced, "I'm having a baby!!!" I guess I've loved making an entrance since day one! They rushed her to a delivery room, and within 20 minutes, all 10 pounds of me came into this world (sans epidural—sorry, Mom), ready for an adventure any way I could get it.

After the drama of my arrival, I lived a low-key life with my three siblings and more cousins than I could count. My mom is one of 10 children and my dad one of four. Travel for us was crisscrossing Long Island visiting family and hitting up Robert Moses State Park all summer long.

In 1990, we moved to Bucks County, Pennsylvania. I got my first computer at age seven and fell in love with computing. I was captivated by what a computer could do, and in 1994, I asked for the internet for Christmas. Santa was good to me that year and left me a Prodigy Internet package under the tree, complete with a modem that I had to install myself and plug into a phone jack. After repeated busy signals, I finally heard a loud screeching noise, and I was magically on the internet. If kids nowadays only knew what we had to do to get online back then!

In 1995, my dad got an opportunity to work for a healthcare startup based in California, which meant he would have to work from home and frequently commute to the West Coast. While he had basic computer knowledge, I was the tech-savvy one in the family, so he leaned on me to book his travel.

It was my first job at age 12: booking travel for my dad. Travelocity had just launched, and I charged him $10 per booking. He thought it was a long and complicated process, but for me, each booking was simple and took only a couple minutes.

As a sales executive, he was on the road a lot. We all understood the sacrifice he was making and made sure not to guilt him when he missed big moments such as sports games or family events. And my dad always made it a point to go on one big family trip a year, usually to Florida but we'd switch things up and rent a lake house in Maine or a beach house in the Outer Banks of North Carolina.

My parents loved taking us places, but they weren't big jet-setters. My dad grew up in a working-class family in Long Island, New York. His dad was a New York City firefighter in Brooklyn, and his family trips growing up in the '50s and '60s were all by car. My mom's father was an accountant in Manhattan and survived one of the most deadly Long Island Rail Road crashes in history, so he refused to take their family of 12 on public transit from that point forward, which included planes. To make the travel logistics even more complicated, my mom's mother didn't have a driver's license, so my grandfather would drive half the family to the Catskills, drop them off, and go back and get the other half of the family. That's what I call dedication!

Growing up in an upscale suburb of Philadelphia, I was always jealous of families that got to go to London or Paris during summer break or the Caribbean at Christmas. My best friend Haley's family loved Hawaii and every year would invite me—all I had to do was pay for the flight. I asked my parents one year if I could pull from my college fund to go to Hawaii, and they incredulously asked me if I was serious. "Yes! Traveling to Hawaii would be an educational experience, therefore I should be able to use college funds to pay for it." They weren't buying it. Hawaii would have to wait. While I resented my parents for being "cheap," their insistence that I learn how to work for whatever I wanted is one of the best lessons they've taught me.

My dad became a road warrior, and I started to notice our family began traveling differently. My dad started banking a lot of frequent flyer miles, earned elite status, and got hooked on travel perks like lounge access. Being treated well while traveling for work took the sting out of being away from home.

Traveling with my dad was always an experience. He exuded confidence and he taught us early on to not misbehave in the airport as it was a privilege to be able to travel. I remember going into the US Airways club with him at the Philadelphia airport. You would have to buzz a fancy doorbell and wait to be allowed in. I remember the lounges were much more exclusive in those days, but all they really had was coffee and peanuts. I never got the fuss and much preferred to be in the chaotic terminal, watching the planes come and go and trying to guess where each one was going based on how the passengers looked.

In 1995, my dad challenged me to use his assortment of airline miles to take our family of six on vacation. He thought we'd be lucky to get to Florida one way using his points and that maybe we could road-trip home if that was the case.

I started to solve the Rubik's Cube that is booking travel with multiple points currencies and a tight budget. What are the odds that the award availability on two different airlines could line up and we could find affordable lodging?

I accepted this challenge, calling the airlines and deepening my 12-year-old prepubescent boy voice to sound like my dad. I'll never know if the phone agents knew I was a 12-year-old and decided to be helpful or whether it was pure luck, but I realized that being sweet to phone agents was the key to getting what you wanted. That's still true today.

I hadn't told my dad, but my dream destination was the Cayman Islands. I had just read *The Firm* by John Grisham, and a portion of the story takes place in the Cayman Islands, which sounded exotic and dreamy. So when I was given the freedom to plan the trip, I decided Grand Cayman was the goal. Doesn't every 12-year-old dream of visiting a Caribbean island known mostly for being a tax-safe haven?

An agent on the phone told me that in January, US Airways flies nonstop from Philadelphia to GCM, the main airport on Grand Cayman. With some flexibility, she could get four of us on the nonstop if we left on a Saturday and returned the following Sunday. My dad had said a week, but eight nights is the same, right?

But this still left two of us stuck in Philly with a small pile of AA miles. I hopped on the phone with American Airlines, and an agent was able to find flights via Miami that roughly aligned with the US Airways flights, but we would arrive a couple hours later. I figured my mom and I could take the Miami flight while my dad and three siblings took the US Airways flight.

I booked the trip and then told my dad so he wouldn't have the chance to say no. A bold move for a 12-year-old, but it worked. He did briefly panic because we didn't have passports, and he wanted to make sure Grand Cayman was safe, but after some research, he got on board with what would be the first of many trips I would book for my family using his points.

Next came lodging. My dad only had enough Marriott points for one room for seven nights. Luckily I was also savvy at AOL searching, and I found a website called Vrbo—Vacation Rentals By Owner—that had just launched. It was a groundbreaking marketplace that would match vacation homeowners with guests. I searched until I found the perfect two-bedroom house, Maiden Plum Kai, that was on the beach and just

$1,300 for eight days, which was less than half the price of what two mediocre hotel rooms would cost.

The night before the trip, I panicked. What if it all went wrong? I was *12 years old*, and my parents let me book an international trip to a new destination to stay at some random person from New Jersey's vacation house. I remember going to bed thinking, "Either this is going to be epic or I'm grounded for a long time."

When we landed at Owen Roberts International, the hot, humid tropical air hugged us. My blood pressure started rising. When we saw my dad on the other side of immigration, would he be furious at me for screwing up what would have been an easy and predictable Florida trip? Or would I be hailed as a hero?

After a seemingly endless line to get through immigration and get our bags, we walked through the doors to the terminal, and my dad was standing there with the biggest smile I think I've ever seen. I ran up and hugged him, and he hugged me back and said, "Brian, you knocked it out of the park. It's like a dream here."

We spent the next eight nights in our cozy beach cottage, bonding as a family and learning that you shouldn't forget to put sunscreen on your back when snorkeling!

We cooked dinner most nights and played cards until we couldn't keep our eyes open. The villa didn't have air-conditioning, but we didn't care. We fell asleep with the waves crashing in the background on humid Caribbean nights. On numerous occasions, my dad said, "I just can't believe we get to experience this for less than what most people pay to go to the Jersey Shore."

To this day, after visiting 80-plus countries, that trip lives on as one of my most memorable vacations. I'll always remember January 1996 as my first successful points redemption of many to come, though little did I know how much this niche would change my life.

Fast-forward to my college years. My second week of freshman year at the University of Pittsburgh was in September of 2001 and I remember the horrific events of September 11 clearly. Rumors spread around campus that the hijackers were aiming for skyscrapers in Pittsburgh. Being a resident of Tower B, the tallest dorm on campus, I encamped to my brother's house off campus as we as a nation watched the events unfold.

Aviation changed forever that day. Many of the big airlines faced funding shortages and 9/11 was one of the events that triggered the consolidation of the aviation industry in the 15 years to follow.

This shock to the aviation industry also allowed a new crop of low-cost carriers to fill the void. Southwest Airlines expanded to Philly, and, as a college student, I started using the airline to take flights that cost $40 each way, down from the $300-plus US Airways would charge when it had a near monopoly on the route.

Back then, Southwest's frequent flyer program was rather straightforward: fly four round trips, get the fifth one free. So, my own loyalty program hacking started in 2002. I would take eight $40 one-way trips then use my free trip to get a pricey $400 trip, like going to Tucson, Arizona, to see friends. I got more value from my rewards than it cost to accrue them!

My junior year I found a cheap fare to Dublin for spring break and then studied abroad in Spain that summer. Somehow, I ended up with US Airways account Gold status. Surely this was a mistake, as I had booked super-cheap fares and was flying on a handful of inexpensive flights from Pittsburgh to Philadelphia. How could I, a broke college student flying on the cheapest fares, have mid-tier elite status?

Curious as to what "Gold status" meant, I started searching on the internet and stumbled onto FlyerTalk, an online community of people obsessed with maximizing airline miles, hotel points, and credit card points and miles. I threw myself full force into the points and miles world, which wasn't the easiest task, as there was (and still is) significant gatekeeping. But somehow, I always managed to weasel my way into the forums that had the juiciest information. I also learned that you had to give to get.

I would share whatever I could, like my experiences applying for credit cards as a college student, taking advantage of low-cost carriers, such as Independence Air (which folded during my college years), and more. Even though I wasn't a road warrior, people appreciated me helping where I could, and I was bestowed with a lot of information on how to maximize the loyalty world.

I graduated in 2005 and moved to NYC to "make it," whatever that meant. I ended up getting a job at Morgan Stanley in 2007, thinking I would make a ton of money. But shortly after I started, the 2008 financial crisis hit, which did not bode well for my compensation (especially being in HR, far from the trading desk or investment bank). My yearly bonuses were, "Congratulations, you weren't laid off. Come back again next year." What was a twenty-six-year-old to do?

I was a pretty efficient recruiter, but it was a challenging sell to try to get a top-tier MIT computer science graduate student to join a bank when the industry was melting down. The bank was going through mass layoffs, and compensation was grim year after year. But I learned I could increase my compensation in a different way—through maximizing my work travel. I was already earning airline miles and hotel points for my travel, but I wasn't earning any points by spending on my corporate American Express card.

My favorite tip in life is "It never hurts to ask," so I called American Express and asked if I could earn points on my corporate card, and they said, "Yes, Mr. Kelly, but it's $95 and you need to have a personal card enrolled in Membership Rewards, so most people decline this option." I knew I was spending $50,000 per month on career fairs and travel alone, so I signed up after doing the quick math of 600,000 points a year at a conservative 2 cents per point valuation = $12,000 a year for $95. Yes, yes, yes, yes, and yes!

As my Amex points balance boomed, so did my other balances. From 2008 to 2011, major travel companies like Starwood Hotels (my forever loyalty program love that later merged with Marriott, RIP), Hyatt, and Delta launched lucrative promotions, battling to gain loyalty from whatever business travelers were still traveling.

Hyatt used to give a free night at *any* hotel after two stays at *any* hotel. Two nights at a rural $79/night Hyatt Place got you a free night at a top-tier property, like the famed Park Hyatt Paris-Vendôme, which was an $800-plus per night. You could easily get four times the return on capital for relatively minimum work since you didn't actually need to sleep in the cheap hotel after check-in.

As the banking crisis got worse, my recruiting never slowed down, because the bank knew it had to build the future tech talent of the company or else they'd never be able to compete when the crisis was over.

This is probably why I never lost my job and even started traveling more after Morgan Stanley opened a technology center in Montreal. They needed someone from New York to help build a technology college recruiting program in Canada. I started taking weekly trips to Montreal, becoming a VIP guest at the W Montreal and raking in more valuable Starwood points than ever before.

I was banking over a million points a year by maximizing promotions and my corporate card spend, which began covering the travel expenses for the hundreds of college students we would fly in for interview days. I gladly put down my Amex for 50 broke college kids staying in hotels in New York City, getting reimbursed for the expenses. It was chaotic chasing down the folios, but I knew each one I expensed got me one step closer to my next free luxury vacation.

This era is what I call the points-rich, cash-poor period of my life, which certainly beat being just poor. I was able to fund a separate lifestyle of flying in first class and staying in hotel suites on weekends, but my bank account was often in the red. Everyone at work started to ask questions. "Are you a trust fund baby and didn't tell us?" And I even had a fellow colleague ask, "Tell the truth, you've got a sugar daddy! Does he have a brother?"

I laughed and responded that Amex was my sugar daddy. And no, I wasn't racking up huge credit card bills to fund my travels; I used points.

I had a reputation in the HR division for being "the guy who will do expenses," which they all thought was because I was being nice. Back in 2008, I had to fax paper receipts to an expense division, which would then pay Amex directly. It was excellent for me since I didn't have a single dollar to float until getting reimbursed, so I was able to rack up huge points without any financial hit.

All day long, I would hear, "Hey Brian, do you mind putting this $25,000 career fair on your card since you don't mind doing expenses? You're the best!" "No, *you're* the best, Karina, because you just paid for a free flight to Los Angeles with that single expense," is what I said in my head. I knew if I told them how valuable the points were, my gravy train would be over.

I did eventually "pay back" my coworkers by sharing my points expertise and helping them book trips for free using their points. As young 20-somethings, we all had more weddings than we could afford to attend, and I remember getting hugged so hard after helping one colleague book a simple trip to Savannah, Georgia, when she said, "Thank god this flight is free, now I can afford to buy the hideous bridesmaid dress." I laughed, but it felt amazing to help people travel and save money so they could make room for the other expenses in their lives.

Soon enough, I had the managing director of the technology division coming to my cubicle for points consultations. I remember him bragging about using his Amex points to buy a grill.

Yes, a Weber grill, one of the worst value redemptions I had ever seen. This was a computer scientist and managing director of the most high-tech division at Morgan Stanley with a PhD, and even he was confused about how to use points. I started to realize that something that came so easily and naturally to me was foreign to so many. I knew there was an opportunity for me to take this skill and do something with it.

I started a blog called ThePointsGuy.com in June 2010, and by the spring of 2011, I had about 50,000 unique visitors per month. While I started blogging about points, I expanded to all matter of travel and how to maximize the entire travel ecosystem to your advantage.

One day when I was randomly checking my spam inbox, I saw an email from Seth Kugel at the *New York Times*. He was the "Frugal Travel" columnist and was a staunch opponent of frequent flyer miles and credit cards, telling his huge audience to book the cheapest flights and don't even bother with loyalty. He was reaching out because his audience was increasingly telling him about *The Points Guy*. I implored him to meet me so I could change his mind.

We met in March 2011 for about three hours, and I changed his mindset on points and miles. I even helped him book a free flight to Brazil with miles he had (that he thought were useless). I didn't know if he'd end up writing anything.

The next month, he wrote an article about how reading *The Points Guy* should be a key step for anyone who wants to get in on the points game. He even included a screenshot of the site and a valuable link, which temporarily crashed the site but, more important, gave the website valuable Google SEO juice. The *New York Times* had essentially endorsed *The Points Guy* as an expert in travel, increasing the website's search ranking and traffic for many years to come.

I resigned from my job at Morgan Stanley that day, April 12, 2011, just nine months from hitting publish on my first blog post, and I remember my boss at the time saying, "Good for you; this is your calling." She was right.

Since the day I left my job in corporate America, in 2011, this fun side project, ThePointsGuy.com, has grown into a powerhouse consumer travel site. Since the first blog post in 2010, over 100 million people globally have consumed *TPG* content on the website, plus countless millions more on social media.

The purview of *The Points Guy* has expanded greatly over the years to include budget, family, theme parks, cruises, and so much more. I couldn't be prouder of the billions of dollars the site has saved consumers by sharing the best deals and strategies for maximizing every aspect of the travel system. But there's still more work to do.

My goal for this book is to be that starting place and explain the foundations of the travel industry so you can better navigate it. I've brought in experts to help me explain certain points, especially in areas where I have little expertise, such as the fear of flying.

To my fellow travelers, this book isn't just for newbies. There are many tips and strategies that will save you time and money, so don't close the book just yet.

Turning Travel Goals into Reality: How to Budget, Research, Plan, and Protect Your Dream Trip

Travel is the only expense that makes you richer.

—UNKNOWN

One of the biggest generational mentality shifts I've seen that shows no signs of changing is the emphasis on valuing experiences over things. Young people more than ever are willing to spend on concerts and trips even if it means buying cheap clothes or foregoing buying a first home. Posting a picture of a Birkin bag on social media is showy, but posting a reel jumping off a boat in Croatia is cool (and may even inspire people to book their next trip to Croatia). Even a bad trip can make you appreciate what you have at home and give you a much-needed perspective change. And an amazing trip can change your life in so many ways, like introducing you to a new hobby or even a future spouse. I believe the best gift we can give ourselves is the ability to explore this great earth and make deep connections with people from different backgrounds.

But turning ideas into vacations takes time, effort, and money. Here's how to begin.

How to Set a Yearly Budget for Travel

There are countless philosophies on how you should spend your money, but one of the most widely accepted is the 50/30/20 budget. This model suggests that you should spend up to 50% of your after-tax income on needs and obligations (rent, mortgage, groceries, schooling or daycare, and other necessities), and the rest should be split between savings and debt repayment (20%), and then everything else that you might want (30%).

But how much of that 30% should be on travel?

Only you can make that decision, but according to a Cornell University study, people get greater satisfaction from buying experiences than they do from material objects.[1] A trip, even one that just lasts a weekend, may be more happy-making than a stereo or a pile of new clothes. Taking trips to new destinations can not only give you that needed mood boost but also foster creativity, empathy, energy, and focus.

So when thinking about where travel should be when you prioritize your budget, remember that taking a trip can be an investment in your mental and physical health. I reached out to my friend Haley Sacks, aka Mrs. Dow Jones (@mrsdowjones), a Zillennial finance expert, for her advice.

"The best way to spend your money is on experiences . . . which is why travel is so thrilling. It makes you happy to look forward to a trip and of course, to actually get away! But please don't get into debt for a trip."

Sacks also recommends using the 50/30/20 budget, and in order to get the most out of your travel spend, she suggests keeping that money in a high-yield savings account so it accrues interest at a much higher rate than a savings account. Set a budget for your trip from the time you leave your house to when you return, and try to stick with it. Even if you don't stick to it exactly, having a visualization of what you want to spend will help you stay on track and not overspend.

Based on this rubric, I'll calculate spending 10% of your income on travel. I'll break it down for someone earning $50,000 per year in after-tax income.

If you're taking home $50,000, that means, by allocating 10% for travel, you'll have $5,000, which goes quickly considering the average domestic flight in 2024 was $370 and that can increase dramatically if you live near a less competitive airport or travel internationally. I'll get into the details more in the points chapters, but getting a single travel credit card can often net at least $750 in tax-free travel, increasing your yearly travel budget by 15% with just a few clicks. If you wanted to increase your travel budget by $750 keeping your 10% of take-home rule, you'd have to make $7,500 more in take-home salary, which at a 30% tax rate would be $10,714 extra in your pretax salary. I would argue it is much more efficient to get a credit card sign-up bonus than to figure out how to boost your salary by over $10,000, but more on that in chapter 6.

Tips for Sticking to Your Travel Budget

In order to stick to a budget, you need to first track your income and expenses. There are many money-tracking apps out there that can help with this. I'd include taking a good look at your points and miles account balances during those sessions. Sacks also explains the importance of not dipping into other areas of your finances for travel.

"This will lead to unmet financial goals or bills not getting paid. On social media, there's a YOLO mentality around spending on travel. All over your feed, you see influencers encouraging you to just spend whatever now because the memories are priceless. And I am here to assure you, memories are not *priceless*. They are, in fact, *pricey*. So follow the 50/30/20 budget to make sure you save ahead for your trip and can fully afford your next adventure," Sacks advised.

I polled my Instagram audience recently, which tends to skew 35-plus with six-figure incomes (mostly people that are skilled with leveraging credit card points and miles), about how they budget for travel, and the most common response I got was, "I have no set number because I spend what I need to spend to travel how I want. I can do that because my frequent flyer miles and credit card points do the heavy lifting and pay for a majority of travel, so I'm able to travel as much as I have the time and will splurge on the things that matter most to me."

Sounds nice, right? The goal of this book is to get more of you in that camp—accruing enough points to pay for travel without having to go into debt or make huge sacrifices to the quality of your everyday living.

Leverage the Strong US Dollar and Avoid Currency Scams

It's important to pick a destination where the US dollar stretches far to make the most of your money. Sometimes, it can be cheaper to take a vacation to a destination like Argentina or the Dominican Republic than it is to go to Florida, especially if you've used points and miles for the flight. Once you're there, everything is cheaper as your US dollars go further.

The dollar has remained strong globally, but here are some top destinations that allow you to maximize a weaker local currency and incredible travel experiences: Thailand, Vietnam, Cambodia, Egypt, Indonesia, India, South Africa, Turkey, Hungary, Argentina, Ecuador, Peru, and Colombia.

Save by considering what style of trip you want to have and picking the right type and level of accommodation. If you want a relaxing beach trip where you really chill out and recharge, it may be worth spending on that fancier hotel. But if you plan to be out of the hotel, touring and taking excursions, you might get away with booking somewhere less fancy and more affordable. Weighing how much you want to eat out and cook can also be the deciding factor between a hotel or home rental.

When spending abroad, make sure to use a US credit card that doesn't have foreign transaction fees. Most travel credit cards have gotten rid of them, but some credit cards still have them, and they'll charge an extra 3% of the transaction, which adds up and is avoidable.

Retailers and hotels often give the option to make the purchase in US dollars or the local currency. When in a foreign country always choose to have a purchase processed in the local currency and *not* in USD. For example, if you're in Spain and you have the choice to buy an item in euros or dollars always choose euros. This way, the bank runs the conversion, giving you the best rate.

I always recommend having some local currency in cash, especially in small bills, so you can tip or buy small items as needed. It's a major nuisance to get caught with no cash and need to pay a park or museum entry fee, and the credit card machine isn't working.

You can take out foreign currency at your bank before you leave, but you'll usually get the best exchange rate when using your debit card abroad at an ATM. Just watch out for conversion scams where they ask you to run the ATM withdrawal in your home currency—it's a horrible deal. Always let your bank do the conversion and withdraw in the local currency. So when withdrawing yen in Japan from an ATM, if the machine gives you a conversion option in dollars, reject it and withdraw in yen. *Always* reject the conversion, whether you're at a store, hotel, or ATM. It's best to withdraw just once (perhaps a larger quantity) to avoid multiple ATM trips and extra fees.

Travel Insurance Versus Credit Card Protections

Deciding how to protect your vacation comes down to many factors, including your age, risk factors, cost of trip, destination, and style of trip. The biggest mistake you can make as a traveler is assuming that the travel provider, whether that is airline, hotel, cruise, or tour operator, will automatically refund you if things go wrong, like a natural disaster. I listen to endless stories of people railing against airlines: "How dare they not give me a refund! My grandmother is sick!"

What people don't realize is that when you buy nonrefundable airfare, you agree to restrictions, including that you'll eat the ticket (or get a lesser-valued voucher) if you can't use it—even if something bad happens to you, like you get sick, or a family member goes into the hospital. Some airline agents might be nice and have mercy, but it isn't the standard on nonrefundable tickets. The same thing happens when natural disasters break out, like in Hawaii. Hotels don't have to refund you if you can't make it to the hotel due to a storm or natural disaster. This is where travel insurance and credit card protections come into play. You cannot expect to buy the cheapest travel packages and then be upset when incidents happen that are your responsibility to pay for.

Generally, airlines have gotten much more flexible with flights, even in basic economy, so if you need to change or cancel you can usually get a voucher. If you want a full refund on a nonrefundable ticket, it is your responsibility to either protect your trip by buying travel insurance or using a credit card with trip cancellation coverage. These protections will cover most emergency expenses and refund you for nonrefundable flights, hotels, and tours should a covered incident occur.

If you can afford it, buy travel insurance for peace of mind. Comprehensive coverage that protects from most incidents that will derail a trip (such as sickness, death of a family member, strikes, weather) will cost about 5% to 10% of your trip. Frequent travelers might want to buy a yearly policy, which can be as cheap as $250.

If you use frequent flyer miles and hotel points and have elite status that allows you to make frequent changes, I wouldn't pay for insurance on domestic trips as your elite status and credit card coverage will cover most incidents. However, I would recommend medical insurance for all trips abroad, especially to countries with poor public healthcare systems where you'd want evacuation coverage if anything went wrong. I would still buy a comprehensive policy for trips that have huge nonrefundable portions, such as cruising, a safari, and other expeditions.

Remember: The point of insurance is that you hope not to have to use it and that it gives you peace of mind in case something unexpected were to derail your plans. When you need it, you will *really* wish you had it. Even young, healthy people will likely need it at some point. For much of my life, I felt invincible, and for the most part, I was lucky, but now that I am a dad, I buy a yearly comprehensive policy, especially since I frequently travel internationally.

However, don't buy travel protections through airlines, hotels, and credit card companies. You're almost always better off buying a policy with a reputable provider through an insurance marketplace, such as InsureMyTrip .com, where you can compare and contrast policies and read the fine print. Take the time and read the policies as the most expensive policies often don't have the best coverage.

Spending the additional 5 to 10% to protect yourself from an increasingly unstable geopolitical world with a rise in unpredictable weather patterns that can upend even the most well-laid-out plans can be a good idea.

In general, travel insurance will reimburse you for expenses if you need to cancel a trip due to a covered reason or get you home, should that be necessary. It often covers nonrefundable aspects of your trip, as well as medical insurance if you get sick or have an accident abroad.

Every policy is different, but a good policy should cover:

- Sickness/death (you or a close family member)
- Airline/tour goes bankrupt
- Job loss

- Strikes
- Weather
- Jury and military duty
- Stolen passport

It often doesn't cover:

- Preexisting conditions, including pregnancy issues (if you knew you were pregnant when you purchased the trip)
- Incoming storm (a storm named before the policy is created)
- Accidents from being drunk or doing drugs
- Extreme sports (such as scuba diving, skydiving, and parasailing, though you can purchase special policies for these)
- Fear of flying
- Elective medical procedures (your hair transplant in Turkey goes left)

You'll want to consider risk assessment here. Are you traveling abroad with elderly people who could easily become ill? Does your destination have unstable weather patterns, or is it prone to strikes (Europe, especially in the summer)?

If you want the ability to cancel your trip for any reason, that coverage is called CFAR—Cancel for Any Reason—and will generally cost 25% of the trip price that you are insuring. I would only recommend this kind of policy if you have a number of known variables that could cancel a trip, such as sick family members or if you are interviewing for new jobs that would potentially require you to cancel your trip if you got the job.

If you do want to buy a policy, it's best to do it sooner than later—shortly after booking. This way, you can take advantage of all the coverage you get before you even travel, which may include trip cancellation.

Credit Card Insurance

Many credit cards come with various trip protections, such as trip cancellation/interruption, trip delay, lost baggage, baggage delay, car rental insurance, and other helpful protections. Each credit card has its own protections and coverage limits, and it's important to read the fine print on exclusions. Trip delay coverage kicks in when your flight is delayed (usually 6 or 12 hours) or if you have to spend an overnight due to a delay. This coverage will pay for hotels, meals, medication, and transportation as well as any other "reasonable costs." Most policies cap coverage at $500 per traveler, though some some credit cards have higher limits, so check on this and then make sure to use that card to pay for the trip.

I find that credit card coverage is often sufficient for cheap trips or domestic trips, but trying to get them to reimburse you if you miss an expensive cruise with multiple family members becomes more complicated. The key is to review the coverage and requirements of the credit card, as some will make you pay for all related travel on that credit card.

If you're using points, make sure you at least put any taxes or fees on that credit card, and the coverage should kick in. In general, it is harder to get reimbursed by a credit card company than a reputable travel insurer, so just understand the risk you are taking, especially when you book nonrefundable hotels and tours. Paying a 5% premium to know you're covered for most instances is generally a cost I would recommend building into your travel budget, as the world is becoming more and more unpredictable, especially with extreme weather events.

How Long to Travel

Even if you can afford to travel, finding the time to do it can be the biggest challenge. The United States doesn't mandate paid time off on a national level like most countries, and the countrywide average for paid time off is a measly 11 working days, just over two weeks. Our European friends have the most flexible policies, with solid base time off plus many public holidays. The United Arab Emirates grants most workers 30 days plus 14 paid holidays. Taiwan offers 30 days of paid leave for those with 10 years in the job; Finland, 25; Iceland, 24; and Denmark, 20. Zimbabwe offers 22 days base, and Mongolians get 15 days, while Mexico requires 12 days off of paid leave.

Don't feel bad about taking what little time you have off. Trust me, the company will survive, even if you think your job is important. I know so many people who stress about "letting their teams down," but know that you'll be a better employee once you've had time to step away and reset.

I suggest taking two full weekends for a weeklong trip and incorporating holidays into your trip in smart ways. Traveling to Europe over Thanksgiving is an amazing way to avoid the busiest airport moments at US airports by taking a bit of extra time off but maximizing the days you do have off. Traveling on Christmas Day is another way to save money and avoid crowds but also take advantage of the time you already have off work.

You can stretch 11 days of paid time off by combining them with weekends and public holidays. In 2024, since many public holidays were on Mondays, you could turn 11 days into 44 with the right selection of PTO on the Friday before the holidays, or Tuesday after, or the Friday after Thanksgiving.

If you aren't boxed in by school calendars, traveling even just a week after the peak holiday dates can mean you'll get much better prices. Mid-December and mid-January often see massive drops in airfare. And, if you're traveling abroad with a foreign air carrier on points, remember to check its peak calendar. Thanksgiving won't mean peak dates on many international airlines, so you may be able to get some excellent award deals.

Make sure to give yourself time to adjust after coming back. I don't recommend the late Sunday night flight. While I recommend maximizing your time, you should also consider a transition day at home as part of your vacation. Getting back late on a Sunday and going straight into work on a Monday can undo much of the relaxation you built up during your vacation.

For shorter trips, be mindful of jet lag. While it may be tempting to do long weekends in Europe or a quick week in Asia, understand that the quality of your trip could be impacted by the time difference, which I'll cover more in chapter 12. I try to travel for longer if I'm heading to a time zone farther from home.

If you're all about a long weekend trip or one shorter than a week, consider destinations within the US, Mexico, Canada, or the Caribbean—perhaps even some spots in Latin America, especially if you're located in a southern hub such as Miami or Dallas, which offers lots of nonstop flights to destinations in Central and South America. You won't have to deal with as much jet lag and can better maximize your time.

How to Pick Travel Companions

Who you travel with can make or break a trip. I've learned after many group trips (some wildly successful, some epic disasters, and many a bit of both) to be selective with your travel companions. Once I realized that, no, I didn't have to travel with my friends or even my family, I found even more joy in travel.

How to Handle Group Trips

In my 20s, I used to take a yearly party trip to Mykonos, with a group that got bigger and bigger every year. Eventually, the trip got too crazy—it was like herding cattle, nearly impossible to handle the logistics on an overcrowded island in the peak summer season. There were couples fighting, drunken blowouts, and just general irritation on every step of the trip, from getting taxis to finding beach club reservations. I gave myself permission to bow out as I reached my 30s, and felt relief and happiness. Travel with people that like the same things as you and make travel easy, restorative, and fulfilling.

You don't have to say yes to every trip or take trips with people out of convenience. Take trips with people whom you love and enjoy spending time with. Don't just go on a trip because someone is organizing one.

The key to the best group trips is to make sure everyone is on the same page (preferably before you even leave) and that your own needs are met. Here's how to do it.

Agree on a philosophy on scheduling and flexibility.

Some of the best trips are easily ruined when over-planners and under-planners don't communicate or agree on trip organization ahead of time. Get it in writing. Send a group email out with a proposed schedule, including where there's flexibility and where there's not (e.g., this tour starts at 8 a.m. sharp, but the next day is an entirely free day). Have everyone respond, "I commit."

Don't travel with friends who are perpetually late to everything. If you're this person, try to be respectful and show up for dinner reservations on time. And remember, be kind to the planner, even if everything doesn't go perfectly or it isn't the way you would have planned the itinerary. The planner is doing a lot of work and deserves a big thank-you.

Agree on a budget.

You don't want to be forced out of your comfort zone financially or, on the other end of the spectrum, not be able to enjoy the luxuries of vacation the way you want. Travel with people committed to the same style of trip as you. Don't be the person who orders the lobster then wants to split the bill.

Try to find travel companions that not only respect your financial boundaries but have similar ones. Decide what splurges you'll do as a group on the trip and where you can save. Using an app such as Tricount, Splitwise, Tripcoin, or PocketGuard can help you stay organized with money and who owes whom what during group travel.

And remember, a great way to earn more points is to pay for it all and then have everyone pay you back for their portion.

Set personal boundaries.

Even if you're taking a group trip, you don't have to share a room or even stay in the same house as the group. I once took a group trip to Thailand, where the other nine people stayed in a shared villa, and I booked a hotel room for myself. I had the best of both worlds: a place to retreat when I needed quiet or alone time and a fun spot to hang out with the group at the shared house.

Protecting your space is especially important as you get older, as you often are able to recognize your nonnegotiable needs—extra sleep, alone time. Sleep is especially delicate, and you don't want to end up sharing a room with someone who snores or watches TV and keeps you up, which takes away from your ability to be rested and enjoy your trip.

Traveling Alone Can Be Amazing

The joy of a solo trip is real, even if you have a family or are in a relationship. Solo trips build confidence and allow you to focus on whatever you want to do. An easy way not to feel alone when taking a solo trip is to sign up for group tours and activities that allow you to be with others while still enjoying your time how you want.

Every year, I take at least one week to do an absolute "me" trip on my own. I find solo vacations especially helpful when needing to make big life decisions, as these types of trips give me the space and insight to consider my next steps and choose the right path.

The Joy of a Multigenerational Trip

Some of my most memorable vacations have been taking my parents and my son on vacation. Spoiling my parents with luxury travel is a gift I never imagined I could give them. From a trip with my dad to Jordan to taking my mom to Easter Island, traveling with family is special and something I never take for granted.

I'm also getting real joy out of taking my son to new places such as Portugal and Japan. He's still probably too little to remember, but I'll always have those memories, and there are plenty of photos to prove it. A great gift for your young children is to create a journal from all of your travels and include pictures and key memories that you can give them when they're older.

How to Choose the Right Destination and Time to Travel

It's hard to balance trying something new versus doing what you know will be a good time. However, travel is also about pushing yourself, leaning into uncomfortable moments, staying open-minded, and experiencing new things. Many of us plan travel based on what's easy and comfortable and what we know or what our friends are doing. But maybe that's because we don't know what else is out there, or it feels scary to do something new.

Picking the Right Season

You can save money, avoid crowds, and have an easier travel experience by visiting destinations during their shoulder season. The high season is summer in the Mediterranean or winter in the Caribbean. The low season is winter in the Mediterranean (cold, with seasonal concessions closed) and summer and early fall in the Caribbean (rainy and muggy with the possibility of hurricanes). Remember, the southern hemisphere's seasons are flipped. Summer in Sydney, Australia; Cape Town, South Africa; and Buenos Aires, Argentina, is from December to March.

The season in between high or peak season and low season is called shoulder season. It's when you can often count on decent weather, but it's not high season, which brings crowds and higher prices, or low season, where weather can be unpleasant and you may not even get a feel for the destination because many seasonal spots are closed. It's much more enjoyable to tour cultural sites in temperate weather and getting into top restaurants is easier in the shoulder season. In my experience, whether it's Disney World over Easter or Tulum over New Year's Eve, you're paying a huge premium to get a worse experience than what you'd get just a couple weeks before or after.

Think about climate change and how locals live. Visiting a European city like Madrid or Paris in August not only means you'll be met with extreme heat but also the absence of many locals, who flee the city in search of the beach. Many smaller shops and businesses close for the entire month, and you may end up having an uncomfortable experience that doesn't allow you to enjoy the more authentic delights of these cities.

Off-season can be cheaper, too. If you look at prices for a trip to Mexico over Christmas and New Year's, then check pricing for the following weeks in January, you might be able to save hundreds, even thousands, of dollars.

Traveling in the shoulder season brings perks you might not even realize, besides being more affordable with fewer crowds. It also means, in many cases, that you can travel on what airlines and hotels consider off-peak dates, and you may find better and more affordable award availability, especially with loyalty programs that don't bother with dynamic pricing and have published award charts with peak and off-peak rates.

Betting Against Mother Nature: Rainy, Hurricane, and Monsoon Seasons

Do your research because some destinations have cheap low-season rates because you're taking a gamble on Mother Nature. I don't recommend planning an advance special occasion, like a honeymoon, to the Caribbean in September. However, I've booked last-minute trips to the Caribbean during hurricane season and had a fabulous time with few crowds and cheap hotel rates, so it's all about the occasion and the perspective—and booking refundable travel whenever possible.

It's important to really understand what the high, shoulder, and low seasons in certain destinations mean. How bad is monsoon season, really? Does hurricane season just mean a heavy tropical shower at 4 p.m. every day or possible catastrophic consequences to an area without proper infrastructure to handle severe storms?

The first time I went to the Maldives in October, it rained five out of six days. While I didn't mind (I could still scuba dive in the rain), my traveling companion was not so pleased we flew halfway around the world to get rained on.

Weather can be a bummer, and even wreak havoc on getting home. I generally don't recommend using precious vacation time during hurricane/monsoon season. But know that in many destinations, weather patterns are changing, so even if you go during a "normal" season, it doesn't guarantee a perfect trip. And if bad weather disrupts your destination before your trip, many travel insurance policies will allow you to cancel or rebook free of charge.

How to Assess Risk and Safety When Planning Travel (and Traveling)

I'm often asked by travelers, from beginner to advanced, if certain destinations are safe to visit. I'm not an expert on every country in the world, but what I can tell you is that America is one of the more dangerous industrialized countries in the world.[2] Do you find it scary to travel around most places in America? I don't. I know that there are places I should avoid and I should do my research before going to any new city to make sure I don't put myself at risk for areas known for violent activity. Use the same logic for other countries and you should generally be okay.

. . . .

I haven't been to every country, but I'm friends with a bunch of people who have, including Jessica Nabongo, the first Black woman to visit every country in the world. I wanted her perspective on how to assess risk when traveling.

After working for the UN and visiting every country on Earth, Nabongo found the world to be much safer than many people think. Here's some of the advice I gleaned from our conversation.

Lean on Locals

Nabongo often uses Google as a resource to find local, on-the-ground tour guides for countries, especially those with reputations for being "dangerous." "At the end of the day, the people living in those countries are the experts. That person will know more about their country than anyone else."

Remember, people and politics are two different things. People are people, no matter where you are in the world. She references a specific experience when visiting Afghanistan, a country many people would balk at visiting due to safety concerns. But Nabongo knew the way to go would be to experience it through the eyes (and help) of locals.

"I found a guy who started a tour company—the name was Let's Be Friends—so cute. He once worked as a security advisor for the UN. He met me at the border and brought me clothes to change into. We went to breakfast and the car broke down. We waited 30 minutes, and I said that I could just pay for a new car. The guide said no. He trusted this driver, and he wasn't going to hire a driver he didn't know. He never told me I was in danger, but I could tell he was controlling the situation in the way that he could to ensure our safety. The moral of the story is you have to trust the right local people to help keep you safe."

Use Your Intuition

She also suggests using intuition as a key way to figure out if something is wrong, which has occasionally happened to her. "If something doesn't feel right, trust that energy and get out," she advises. I couldn't agree more and some of my friends call me callous, but I generally don't interact with people on the street in crowded tourist destinations. I like to think of high tourist areas as the African savanna and the tourists are prey for the predators who constantly analyze the pack and decide to go for the weakest links. Often pickpockets will distract you while their counterparts quickly bump into you and steal your belongings before you even realize what happened. By all means I encourage you to meet locals wherever you go, just avoid it at most tourist traps, which are where most pickpocketing and criminal activity happens (like the Trevi Fountain in Rome and Las Ramblas in Barcelona). Scammers will often ask you innocent questions like where you're from and before you know it you're having drinks with them at a local bar where they're in cahoots with the bar owner and they charge you $1,000 per drink or else they'll threaten to call the cops on you (who may or may not be in on the scam). This happens more often than you'd think, so I highly recommend keeping to yourself and avoiding contact with random people in high tourist areas. Here are some other tips to avoid being pickpocketed:

1. Use a money belt around your chest under your shirt for your valuables.
2. Never use your cell phone in public in a high tourist area—someone could come up on a bike or motorcycle and snatch it out of your hand.
3. Never store anything in your back pockets.
4. Backpacks should be turned forward on your chest when worn in public areas (thieves will slice the bottom of your bag and you'll never know it's been emptied).
5. No expensive watches or jewelry—organized crime rings will steal it off your hand in a matter of seconds—in broad daylight in major cities.
6. Always leave your passport and extra credit cards/cash in your hotel room safe when possible. (However, this isn't 100% secure as hotel safes can be breeched by employees and thieves.)

7. Never hire random cars—always use a ride service app or arrange through a hotel.

Stay at Hotels

Stay at hotels if safety is a concern or if you're traveling alone. "If I have to run in, I know there's going to be someone at the front desk. If you're solo, I recommend a hotel or hostel because there are other people there," Nabongo said.

Make Smart Choices and Be Prepared

When it comes to general travel safety, use your head. Don't be showy with jewelry or cash, especially in certain destinations. And know that much of what could happen abroad could happen at home.

During Carnival celebrations in Rio de Janeiro in 2019, I was at a local outdoor party in Ipanema (the neighborhood near the famous beach) and heard gunshots that were very close by. My group of friends had to scatter and run as the shots kept happening, which was pretty traumatic. We eventually found each other, and luckily none of us were harmed and we just happened to be in the wrong place at the wrong time—a robbery went awry near us and fortunately the victim lived. If you're being robbed, don't try to be a hero and fight back—things can be replaced, your life can't.

If you are approached by a group of young people, don't underestimate them, as coordinated youth gangs can inflict damage quickly. And just as this can happen abroad, it can also happen in the US, so it's best to take precautions no matter your location. I recommend always being aware of the exits, especially in hotels. Imagine smoke filling the hallway and you have to crawl to find the exit. Whenever you check into a hotel, make a mental note of where the stairwell is from your room. Hopefully you never have to know, but in the off chance you do, that piece of information could save your life. Also, 911 is not the global number for emergency services; finding the local emergency phone number in the country you're visiting takes a minute and having it on hand will be useful if you need to call it quickly.

Strike the Right Balance Between Getting Scammed and Supporting Locals

There's a tricky balance between being a gracious tourist and holding your ground, especially in countries that are wildly different from the United States.

Nabongo suggests playing the cultural game, like bartering at local markets, because, well, it's fun. "I often talk to guides or drivers to understand more about a price range. I didn't do this on a trip to Morocco, and I went in blind. They really got me at the leather tannery and, later, at the souks. When I realized they'd overcharged me three times as much as normal prices, I went back. And they gave me money back, plus other goods. Negotiate, but also tip and don't try to cheat locals. I tip a lot, like if someone walks me somewhere or offers kind service. I recognize the economic disparity. Always have the local equivalent of one US dollar, so that if you want to tip, you can."

Travel Safety Resources

The US State Department travel advisories are valid resources, but you must use the information and warnings offered with a knowledgeable outlook. In many cases, countries as a whole are marked with high-level travel warnings due to public health concerns such as outbreaks of infectious diseases or violence in a specific area that's nowhere near where you might be headed. Familiarize yourself with the regions of a country and understand that an issue in one area doesn't necessarily mean you can't safely visit other parts.

Nabongo also says to think carefully about certain travel advisories, as sometimes the dangers are irrelevant to tourists and are "politically charged/biased or based on specific local violence."

She suggests some "starter" countries in the Middle East and Africa that those who want to explore, but not get in too deep, can try: "Jordan and Oman are great starter Middle Eastern countries. In Africa, Kenya, Tanzania, Egypt, Morocco, and Ghana. For something more off the beaten path, Algeria and Tunisia."

Natural Disasters

When it comes to natural disasters, do the research, and don't just count on one source or hearsay from friends. Find out where the flooding or wildfires are, take serious considerations if a country is facing political instability, but try to find unbiased information. If you can reach someone on the ground there or someone who's visited recently, this work can help you get more accurate information.

You should never go to a disaster area where your visit would detract from the welfare of the local population. Once in recovery, however, your visit may do some good, so try to support local businesses as much as possible so your tourism dollars go into the local community more than a publicly traded company's bottom line.

I took a trip to Puerto Rico 90 days after Hurricane Maria to assist with the recovery, and the island was in desperate need of tourism again. Visiting these destinations can aid in recovery, but it can be a fine balance. I recommend talking to locals, but even then, you'll find differing opinions. In general, if you're torn on whether to visit a destination, I recommend doing it in the future and going somewhere else this trip instead. There's no shortage of incredible places to visit where your presence won't be a drag on limited resources.

Understanding Your Personal Risk Profile

There is always risk in traveling, and you need to make the best decision for yourself and your family. At the most extreme, you don't want to become a political prisoner, because we've seen adversarial nations such as North Korea and Russia detain American citizens to use them as bargaining chips. Don't be naive and downplay the risk of kidnapping in countries with elevated risk warnings.

If you have a medical condition that might require specific doctors or equipment, it's on you to make sure that it's available at your destination. If you love scuba diving like me, you should understand where the nearest hyperbaric chamber is in case you get decompression sickness, which can happen on a normal dive.

As a single gay father, I research each destination I visit, especially with my son, and I always have proof that I'm the only parent on his birth certificate. I understand that this is not the norm in most countries, and immigration agents may want to screen me more to make sure I'm not trafficking a child.

A destination may have a low level of violent crime, but there may be a large amount of undocumented crime against women or LGBTQ+ people. As an openly gay traveler, I always do my due diligence and understand both the laws and societal norms of where I'm going. It's my perspective that it's not my duty to be an activist everywhere I go, and as a visitor, I agree to abide by the local laws and customs while visiting.

While I don't agree with the laws of many countries I visit, I'll still abide by them. I fully understand those LGBTQ+ travelers who don't want to do that, and I respect that. But I also disagree with boycotting countries that have anti-LGBTQ+ laws, as I have traveled to many and often the tourism industry is the only place where the most marginalized LGBTQ+ members can work, so boycotting directly harms the people you're trying to help.

You never want to put yourself in a situation where you could be at risk of violating local laws. While the US government may help connect you with a local lawyer, never expect the local embassy to rush to your defense, especially if you do something avoidable. The freedom of speech we enjoy in the US is not universal, and many American tourists have learned this lesson the hard way.

In 2020, traveler Wesley Barnes, who was working in Thailand, faced up to two years in prison in Thailand for violating their strict anti-defamation laws. He left a 1-star Tripadvisor review on the Sea View Resort on Koh Chang Island, stating, "The staff was not friendly. Nobody could smile. The restaurant manager was rude and very full of himself. There are other hotels with better, friendlier staff. Avoid this place as if it were the Coronavirus!" Thankfully the authorities released him after a short detainment (he had to issue a public apology), but it serves as a warning that your sense of humor may not translate abroad, especially on social media, where it can be quickly misconstrued, so your best bet is to keep your mouth shut and at least wait until you're back in the US to voice your potentially controversial opinions.

This should go without saying, but *never* get mouthy or handsy with airport workers. Elizabeth Polanco De Los Santos learned that the hard way when she allegedly tapped a security guard's arm when they asked her to take off a compression garment when undergoing security at Dubai airport. The guard perceived it as assault, and the 21-year-old college student was fined and detained for months while her case worked its way through the UAE's complicated legal system. Fifty thousand dollars and two months later, she was allowed to leave, but she could have faced up to a year in jail.

While these two cases are outliers—they are reminders that international travel can bring many positives—it is still your responsibility to act respectfully.

When traveling to a foreign country, take two minutes and register with the US Department of State's STEP, Smart Traveler Enrollment Program (https://mytravel.state.gov/s/step), so you can receive important updates. This program allows the US government to contact you should any geopolitical or weather situations arise. I was recently in Guatemala and was notified about national protests that would close major highways around the airport. Luckily I had several days' notice and moved my return flight up by a day, which saved me from being stranded in the country for five days as airport operations ground to a halt because employees couldn't arrive or depart. If there are natural disasters or political unrest, STEP will connect you with critical government resources, and in dire situations the US government may even expatriate you. I highly recommend registering even when you're in "safe" countries, as situations can arise out of nowhere and escalate quickly. Getting the right information is critical and being registered in STEP is easy to do.

If you're still feeling apprehensive about a destination even after you research or connect with a local, save the trip for another time. There are plenty of places to visit and some destinations will require a higher tolerance for risk that might be more suitable to visit after you've traveled more.

My Points Bucket List with Top Points Hotels

These are some of my favorite destinations to visit on points that are a great value and have changed the way I view the world and travel.

Culture and Food

1. **Japan:** Tokyo, Kyoto, Osaka (bonus winter add-on: skiing in Niseko)
   Edition Ginza, Park Hyatt Kyoto, St. Regis Osaka
2. **Thailand:** Bangkok and Koh Samui
   JW Marriott Bangkok, Conrad Koh Samui
3. **Argentina:** Buenos Aires and Mendoza for wine
   Palacio Duhau - Park Hyatt Buenos Aires and Park Hyatt Mendoza
4. **Paris, France:**
   Park Hyatt Paris-Vendôme, Prince de Galles, a Luxury Collection Hotel, The Westin Paris-Vendôme, or the Kimpton St Honoré

Relaxation

1. **The Maldives:**
   The Ritz-Carlton Maldives, Fari Islands, the St. Regis Maldives Vommuli Resort, and the Waldorf Astoria Maldives Ithaafushi
2. **Hawaii:** Kauai or Maui
   Grand Hyatt Kauai Resort or the Andaz Maui at Wailea Resort - A Concept by Hyatt
3. **Cabo San Lucas:**
   Waldorf Astoria Los Cabos Pedregal or The Cape, A Thompson Hotel, by Hyatt

Adventure

1. **Dubai:**
   Park Hyatt Dubai or Conrad Dubai plus a desert safari with a stay at Al Maha, a Luxury Collection Desert Resort & Spa
2. **South Africa:** Cape Town and safari at Kruger or wine country (Stellenbosch or Franschhoek)
   Westin Cape Town and Hyatt Regency Cape Town (there aren't any luxury traditional points hotels in the bush but splurge on any Singita; I love Sabi Sand). Or, tack on a safari at Cheetah Plains or at the JW Marriott Masai Mara Lodge in Kenya
3. **Iceland:**
   Edition Reykjavik, Hotel Ranga (Hilton)

Chapter 4

How to Win at Booking Travel

The key is flexibility and knowing when and where to purchase travel.

first became fascinated with airfare during a segment on *60 Minutes* where the reporter interviewed everyone on a plane and showed the widely varying amounts passengers paid for essentially the exact same thing. I couldn't believe how much airfare cost and I vowed to never be the poor guy who paid three times as much as the person sitting next to him did. What a fool! (And what a fool I would become many times in my life when left to buy expensive fares due to my loathing of planning in advance.) While airfare seems to make no sense, once you understand how it works you can then begin to hunt for the cheapest deals and avoid the things that make airfare so expensive. There are so many factors that go into the price of an airline ticket and if you watch fake experts on social media, they'll spread false tips like "using incognito browsing" or shopping on a certain day to get the cheapest fares (that used to be the case many years ago, but modern computing now allows airlines to update pricing almost immediately). While I love a conspiracy theory, airlines do not price airfare based on your individual session—they use much larger datasets, primarily demand, which is triggered when someone buys a ticket. And if it's the last ticket in a fare class, the price will likely rise. Your simple act of browsing didn't trigger the change—it's very likely that someone else bought (or canceled) a ticket that caused the price change. To become a pro at finding cheap fares, you need to understand the basics of airfare.

As stressful as it can be, there's nothing more satisfying than getting an amazing deal on a trip. I remember my first cheap flight booking as if it were yesterday: the excitement of seeing something too good to be true, the frantic call to my college roommate to see if he wanted to go to Ireland on spring break for $300. Everyone that year was going to Acapulco, but those pricey packages were too steep for me. But $300 was doable, especially since I had a friend studying abroad in Ireland who assured me we would "pregame" (drink cheap booze in his dorm room) before going out to minimize how much we spent at the pubs. Frat boy math at its finest! We would be staying in hostels, so we figured we could do it all for $800.

After squeezing into a regular US Airways 767 economy seat (window seat, always) and taking NyQuil to distract me from the imprints my knees made in the seatback in front of me, I remember landing in the Manchester airport on a grim March morning but thinking it the most magical place in the world. A utopia where *everyone* was drinking at the airport at 9 a.m.! I hadn't even gotten off the plane when I declared my undying love for international travel.

After arriving in Dublin, we packed into a double-decker bus that took us straight to our hostel in Temple Bar. Everyone was so nice! Everything was so green! I could live here!

The Ireland trip was an epic success, and I craved more of Europe. I decided to squeeze in a six-week study abroad that summer in Madrid, and I aimed to find another flight deal. But unlike my flight to Dublin (via Philadelphia and Manchester) in March, the dates—May to early July—contributed to the wild seasonality of fares, especially when the study abroad department sent the bill: $1,800 for airfare for the "discounted group rate." Luckily, they said, "Feel free to book on your own, but you won't find better than this." Challenge accepted.

I ended up searching and found round-trip airfare for $472.75 from May 24 to July 4 between Philly and Madrid. Flying on the July Fourth holiday would save me money. I emailed all of my fellow study abroad participants, who granted me hero status. "That's so cheap. I'm going to take that $1,300 you saved me and travel around Europe for a month. You're a legend!" And so began my unofficial career as the cheap-flight guy.

After I started ThePointsGuy.com as a fun blog while working at Morgan Stanley, I helped spread some epic deals. In 2011, there was a Delta fare mistake: $150 nonstop round trip from JFK to Stockholm and Copenhagen with the ability to layover in Amsterdam. I once took my mom on a cheap business-class fare ($800) to Easter Island, and when blog readers came up to me on remote Easter Island and high-fived me while screaming, "Oh my god, it's the Points Guy!," she stopped questioning why I quit my stable job on Wall Street and looked me in the eye and said, "You have fans in . . . Easter Island? This is way bigger than even I realize." My thoughts, too, Mom!

The Deals Are There, but Buyer Beware

You can find great deals on travel if you're flexible, use technology, take the time to research, and weigh costs logically. But cheap can be expensive, so it's important to look at the big picture and not just the cost of the fare. The fare is just one component of the total price you'll pay to fly as airlines are adding more fees, even for elite and business-class travelers. When deciding if a flight is a good deal, I weigh five pieces of information:

1. Is this a good fare based on historical fare data for this route? I usually use Google Flights or Hopper for their data, which will show pricing history for that fare and tell you their opinion if its low, average, or high.
2. Can I earn frequent flyer miles or elite status that will bring me value in the future?
3. What fees or exclusions come along with this fare—for example, can I cancel and recoup the value in the form of a voucher? Does this fare allow me to access the lounge or change to other flights on the airline?
4. Is the airline reputable or will I end up being delayed or canceled? Time is money (generally as you get older you value your time more), so flying on unreliable carriers has a cost. I recommend booking directly with the airline whenever possible to avoid costly cancellation or delay situations, earn miles, and make sure your trip runs smoothly.
5. Can I book this directly with the airline so I can avoid involving

an online travel agency, which can complicate things if my flight is delayed or canceled?

I wish there was one single tip that would give you the best price on a flight or hotel every time, but there isn't. The travel booking space has evolved, and for you to understand how to get the best deals, you need to understand the seismic shifts happening in travel. Understanding how an industry functions is critical to understanding how you can benefit from it—meaning, getting the best deals.

Interestingly, the airlines don't really make money selling you airfare; they make it on lucrative add-ons, such as fees, and by selling miles to credit card companies. Then, you use their co-brand credit cards for all your purchases. This evolution is important to understand as you start to master the booking landscape.

Booking Flights: Tricks and Ways to Save

When purchasing airfare, you have five main options:

- Google Flights
- Directly from the airline
- An online travel agency (OTA) like Expedia, Orbitz, and Hopper
- A credit card travel portal (American Express Travel, Capital One Travel, Chase Travel)
- A travel agent/luxury travel advisor

Use Google Flights

Google.com/travel/flights is the first place to do your initial research on what flights are available, along with the times, airlines, and prices. It's free, fast, and easy, you can include multi-airport searches, find flights by airline alliance, and even search for the cheapest fares to a country, or even to an entire continent. You don't actually purchase the airfare from Google, but you can see pricing from both airlines and OTAs, so it's my preferred place to comparison shop.

It does have a few drawbacks. You won't find flights on some foreign carriers, especially budget airlines. And occasionally, you'll find that deals shown on Google Flights are no longer available. So before you get too excited, you'll want to click through the fare to make sure it appears on the airline or the online travel agency website. Prices can sometimes change when you click through to check them out as many travel sites store, or cache, airfares for ease of search but then only pull them when it's time to buy the fare.

Just like searching a single airline's website, you'll need to put in your origin, your destination, your travel dates, the number of travelers, and your class of service (economy, business class, and so on). Once you have results, you can narrow it down by airline, connecting airports, flight times, and duration. Clean up your results by filtering in the number of stops or connection times.

You can also view historic pricing data (fare graphs go back 60 days) to give you an idea of how the fare has changed. If you see that it has been increasing steadily, chances are that it will continue to do so. Fares tend to increase more than they decrease.

And if you're looking for the cheapest times to travel, you can show all the options in a calendar view, which allows you to scan multiple days at a time. Sometimes varying your travel dates a little can make a big difference in the price you pay. Make sure to see if Google "predicts" the price will drop or go up in the "fare predict" section so you can figure out if you're getting a good deal, or if it may be better to wait. While not perfect, Google has billions of datasets from which to base its predictions, which will be much more accurate than asking your travel expert friend if it's a good deal or not.

Another helpful feature in Google Flights is the "Explore" button on the toolbar. This allows you to enter your home city and then search by region. One example: New York City to Caribbean over a certain time period or even parameters like "weekend or one week" over a monthlong period. The more flexible you are with your search, the better deals you will find.

Customer Service as a Consideration When Booking Airfare

The airlines often make things harder for passengers who choose to book flights via OTAs by forcing them to call the OTA if there's an issue with the flight—even if the airline canceled the flight. Imagine this: You're at the airport and your flight gets canceled. The next flight out leaves in 40 minutes and has one open seat. If you booked through the airline directly, usually, they would put you on that next flight. However, in some instances, if you booked through an OTA, you might have to call them to get rebooked. Sometimes customer service waits can be lengthy, especially during peak times and weather disruptions. The flight may have already taken off by the time you get hold of a representative. If you get caught in a customer service loop, you might not get home that day. On the flip side, you may have long waits when calling an airline, so it is possible that an OTA could have faster service.

Generally, passengers who booked with the airline (or their favored channels, like corporate travel agencies) get to be accommodated seamlessly. Yes, you might have saved a small amount by booking through an OTA, but you might pay for those savings by getting slower customer service if things go wrong.

I'm not saying you should not use OTAs. You should use them to compare pricing and see options. But when it comes to buying your ticket, unless you're saving a massive amount of money, which is rarer and rarer these days, booking through an OTA means you'll often negate these savings through inconvenience if the itinerary gets disrupted.

However, an OTA can sometimes put together an itinerary with multiple carriers that aren't partners, and these are flight options that might never show on an airline website, but will on an OTA. This can be a huge advantage on some international itineraries and potentially save you some money. Some OTAs also have access to special bulk airfare that airlines won't show on their own websites, so it always makes sense to check OTA pricing.

If you book through an OTA, ensure you're getting miles and credit toward elite status from the ticket you purchased through the OTA. And you should always sign up for OTA loyalty programs if you plan to book through them.

If you've never heard of an online travel agency and want to know if they're legitimate, I recommend checking out their reviews on Trustpilot .com or googling to see if there are threads about them on Reddit or FlyerTalk. You should be able to identify a shady operator pretty quickly with some minimal online due diligence. If you can't find any information on a company, that alone is a red flag and I recommend avoiding them (or if you do use them, at least use a credit card with strong purchase protections should anything go wrong).

Does this mean the end of OTAs? Hardly, but I think all companies in travel need to provide more to the consumer than just the ease of booking. I think OTAs should also focus on the customer experience throughout the entire travel journey.

Getting Discounted Fares

When it comes to getting discounted fares, OTAs aren't the only way. Discounts on airfare also exist when you book directly. For example:

- **Student or young adult fares:** United has a 5% off coupon for booking economy seats in its app for 18-to-23-year-olds through the end of 2025 (but keep an eye out for future promos).
- **Child pricing:** Domestically infants fly free on your lap; internationally airlines will charge 10% of the adult ticket price. Many airlines offer discounts ranging from 10 to 50% on child fares for ages 2 to 12.
- **Senior pricing:** Some airlines offer senior fares, but often you have to call to see if you're eligible.
- **Military pricing:** Many airlines offer discounts to active-duty members as well as increased checked baggage allowance.
- **Bereavement fares:** These are usually for direct family members and require proof.
- **AARP:** Membership can sometimes be as low as $12 per year (and most important it is *open to all ages*) but can get you to major discounts on flights and hotels.

- **FoundersCard:** This membership costs $595 per year (plus a $95 initiation fee) and offers discounts on United and numerous other airlines and hotels. At the time of writing, you can save up to 16% on United fares, up to 10% on British Airways fares, and up to 15% on Singapore Airlines, among others. *If you travel and shop frequently, this can pay off.*
- **Airline promos:** Airlines often run discounts and promotions where they're seeing low demand on new routes that they want to get people excited about, so follow major airlines on social media, along with the deal sites I'll outline below.

When It Makes Sense to Use Credit Card Travel Portals

After checking Google Flights, as an Amex Platinum and Centurion credit cardholder, I always then go to Amex Travel to see what special fares they have for the route. It offers a special International Airline Program (IAP) where they partner with airlines to offer lower fare prices. I've saved thousands of dollars booking with Amex, as they often have rates that are lower than what you see on other OTAs (usually, only available for Platinum and Centurion cardholders). A recent trip to Tokyo was $8,500 on Japan Airlines, all OTAs, and Google Flights, but it was $6,200 when I logged in to AmexTravel.com since I have the Platinum and Centurion cards.

If you want to use credit card points to book your ticket (and not transfer them to a partner loyalty program), you'll have to book through the credit card portal (Chase Travel, Amex Travel, Capital One Travel, etc.), which is basically an OTA and at times even powered by the big OTAs. The difference is there's another layer of customer service if things go wrong, and credit card customer service is often more helpful than a regular OTA. They're trying to retain you as a valued customer, and they often have travel concierges that have better training than the average OTA phone rep. Plus, many of these platforms give extra miles or points for booking through them, even though they work using general OTAs. For example, I book most of my airfare directly on airline websites or via Amex Travel using my Amex Platinum, which earns me 5X points per dollar spent. If I were to book through a regular OTA, I would only get 1X point per dollar spent.

Flexibility: The Biggest Money-Saver

Flexibility will be the largest factor that saves you money. The more you expand your search to include more dates and airports, the better deals you'll find. It's a myth that booking travel on Tuesdays and Wednesdays can save you money. The day of the week you book doesn't have much to do with it, but the day you fly does. Airfare is largely based on demand between city pairs, so traveling on days when there are fewer business and leisure travelers (such as Tuesday, Wednesday, and Saturday) or on actual holidays versus days prior and after can help you save.

Flying on off-peak times and dates incurs the best fares. And when you keep tracking the price of your flights, you can rebook them at lower fares now that most of the major airlines no longer charge change fees.

Do Multiple Searches

Although I usually don't recommend booking on OTAs, searching on them, as well as via Google, Amex, and through the airline websites, is a good plan to do before booking. There's no one tool that will show you every single flight option, so understand that you have to do multiple searches to see what's out there.

Mistake Fares and Deals: Act Quickly

One of the thrills of the miles and points world was buying fares when airlines would accidentally "fat finger" or upload a clear mistake. Think $800 round trip from New York to Hong Kong on Cathay Pacific in first class, a ticket that was normally $25,000. Sometimes, the airlines would honor them. Other times, they would offer an alternative that was sometimes still a great deal (such as business class instead), and sometimes they'd deem them invalid.

While rare, these mistakes and deals do still happen, but you need to act quickly when they do. And most of them aren't posted on blogs or forums because they get killed fast.

Use Technology to Your Advantage

I already mentioned using OTAs to compare prices and discussed how to use Google Flights. Many of these websites, including Google Flights, allow you to set alerts to find the best deals. You register, set your departure, destination, and dates, and you'll get alerts when the price drops.

Downloading airline, hotel, and OTA apps can also offer discounts, sometimes ones specific to booking via the app.

These are some of the websites I use to look for deals and compare airfare.

- **Hopper:** This mobile app offers flash deals on travel reservations, including airfare sent as alerts.
- **Kayak:** This tool allows you to compare fares from the airlines as well as those from OTAs. Kayak features useful filter options, allowing you to search by a specific airline, alliance, aircraft, or by layover airports. It also has a calendar grid option that shows pricing up to three days before and after the dates you searched.
- **Momondo:** This tool is ideal for displaying airfares in visual form so that you can choose one based on flexible travel dates. You can also set up price alerts and receive advice on when to purchase based on recent fare trends.
- **Skyscanner:** This site allows you to enter your departure city and select "Explore everywhere" in the "To" field, then receive a list of available destinations ranked by price.
- **The Flight Deal alerts:** This is an X account (@theflightdeal) that allows you to receive real-time deal alerts without having to search for them yourself. This team finds deals, and you might be lucky enough to find one from your home airport.

Subscription Services

Another option is to pay for a subscription service that alerts you to the best deals. These sites scan for cheap deals and you can set parameters and alerts that work for your travel situation. Start by following these services on X, and if you like what you see, you can consider a subscription: Dollar Flight Club, Going (formerly Scott's Cheap Flights), and

Secret Flying. Check out chapter 7 for my favorite services to use for finding award deals.

Book at the Right Time and Do Your Research

Persistence will pay off. If you're impatient and want to book today, I can almost assure you that you're not going to get the best deal. Airlines capitalize on nervous travelers who need to book in advance and extract pain from last-minute bookers. The cheapest airfare is often somewhere in between. I recommend using the Goldilocks strategy for booking domestic travel, which means booking not too early, not too late, but at just the right time.

For domestic travel, book about six to eight weeks before departure, and for international three to six months in advance, on average (though more if you're traveling on peak periods, for special events, or on holidays).

Save Money After You Book a Flight

Even after you book, you should set an alert to see if the price drops. If so, many airlines will give you a voucher for the difference, and if the fare drops within 24 hours, you can cancel free of charge and rebook. Always check the fare for the flight you booked the next day, and if it dropped at all, rebook—you're already winning.

Always Book with a Travel Credit Card That Offers Protections

Most travel credit cards come with certain protections and insurance that can help if travel situations occur. Airlines are cheap when it comes to making things right when disruptions happen (and by law, they're only required to give you a refund if things go really badly), so book with a travel credit card that offers flight delay and cancellation coverage as well as delayed and lost luggage compensation.

Look at the Big Picture: Cheap Can Be Expensive

When making airfare purchases, look at the total costs, including fees for bags and seats, especially with low-cost carriers. You may end up paying way more at the end when you factor in all the fees. If you fly ultra-low-cost carriers such as Ryanair, you must know the rules and luggage requirements, as they aren't like most airlines. I once got charged nearly $200 for not checking in online early enough before a flight. I paid three times the cost of the ticket because I waited until three hours before departure to check in (at least I had a fun weekend in Edinburgh, Scotland, and I'm lucky I even made it to the airport). Some lessons are learned the hard way in travel. I will still fly with Ryanair because they have an incredible route network within Europe, but I just make sure to know all of the rules and I'll buy the more premium fares that have fewer restrictions.

Split Your Group

Airfare is sold in "buckets," which means there are a certain amount of tickets in each fare class. When one sells out, the next-highest-price fare is what is available. So when booking groups, search for the max group size to get the base price. For example, first do a search for four people, then a search for two or three. If it's all the same, it's usually easier to book a group reservation so everyone is on the same booking if a situation occurs and the airline rebooks you. But if there are only three cheap fares left, the airline will price your entire group fare for four at the higher fare. So buying three at the low fare and one at the higher fare can save you money.

Round Trip Versus One Way

Sometimes round trip is cheaper than one way—especially internationally. You can often save money by booking a return flight in the future that you may not even take (and if that flight time ends up changing enough, the airline may let you cancel and get a voucher for the difference).

But if the one-way ticket is half the price (or less) of the round-trip ticket, I prefer booking one-way flights. I do so because if I miss the first part of my round-trip flight, my return flight would be canceled automatically. If I had two one-way flights, my return flight would still be active.

If you're the type of person who changes flights often, booking one-way flights gives you more flexibility. If you change your outbound flight, the entire round-trip ticket reprices, meaning the cost could go up, because if you change the outbound flight to a round trip, the whole trip has to reprice and can often be higher. But if you book a one-way ticket, you only need to reprice that particular flight, which can end up being cheaper.

Positioning Flights

Airfare is generally priced between city pairs and the more wealthy those city pairs are, generally the more people will pay for tickets. For example, one of the most expensive airline routes in the world is New York to Hong Kong, which is $30,000 nonstop in first class. It connects two financial hubs filled with companies and wealthy people who will pay a premium to fly nonstop and not have to make an already-long trip more time-consuming with a layover. It can make sense to buy a cheap flight to get you to a major city to buy affordable airfare from there, which is called positioning (or repositioning) flights. One example: You buy a $100 ticket on Southwest from Oklahoma City to Los Angeles, and then you book Los Angeles to Tokyo for $800 round trip, instead of $1,800 if you booked Oklahoma City to Los Angeles to Tokyo (Southwest doesn't partner with other airlines, so you're paying a premium to book other airlines). Often, people from smaller cities have fewer airline options and competition, so fares can be higher, especially for international journeys.

Repositioning can even be done internationally. One friend of mine, Lays Laraya (@freakwentflyer), who's based in Dubai, loves doing this, especially when flying Emirates. She started repositioning internationally when she needed to take a trip to Geneva but round-trip tickets from Dubai to Geneva were $12,000. Then, a friend told her about flying out of Colombo, Sri Lanka, as it can be significantly cheaper to fly out of certain cities than others.

She checked, and a round-trip flight from Colombo to Geneva (via Dubai on the same Emirates flights that were $12,000) was just 25% of that: $3,000 round trip! She would need to pay $500 to get from Dubai to Colombo where she would start and end her journey. She bought a $500 round-trip flight from Dubai to Colombo. Then she bought the round-trip flight from Colombo to Dubai to Geneva for $3,000. All in she spent $3,500 and earned a large quantity of miles and elite status miles for future travel—all by buying a first class ticket with Colombo as her origin.

Colombo is among a list of other cities that generally offer very low fares, especially in business and first class. Others are Cairo, Karachi, Kathmandu, San Juan, and Johannesburg. However, if you do use repositioning as a trick for affordable flying, make sure you have the right visas to enter any country, even if you're just there on a layover. And, if you don't know how to even begin doing this, start with Google Flights, where you can input up to five origins to your chosen destination.

Book Early Flights to Avoid Delays

Book the earliest flight possible, because as the day goes on, the higher the chances are of your flight being delayed or canceled. Statistically, the earliest flights are less likely to face delays, and after 3 p.m. your flight is 50% more likely to be delayed or canceled. If inclement weather rolls in (often in the afternoon in the summertime or during snowy times of the year), delays start compounding, and your options for getting a flight out that day dwindle as there are fewer to choose from as the day goes on.

Pick Better Airlines

Here's another instance where cheap can be expensive. Not all airlines are equal. Give preference to airlines that have better reliability (time is money!). Delta often charges more, but the odds of you landing on time is greater on Delta than it is on JetBlue. So never forget to factor in reliability when choosing an airline, especially when you have multiple options and need to narrow the pack.

If you're interested in the top airline rankings, I recommend you read *The Points Guy*'s yearly top airline roundup, which takes fees, bumps, timeliness, affordability, baggage, and more into consideration. Delta was the top winner for the sixth year in a row in 2024, followed by Alaska and United.

Baggage Costs

Nearly all airlines will charge you for checked baggage unless you have elite status or their co-brand credit card. It's always smart to consider baggage costs when purchasing a ticket to account for the entire trip cost.

Let's take a look at how the price would compare between Spirit Airlines, which charges for both carry-on and checked bags, and Southwest, which doesn't charge for carry-ons and lets you check two bags for free. Pricing a flight from LaGuardia, New York, to Atlanta, Georgia, I found a round-trip flight on Spirit for $118.18 and a comparable flight for $169.95 on Southwest.

Spirit wins, right? That's just what Spirit wants you to believe, but unless you're traveling without any checked or even carry-on bags, Southwest will end up less expensive in the end. Spirit charges you upward of $79 for each checked or carry-on bag. And if you need to bring both, the added fees far exceed the cost of the ticket. So, Southwest wins on price if you need to check or carry on a bag. Plus, Southwest will offer you two checked bags, a free beverage, and far more legroom.

Understand Class Differences

Always research the aircraft before booking because not all airline economy, business, and first classes are the same. (Historically the site SeatGuru was the best for understanding where to sit on a plane, but it stopped updating in 2020. I recommend AeroLopa.com and SeatMaps.com as well as reading *The Points Guy* flight reviews where available.) Often, you'll see Icelandair business class as the cheapest going to Europe, and it's for a reason. It's basically premium economy: a recliner seat with little legroom compared to lie-flat beds on most other carriers. Meanwhile, intra-European business-class seats are usually the same as economy, with the middle seat blocked off, though this depends on the airline and route.

Basic Economy Versus Standard Economy

Nearly all airlines now sell basic economy tickets. And while the airlines like to say that these tickets offer travelers a less expensive option, these fares were introduced at the same price as before but with fewer options. Today, travelers have to pay up to enjoy the features offered by the standard fares.

While it varies by airline, a basic economy fare will typically lack a checked bag and a full-size carry-on, although a purse, backpack, or "personal item" that can fit under your seat is allowed. You'll also be missing out on seat assignments, frequent flyer miles, and the ability to change your ticket for a fee.

My advice: Avoid basic economy fares, unless you're sure that your plans are fixed and you can get by without a seat assignment or a carry-on bag. Otherwise, you'll end up paying the same or more as a standard economy ticket. But if you buy a basic economy fare for a flight operated by a regional jet, at least you won't have to worry about being assigned a middle seat, as these smaller planes don't have any.

Don't Book Tight Connections and Pad Your Dates

I suggest a minimum of two hours for domestic connections and three hours for international connections. Anything shorter, and you set yourself up for failure, especially if your flight is delayed. Even without cancellations and delays, getting through the airport to a different terminal or a far-off gate can be taxing, and you don't want to have to sprint to catch your next flight.

Even just half a day can make all the difference if you're dealing with a delay. If possible, make plans to arrive at least a day in advance, which can help mitigate the chances of missing your cruise ship departure, event, meeting, or beyond if delays or cancellations occur.

Book on an Airline with High Frequencies

Check how many flights the airline has on your route and choose the one with the most options in case yours gets canceled. This concept is especially reliable during bad weather months, like snowy or rainy times of the year, when weather delays are common.

You should also consider an airline that'll rebook you on a partner airline if there's a cancellation. Many low-cost carriers won't. You can check which US airlines rebook passengers on partner airlines using the US Department of Transportation's (DOT) Airline Customer Service Dashboard.[1] At the time of writing, all major US carriers will, except Allegiant, Frontier, Southwest, and Spirit.

You don't need to memorize every airline route out there, but it's always a good idea to see what other flights are available on the day of your departure in case your flight were to get canceled.

This is where I would pull up Google Flights and put in the route to see if there are seats available on other airlines. Just note that within two hours of departure, some flights won't show as available for sale, so this is when you should check at the airline counter.

Make Sure the Airline Knows How to Contact You

Always make sure the airline has your correct email address and phone number so that they can contact you if there's a flight change. If you book through an OTA, this information often doesn't get passed on, and people show up for flights that may have been canceled long ago.

Check your reservation after booking to make sure your frequent flyer mile number is there, pick seats (or check that they've been assigned), and confirm luggage requirements and allowances. This is especially important for codeshare tickets when booking through OTAs or using partner airlines. It's also key when traveling with a lap infant—they should still always have a ticket number for international flights. Call the airline if they don't have a ticket number because it'll be a hassle if you try to do it at an airport, especially if you're traveling from a small airport and not a major hub. Sometimes, an airline will add your child but not ticket them, and you may be rejected during boarding or have to call the airline to fix it. I recommend checking 30 days, one week, and one day prior to your flight to ensure they haven't changed the aircraft type (and your seats). Doing this on the day of departure is stressful, but confirming in advance means you'll be set. If you do notice a schedule change, you might be able to switch your flight to a better one for free.

Booking Hotels: Tricks, Tips, and Ways to Save

Booking a hotel is significantly easier than purchasing airfare, but you're still faced with the same choices. You can book a stay directly with the hotel, go through an independent online travel agency, or use your credit card issuer's travel portal. Just remember when comparison shopping to compare oranges to oranges. If booking directly is slightly more but gives you free breakfast, consider the advantages and do the calculations to see if you're saving by booking via an OTA, forgoing hotel points and elite status recognition. In general I try to book direct or via a luxury travel advisor. If an OTA has the best price I call the hotel and see if they'll beat it (which they often can).

Free Cancellation Versus Nonrefundable

One of the biggest things to consider is whether to book a stay you can cancel for free or one that's nonrefundable. I think it's worth the money to consider the free cancellation, as you never know what could happen. Plus, hotels sometimes do get cheaper as your stay approaches, so it's nice to have the ability to cancel and rebook for a lower price or just cancel if your plans change. Weigh the probability of your trip going through with the price it costs to book a cancelable rate. It can often be cheaper to buy a nonrefundable rate and buy travel insurance that will reimburse you if you need to cancel or change the trip.

Booking Directly Versus Using OTAs

When it comes to hotels, I believe the best choice is booking directly. This way, you'll earn points or miles and your elite status (if you hold it) is recognized. These days, you won't earn points or miles or have your elite status recognized (in most cases) if you book a hotel through an OTA.

Shawn Newman, a hotel front office manager who has worked for Marriott, Hyatt, and Hilton, told me that the best way to get upgraded at hotels is elite status. "The best way to get upgraded is by rewards status—the highest loyalty is the first option. We would usually do the next room type further for elite status. If there are no higher elite members, we would then upgrade the highest-cash-value-paying guest. Complimentary up-grades are always based on availability on the day of arrival, or we can guarantee an upgrade prior to arrival for a fee. If you are nice and polite, we'll usually attempt to give you a better view," he said.

Having hotel elite status is worth it for upgrades and other perks, and in many cases, booking through hotel programs is the only way it'll be recognized, so skip the OTAs and book directly if you hold a high elite status and are hoping for an upgrade.

Booking your hotel stays through an OTA can sometimes make sense when you get a good package that also includes airfare and a rental car or transfer. Or, it could make sense if you get significant savings for booking a hotel that's not part of a loyalty program. If you do go that route, you might as well take advantage of the OTA's loyalty program, if there is one.

When to Book Hotels Through Credit Card Travel Portals

There are two main ways to book hotels through major credit card portals. There are the general portals (American Express Travel, Chase Travel, and Capital One Travel), where the booking is treated like a normal OTA booking, meaning you won't earn points in the hotel loyalty program or expect to get hotel elite status perks (you will earn credit card points for booking through the portal). Still, it's worth adding your hotel loyalty number to the reservation because it never hurts to try! However, some credit card portals have luxury hotel collections, where premium cardholders get elevated perks at top-notch hotels, such as American Express Fine Hotels.

In these hotels, you'll usually earn points through the hotel loyalty program, get hotel elite status perks, and any additional perks that the program offers, such as room upgrades, late checkout, early check-in, free breakfasts, or hotel credits. And in many cases, you can still earn credit toward elite status. American Express even offers Platinum card-holders a $200 statement credit toward prepaid stays of two nights or more. Amex also offers another hotel collection that's available to Gold card members: The Hotel Collection.

Chase Sapphire Reserve, JPMorgan Reserve, and Chase United card members are eligible for similar benefits through its luxury hotel collection, The Edit, and Capital One offers similar benefits at hotels and vacation rentals that you book through its Premier Collection.

And just as with airfare, you can earn a lot of points by booking your hotel through your card issuer's travel portal. Cardholders can earn 5X points from prepaid hotels booked through Amex Travel using their Platinum cards, and a remarkable 10X from the Capital One Venture X when you book hotels through Capital One Travel. Capital One Venture X cardholders get an annual $300 credit toward Capital One Travel bookings.

Travel Advisors and Agencies: Should You Use Them?

Travel advisors can be particularly helpful when booking hotels, cruises, and tours, especially for complicated destinations that require insider knowledge or group trips. They often have relationships with hotels and can give you access to special discounts as well as valuable perks that can make your trip more enjoyable, such as early check-in, late checkout, free breakfast, upgrades, and other amenities.

Booking through certain luxury travel advisors, such as Hyatt Privé, can offer you select hotel benefits. Since these advisors have special relationships with Hyatt, you'll get special discounts, free nights, and perks.

Where travel advisors shine is helping you if your trip doesn't go as planned. During COVID I used travel advisors because it was almost impossible to get through to airlines. When booking through a travel advisor, you can tell them what changes you want to make and then they handle doing it with the airline and can often make many changes themselves. If you value time and want expert advice on how to plan a trip, travel advisors can be worth every penny (and often you don't have to pay them as they get a commission on most of your bookings). Advisors can do so much more than booking hotels, as they can set up VIP airport arrival, transportation options, and special experiences that aren't usually available to the public.

How do you find an amazing travel planner? Wendy Perrin, one of the top travel journalists who used to work at *Condé Nast Traveler*, curates a list of top planners: the WOW List (www.wendyperrin.com/wow-list/). These are vetted top-tier planners who are best suited for luxury trips. For African safaris I personally recommend ROAR Africa (www.roarafrica .com), as they have inside contacts at all of the major lodges and have helped me plan some of my best trips to the continent. Every safari camp is different, so having an advisor who has personally been to these lodges can help you narrow down your options.

Hotel Promotions, Discounts, and Packages

Double-check to see if your preferred airline offers a package with air and hotel together, which can also help you earn additional miles and credit toward elite status. Many hotels offer sales and promotions when booking directly, which include a free night, discounted rates, or points bonuses for stays. Hotels frequently offer packages that can include amenities such as parking, breakfast, and on-site credits, for less than you would have otherwise paid.

Likewise, AARP, AAA, and FoundersCard all offer discounts on hotels. I'm also a member of the American Bar Association ($150 per year), which offers amazing hotel discounts. The Ritz-Carlton Chicago was charging $563 a night for a flexible rate over Memorial Day week-end last year and $444 for a nonrefundable rate. The ABA rate was $375 a night and refundable up until the day before. And, you usually earn points on ABA bookings if you make them directly through ho-tels. They also offer car rental deals. Note that you have to pay for the membership to access the deals, but just staying a few nights could easily save you well over the membership fee.

When it comes to corporate codes, you'll often be asked for ID, so it's best to only use these if you have proof. In most cases, you can use your corporate codes for a personal stay, assuming you have proof to show if asked.

If you have a group or extended stay, call the hotel. You may get a discounted rate. Just make sure that you're speaking with a front desk manager or supervisor with the ability to grant your request.

You can also submit claims for hotels that offer a "Best Rate Guarantee," which is a promise that you'll get the lowest rate by booking directly. If you find a lower rate, hotels such as Marriott, Hyatt, Hilton, Wyndham, and IHG will price match or offer you a discount, perks, or points.

In most cases, you'll have to submit your claim within 24 hours of making the reservation with the hotel, and the competitor rate has to be available publicly, as well as other requirements, like the dates, room type, and rate type have to be the same. The cancellation policies must also match, and don't expect the hotel to honor a claim matching special rates such as AAA or AARP.

If your claim is successful, you could receive valuable discounts or other compensation, depending on the chain. Here's a brief rundown of what's offered:

- **IHG:** Will match the lower rate and offer you 5X points with a 40,000-point maximum.
- **Hyatt:** Your choice of either an additional 20% off the lower rate or 5,000 bonus points.
- **Hilton:** 25% discount off the lower rate.
- **Marriott:** Your choice of either up to 25% off the lower rate or 5,000 bonus points.
- **Wyndham:** Will match the lower rate and offer you 3,000 bonus points.

Booking Car Rentals: Tricks, Tips, and Ways to Save

After airfare and hotels, car rentals are the next place to save money on travel. A good place to start researching is AutoSlash, which compares prices from all of the major rental car companies. One of the best features is that you'll be alerted if the price of your rental car goes down so you can rebook it and save money for the same exact rental.

Online Travel Agency Versus Credit Card Portals Versus Direct Bookings

Similar to booking flights and hotels, it's best to use OTAs for research but book directly for ease. I tend to avoid booking cars using points through the credit card issuer's travel sites. Redeeming points isn't ideal because you may not get the insurance protection that comes with paying for your rental on a credit card with auto rental protections.

Join the Loyalty Program

You should always sign up for your rental car company's frequent renter program, both to receive upgrades and to earn credits toward free rentals. These programs allow you to add your credit card and driver's license to your reservation and skip the lines at the counter. Booking directly is especially important if you hold elite status with the rental company, which you can often get on a variety of credit cards. Status gives you discounts and perks and will result in a quicker, more hassle-free rental experience at the airport or otherwise.

Use the Right Credit Card

Besides using a credit card that offers bonus points on car rentals (or general travel), make sure the card you use offers car rental insurance, such as collision damage waiver coverage. The gold standard is called primary coverage, which means that you don't have to involve your personal automotive insurer if you have one. The Chase Sapphire Preferred and Sapphire Reserve have primary Auto Rental Coverage for theft and collision damage, as do Chase's United MileagePlus Explorer, Quest and Club cards, Ink, and all Chase-issued business cards (when renting for business purposes), along with the Capital One Venture X.

Another option is the American Express Premium Rental Car Protection program. Once enrolled, you are automatically charged $19.95 or $24.95 per rental. Since it's not a daily charge, it's ideal for longer rentals, and the quality of the coverage makes it a great choice when you rent an expensive car or are renting in a place where damage seems more likely.

Just note that it's not valid in Australia, Ireland, Israel, Italy, Jamaica, and New Zealand due to quirks in these countries' insurance laws.

At the very least, make sure you use a card that offers rental car coverage, even if it's secondary. Secondary coverage is the same as primary if you don't own a car or are renting outside of the US, where your personal policy won't cover you anyway. Most card issuers will offer this coverage, but you should always verify. Discover and Citi are notable exceptions, as these issuers have removed nearly all of their travel and purchase protection benefits, including rental car coverage from many of their credit cards.

Promotions, Discounts, and Packages

As with booking a hotel room, search for discount codes from your company or any organizations to which you belong. If you, your spouse, your partner, or anyone you're traveling with is employed by a government agency or a large company, there's a good chance it has negotiated rates with the major rental car companies. These codes may be valid for leisure use, or there may be no policy preventing you from using them for personal travel. And when you skip the counter, as you always will when you're a member of the company's frequent renter program, it's rare that anyone will ever ask you for proof of employment, let alone anything to document that you're not using it for leisure.

Other sources of discount codes can be personal or professional organizations, as well as discount clubs such as AAA, AARP, Costco, and Sam's Club. Current and former members of the armed services can also qualify for substantial discounts.

I mentioned the savings you'll find with vacation packages offered by airlines or travel agents. These packages can include combinations of airfare, hotels, rental cars, transfers, and activities. They can save you money or not, but the math is pretty simple. The packages can make it faster and easier to book your vacation, but as with any travel agency booking, you may not get the support you need if there's a problem. And you may not get the points and miles you would have if you had bought each piece from the travel provider.

Many people swear by booking vacation packages, which include car rental as well as flights and hotels, through Costco. You can find some incredible savings here, but I only recommend doing it when booking hotels that aren't members of loyalty programs, and only if it nets you significant savings. Keep an eye out for blackout dates and minimum stay requirements.

Chapter 5

What Are Points and Miles?

What are points and miles? They're *currencies*. Unlike the currencies created by governments or blockchains, points and miles are created by companies such as airlines, hotel chains, or credit card issuers. Some of these currencies you earn by flying, staying in hotels, and spending on a credit card. Each currency has a set of rules on how it can be earned and redeemed. Understanding the underlying economics of the travel industry will help you understand the system and how to best use it to your advantage. So many people underestimate loyalty or feel that "the good days are over." That mindset is self-sabotaging and not true. These days, airlines are banks, and their data doesn't lie:

- More revenue from travel than ever is attributed to loyalty.
- More online bookings are direct via loyalty.
- More travel brands are penalizing those who don't play in their ecosystem.

You might have been okay until now, ignoring the points and miles world or living "just fine" with your debit card. It might have seemed worthless or you stopped traveling, so you don't care as much.

But as you'll find out in the coming chapters, loyalty is less about travel and more about personal finance and harnessing the power of your spending. Even if you don't want to travel, the tips you'll learn can save you money that you can then invest and build a stronger financial future or save for your children's education (or pay off those student loans).

Points are real, nonliquid assets. While the IRS doesn't generally consider points as income and won't tax you on them (in most cases), points are an extremely worthwhile currency. Yet, it's challenging to assign an amount of value. It's not a one-size-fits-all process. Perhaps you haven't given them much thought because you don't realize how valuable they can be, and the process of figuring out how they can be valuable to you takes time and education, which is a deterrent for many.

Points and miles are a currency that you can collect for doing the most basic parts of life, such as eating, shopping, and even paying your rent. Choosing to participate in this ecosystem is becoming increasingly easier with technology, and you've come this far by reading this book, so let's get into the evolution of the loyalty world so you can maximize it for your own benefit, starting today.

Points are a point of contention in the court of law, especially when it comes to divorce settlements. "Points are considered nonliquid assets. But there's nothing quite like points. They're unique because they're not necessarily transferable in the same ways money is. And you can't kind of pick up a piece of furniture or sell a house and [always] give somebody half. The valuation issue can be really complicated," said Bonnie Rabin, a prominent New York City family law attorney. She suggests including your own points on your prenup, then getting a joint credit card to accrue points together during a marriage—those points will be joint property. According to Rabin, "Frequent flyer miles are a valuable asset." This is true, and even holds up in a court of law. Points are unique assets that are difficult to transfer, even in death.

When you die, technically most of your points will as well, unless you pass along your account credentials to your loved ones who can then log in and redeem all of your remaining points without having to go through paperwork with the airline. Just remember to also include your email and phone passwords in case any of your accounts have two-factor authorization. I highly recommend that everyone include their loyalty account passwords in their wills so their next of kin can login and use those points. However, assigning an actual value to points is tough for everyone in many contexts, from planning travel at home all the way to divorce court.

While they're valuable, it's difficult to determine a value, and just like any currency, the value fluctuates (though I'll try to give you some valuation examples in the earning and redeeming chapters). Winning at travel has a lot to do with understanding the core concepts of how to value your points and what they mean to you.

Once you cross a certain knowledge threshold, your mentality of "Ugh, this is too complicated and hard" will shift into "Wow, I can't believe I haven't been doing this my whole life." I also don't look at this as "Oh, it's too much work"—I think of it like a game. Some people get great satisfaction out of crossword puzzles or a sudoku; I get mine from cracking the points and miles code and booking incredible travel for a fraction of the price.

Some people thrive on bragging rights, but I thrive on extracting as much value as possible out of the airlines and credit card companies.

Just like anything in life, there are plenty of ways you can take this craft to the extreme, but just know that the loyalty industry has invested heavily in technology that can find the customers who are a net negative to the program, and it's within their right to ban you from doing business with them. Whether that's an airline or a credit card company, I don't recommend testing those limits. It's best to take a slow, measured approach when it comes to points and miles.

What Shouldn't You Do?

- Sell your points and miles.
- Manipulate credit card application links to get offers you're not supposed to get.
- Anything that involves buying items and returning them in hopes of getting "free" points.
- Anything that could create red flags that you are money laundering, such as buying the cash equivalent gift cards and liquidating them into other forms.
- Complain about frivolous issues in hopes of scoring compensation.

- Charge credit cards and default on payments. Make sure to always pay minimums.

In general, it's best to earn rewards in programs that are generous in how they dole out points and miles but are also as flexible and generous with how you can redeem your rewards, offering you as many options as possible. To help readers figure out which points and miles deliver the most value, *The Points Guy* publishes a monthly guide to how much each currency is valued compared to the dollar, just like a foreign currency.

We can all create our own portfolios of points and miles that best serve our needs, and your strategy will likely evolve over time. Advanced points and miles enthusiasts will frequently update their strategies, whether by adding new credit cards, signing up for new promotions, or deciding to switch airline or hotel loyalty. People always ask me which credit card, airline, or hotel program is the best. There isn't one best program for everyone; it's highly personal.

This chapter will teach you the fundamentals of how to assess a loyalty program's earn-and-burn ratios so you can assemble your own strategy that will provide long-term value and flexibility.

My 10 Points Commandments

These are some of my key ground rules for the points game, which have guided me through earning and redeeming points and miles, reaching elite status, and generally helping me grow into the traveler I am today.

1. **Try to accrue points at no additional cost to you.** Avoid paying fees to earn points and by all means avoid any interest or late fees as they will negate the value of any points earned.

2. **Aim to earn more than 1 point per dollar spent.** There are many ways you can double and triple dip earning of points for a single purchase, so try not to leave free points on the table.

3. **Points are more valuable when you are flexible with where and when you want to travel.** When possible, be flexible with your dates,

destinations, and overall goals and let deals guide where you go. The more money you can avoid paying to get to a destination, the more you can spend on the things you love while there.

4. **Don't hoard points! Use them.** Save your hard-earned cash for activities and experiences, and use points and miles for flights and hotels.

5. **It never hurts to ask.** Program rules are often more flexible than they're written and if you're nice to an agent, they can often make exceptions. Don't expect them, but ask nicely and you never know what might be possible.

6. **Remain cool under pressure.** We often resort to panic buying. Even when deals or changes come, stay calm and think. If something goes wrong, think of it as an opportunity to obtain something even better.

7. **See travel "problems" as opportunities.** Turn changes and cancellations into situations that get you a more favorable outcome. Recently, an Air France award cancellation threw a big wrench in my travel plans just as I was getting into the taxi to head to the airport. I turned around, headed right back inside the hotel, and took out my phone and computer to troubleshoot. I ended up with an even better deal (and cash compensation from EU261): a nonstop flight on Emirates, which saved me time and earned me miles.

8. **Leverage technology and resources.** No human can know how to do it all, so don't try to be a superhero. Use the apps and tools that I provide in this book. If it all seems complex—it is! But I assure you, once you get the hang of maximizing points and miles, you'll wish you'd have known all this sooner.

9. **The pursuit of perfection is your enemy.** Stop trying to maximize travel and points to the point that you may end up losing out. Maybe you waited so long to use your points that they expired or were devalued. Perhaps you sat too long pondering if a deal would work, and then the award availability disappeared. Maybe an iconic trip you organized didn't turn out as planned, or you ended up downgraded due to an aircraft change. You won't win them all, and that's okay. Don't let small issues ruin a trip.

10. **Go with the flow and embrace change.** It may be the beginning, an opportunity to try something new. If a frequent flyer program has devalued its rewards, your favorite hotel program merged, or you were denied for a credit card, it's okay. You'll figure out a new way to play the points game. Only you can decide your own points and miles strategy and what winning at travel means to you. Your definition will change over time as your life changes and flows. Tune out what others are doing and focus on your personal happiness. If you're happy with your travel style, how you earn and burn points, and the airlines and hotels you choose, that's all that matters.

Chapter 6

How to Win at Earning Rewards

Winning at rewards means having a strong foundation and a constant influx of earning points to fund your travels (and life) for years to come.

Some people collect watches. Some collect stamps. I collect points, and unlike most hobbies that cost a lot of time and money, mine pays *me*. Not only that, but it has improved my credit score, I can do it from home, and it was free to start. It's allowed me to visit over 80 countries, mostly in first class, for a mere fraction of the cost. How many other hobbies can claim those benefits?

In addition to deeply discounted vacations, I also view my rewards portfolio as an insurance policy. It's empowering to know that on a minute's notice, I can get anywhere in the world inexpensively.

The ability to earn rewards is simple, as it's built into everything we do, such as trips to the grocery store, flying to visit family, or shopping online. You can earn rewards for all of these things while paying the same price—all it takes is a little extra knowledge and an additional click or two. There's no other country in the world where this works as well as it does in the United States. But for my readers outside of the US, don't worry—you can make it work for you, too.

By the end of this chapter, you'll be able to identify where you've been missing out and how to maximize your spending on everyday purchases so your earning potential will skyrocket.

The Three Core Concepts for Earning Rewards

1. Create a credit card strategy that works for you and creates a sustainable flow of rewards that can allow you to take more trips for less cash.

2. Don't overlook the non-credit-card ways to earn rewards, including shopping portals, partnerships, and promotions. By maximizing all channels, you can often earn multiple currencies for every purchase, increasing your net rewards income.

3. While earning miles and points for free is ideal, buying miles and points can still create opportunities to travel at a fraction of the cost, especially for those who like to fly first and business class and stay in luxury hotels.

Perhaps what I love most about points and miles is that you can often earn them without having to pay for them. They're frequently built into the cost of goods, whether that's an airline ticket or buying groceries with a points-earning credit card, and you'll earn them with no extra fee, so choosing not to collect them is like having cash in your hand and deciding to throw it away.

And perhaps the magic of many rewards currencies is that they can grow in value the more you increase your knowledge of them. Most fiat or cryptocurrencies fluctuate in value based on market forces outside of our control, but the rewards that you have in your airline, hotel, and credit card accounts may increase in value due to your ability to educate yourself on how you should best redeem them.

The Points-Earning Hierarchy

There are many ways to earn points and miles, and some are easier than others. One way to think about it is as a hierarchy, with the easiest and most valuable ways at the base and the harder and less common ways at the top.

The Strong Foundation: Credit Cards

Credit cards are the quickest and cheapest way to accrue miles and points—at least in the US, where 99% of merchants accept credit cards as payment, and a vast majority of those merchants don't assess a fee for using credit cards (though it's becoming more common).

Credit cards are a part of being American. The average American has 3.84 credit cards, but the average person in Germany doesn't have a credit card—the most popular way there to pay for online purchases is PayPal, followed by direct debit, and then credit cards. Why are Americans obsessed with credit? The obvious answer might be that we are a materialistic and capitalistic society that's obsessed with competing with our neighbors, and social media means "the neighbors" are everyone on the internet. Although there's a certain truth to that, the real reason Americans love credit is due to something called interchange.

The interchange fee is the amount a merchant pays to process a credit card transaction. On average, that amount is just under 2%, with a small portion of that fee kept by the credit card network (Visa, Mastercard, Discover, American Express) and the majority passed along to the bank that issues the credit card.

The bank then kicks back a portion of the interchange fee to the consumer in the form of rewards, whether that's in a loyalty currency (like airline miles) or cashback. Interchange is one of the major ways banks make money from credit cards and use it to fund valuable rewards and promotions to incentivize consumers to spend. On average, interchange is higher in the US, meaning that banks can give more rewards to consumers for each purchase. The other ways they make money on credit cards are the interest paid on balances and annual and late payment fees.

How to Make Credit Cards Work for You: Start and Stay Debt-Free

To win at credit cards, it's essential to pay your credit card bills in full every month so that you never pay any interest. If your credit card interest rate is high, the rewards you earn will be negated in value if you pay interest to receive them. You lose at rewards when you pay interest.

If you carry a balance of $5,000 at 28% APY, you'll incur interest charges of about $116 *a month*. If you earned one point per dollar spent, even at 2% back, you'd only earn rewards worth $100. So you're already losing on month one and getting clobbered with fees if you let that balance revolve any longer, as the balance and interest will compound.

You should always pay your balance in full and on time to avoid interest charges and late fees. In a worst-case scenario where you can't pay the full bill, at least pay the minimum and as much of the balance as possible to limit your interest. If you don't pay it at all, not only will you get hit with fees, but your credit will take a hit, and you should do everything possible to keep your credit in good shape. Before you start opening up credit cards to earn points and miles, agree to the following:

1. I won't make purchases I can't afford for the sake of earning points.
2. I have the money available now to pay for any charges I make.
3. I'll pay my balance in full to avoid interest.
4. I won't use the spending power of credit cards to incur debt.

Be disciplined with your spending and maniacal on your bills and balances (the second you get a credit card, set up auto-pay, at least for the minimum payment due), and you'll have the keys to the kingdom of a lucrative side hustle of credit card points.

If you don't have any rewards cards today, you've lost out on a lot of value over the years, but look on the bright side—you have so many options to choose from. And contrary to what most people think, your credit score will increase long-term as you get new credit cards and pay off the balances on time and in full each month.

Understanding Your Credit Score: Key Definitions

Credit Score: In the US, a credit score is a number between 280 and 850 that's designed to predict whether or not you'll repay a loan. There are two main types of credit scores FICO (Fair Isaac Corporation) and VantageScore. A score between 800 and 850 is excellent, a score between 740 and 799 is very good, 670–739 is good, 580–669 is fair, and anything below 580 is poor.

Credit Reporting Agencies: There are three credit reporting agencies that companies such as credit card companies, cell phone providers, and hospitals use to report debts owed to them: Experian, TransUnion, and Equifax. Not all lenders report to each, which is why your scores with each will vary.

Each collects similar data, but there are key differences. Experian is the only bureau that collects landlord data. Equifax has its own credit scoring model that is 280–850 (vs. 300 with the others). Basically, all three are similar, so getting your free score from each will give you a good sense of what most lenders are probably seeing when they pull your report (since you rarely know which bureau they'll use).

Credit card companies pay them each time they pull someone's score and feed them into their own proprietary underwriting analysis to decide whether to give you credit, and if so, how much. There are scenarios where even if you have a near perfect score, you might still get denied for credit, like if you've applied for too many credit cards lately or have maxed out on the total number of credit cards that bank is willing to give you.

How to Check Your Credit Score

Before you start applying for cards, check your credit score to get a baseline reading. I recommend visiting AnnualCreditReport.com, which pulls in data from the three major consumer credit bureaus. This service is free. Just watch out for scam sites that'll ask you to pay to access your credit report. You can also get free credit reports from credit card companies (sometimes even if you're not a cardholder).

The following companies offer free FICO scores: American Express, Bank of America, Barclaycard, Citi, Discover, and Wells Fargo. Capital One, Chase, and US Bank offer free VantageScores.

Credit Cards and Your Credit Score

Your credit score is the most important (but not the only) factor credit card companies use to determine whether or not you'll be approved for a credit card. FICO, which is pulled for 90% of credit applications, states what goes into your credit score:

- 35% payment history: Do you pay your bills on time?
- 30% amounts owed: Better known as utilization, the bureaus look at all of the credit made available to you and see how much of that you're using. They reward people who pay off their balances in full because if you have a large amount of credit available to you and

you're only using a small portion, it shows that you are responsible. What they're trying to assess are people who will be responsible with credit and not those who are on the path to bankruptcy and might be compelled to run up huge balances before declaring bankruptcy. In general, the more available credit you have and the less you use, the more your score will benefit.

- 15% length of credit history: The longer you have a credit file the better, so it's never too late to start.
- 10% new credit
- 10% credit mix

VantageScore has similar metrics but with different percentages:

- Payment history: 41%
- Depth of credit: 20%
- Credit utilization: 20%
- Recent credit: 11%
- Balances: 6%
- Available credit: 2%

You'll often see in your credit card accounts free access to your credit score and on any given day, these scores can vary. Not only because some are FICO and some Vantage, but each credit card company uses different credit reporting agencies for different reports and some will pull balances on different days. There are also different models of VantageScore, some lenders use the 3.0, which is from 2016 and prior and some use 4.0, which is from 2017 and onward. But generally, you'll get a sense of what lenders see, and if you ever see any inaccuracies reported on your account, take action to remove them as soon as possible.

What Credit Score Do You Need to Get Approved for a Credit Card?

For most credit cards, you'll want to have a score of 680 or higher. However, there are certainly people who have been approved with lower scores. If you have a thin credit file, I recommend starting with more beginner, no-annual-fee cashback cards. If your score is lower than 680, you may want to focus on building your credit score, which can be done with the right approach.

How to Build and Improve Your Credit Score
Fix Negative Items on Your Credit Report

If you notice negative items on your credit score, the first thing you should do is try to correct or rectify them with the lender. Most lenders won't report late payments right away, so if you ever realize you missed a payment, always ask to have them not report it and also ask them to reinstate any points you may have forfeited due to the late payment. If it's your first time, many will waive any fees or penalties. The sooner you catch the mistake, the better.

If you have negative items from the past, you can try to ask for something called forbearance, asking the card issuer or other creditor to remove your late payment history. This works best when you've suffered from circumstances outside of your control, such as a serious illness or being part of a disaster.

If they refuse, you can dispute items on your credit report, and the lender then has to prove that they're accurate (and many won't, especially for older debts, since it takes time to do this and they may have written off the debt). It never hurts to dispute items since it is easy and free to do online.

There are also credit repair companies out there that are as sophisticated at helping improve your credit as points and miles people are at earning free travel. Just be careful because there are predatory companies out there that will promise the world, but they have the same tools as you to fix your credit, so I would only recommend using them once you've exhausted all available resources.

Decrease Your Debt

"Amounts owed" is the second biggest factor of your credit score, so getting that balance down as much as possible will directly correlate with your credit score increasing.

Even if you pay your bills in full every month, the way credit card reporting agencies work is that they pull balances at random times throughout the month, so even if you pay on your due date, they can pull your balances the day prior, and it will look like you are using more of your available credit and your score will go down. So if you're about to apply for a mortgage, I recommend paying all of your bills off in advance of their due date and making sure your balances are near zero so that when your credit is reported, your balances are low. If your utilization is low, your credit score should increase.

The more available credit you have helps by increasing your total amount of credit extended, so you'll lower your ratio of debt to credit.

If you're currently paying high interest on a credit card, you might want to consider a balance transfer to a credit card with a 0% intro APR rate, sometimes as long as 18 months or even longer. This can save thousands of dollars in interest that you can then instead use to pay off the principal.

Consider Adding an Authorized User

Adding someone as an authorized user to your credit card has its pros and cons. The cons are that you're responsible for whatever is spent on that card, so only add an authorized user that you trust (and also make sure you set their spend limit to something you're okay with).

If you add an authorized user to your card, your positive credit history with that card will, in most cases, transfer over to the authorized user. This is especially helpful for young people with limited credit histories, but just note that most credit card companies won't report the card to credit agencies until the authorized user is of a certain age, usually between 15 and 18. But this is an excellent way to help teens get started on building solid credit habits and a lucrative financial future.

Get a Secured Credit Card

If your credit is too new or has blemishes, get a secured credit card, where you will have to prepay your credit line in the form of a cash deposit. Then, make sure to pay it off in full every month, and it will increase your score over time. Just make sure your chosen secured credit card reports monthly to the major credit bureaus, as some don't. Once your score is high enough to get a rewards credit card, you can stop using the secured card since the rewards one will accomplish the same mission and earn you rewards.

Get a Personal or Credit-Builder Loan
Many banks will give small loans to help creditors build credit. There are high fees associated, so I would only recommend this if the other options don't work fast enough, but this can add a mix to your credit portfolio and more on-time payments to your score, which we know is the top factor of your FICO score.

Getting Started with Credit Cards
Here I'll debunk (or validate) some myths about credit cards:

- **Having too many credit cards will hurt your credit score.** While it's true that when you apply for a new credit line, there will usually be a two-to-five-point decrease in your score, that temporary drop is counterbalanced by the fact that the new credit line will increase your total credit. When your debt-to-credit ratio (amounts owed) is 30% of your score, as long as you pay on time your score will continue to rise. Those two factors are 65% of your score, while new credit is only 10%.
- **Credit is the devil.** Many financial experts rail against credit. It's bad financial practice to give one-size-fits-all advice, especially when it comes to personal finance. I would agree credit can be bad for consumers who don't know how to manage it, but for the millions of people who do, I think that *not* using credit cards is financial mispractice. Not just because you're losing real value on forgoing rewards, but you're also giving up free float from the bank (you can keep your cash in an interest-earning account and wait to pay off a balance until it's due, which is often up to 60 days from the purchase) as well as getting a host of valuable protections. Imagine

getting defrauded from a vacation rental where you paid in wire, and you show up, and the home doesn't exist. Who would you turn to for help? Your bank will tell you they warned you about wire fraud. But if that charge were on a credit card, you could reverse it from your account almost immediately.

- **Checking your credit will hurt your score.** False. Only applying for new credit lines will incur a temporary two-to-five-point drop.
- **Getting declined for a credit card will hurt your score.** This is somewhat true but technically false. It isn't getting declined that harms your score, it's applying for credit that causes a temporary two-to-five-point ding on your score. So whether you get approved or declined, the impact is the same.
- **There are certain times you shouldn't apply for a credit card.** This one is true. I don't recommend applying for new cards if you're applying for a loan, specifically a mortgage. Recent inquiries can raise red flags, so always wait for a mortgage to close before applying for cards (unless you can confirm with your mortgage broker that a new credit application won't impact your mortgage).

Debit Cards

Due to legislation that US Congress passed in 2012, most banks stopped offering rewards on debit cards. Over the last several years many rewards debit cards have popped up, like the PayPal debit card that offers rotating cashback categories. You can get a Membership Rewards–earning debit card with an Amex Rewards Checking Account. American Express also offers a business debit card that earns 1 Membership Rewards point for every two dollars in eligible purchases. If you're going to use a debit card, you might as well get one with rewards, though just beware of any banking requirements and avoid paying annual or monthly fees.

The Lucrative World of Rewards Credit Cards

There are three main types of rewards credit cards: cashback, co-brand, and transferable bank rewards. Each type of card has its pros and cons based on the type of rewards you want to earn and how you want to travel.

Cashback

As the name implies, you earn rewards that are a cash rebate based on the amount of money you spend. Within cashback, you have two main types:

- **Fixed cashback:** This is a fixed amount of cashback you earn on all purchases, usually between 1 and 2%. This type of card is for people who don't want to bother with using different credit cards for different purchases and want a simple earning structure. Over the last decade, the earnings on these cards has increased, with several no-annual-fee options offering a 2% return. Some even offer 0% APR on balance transfers, so if you're focused on paying off debt to improve your credit score, it might make sense to switch to a 2% cashback card with a 0% APR so you save massively on the interest you would have paid and also earn rich rewards on the spending that you can then use to directly pay off your balance (just know you may have to pay a balance transfer fee to do this). Some examples are the Citi Double Cash, Chase Freedom Unlimited, and the Capital One Quicksilver. Online brokerage Robinhood just launched an industry-leading 3% cashback on all purchases for their Robinhood Gold ($50/year) members. Time will tell if they are able to sustain that lucrative level of rewards, but it launched in 2024 and is the most notable new entry in the cashback credit card space.

- **Rotating category cashback cards:** There are many cashback cards that will offer lower base earnings of 1–1.5% but bonus categories (like 3–5% on restaurants or drugstores) or rotating quarterly categories that change. Depending on how much you spend on these special categories, you might be able to get even more than 2% back, but it takes work. Some examples are the Chase Freedom Flex and Discover it. Some cashback credit cards like Chase Freedom cards have a special perk: that the cashback "points" you earn can be transferred to valuable airline and hotel transfer partners if you have one of their more premium cards, such as the Sapphire Preferred or Reserve and certain Ink business cards. So, for anyone who wants the option to turn cashback rewards into valuable transferable rewards, it might make sense to earn a little less but have more flexibility with being able to transfer them if you have another credit card that allows transfers (more on transfer programs later in this chapter).

Pros of cashback cards: For those who don't want to travel, the most flexible rewards currency is cash. Even for those who do want to travel, earning 2% back might be more lucrative than earning travel currencies (airline miles or hotel points) that have seen steady devaluations as airlines and hotels make them more expensive to redeem.

Cons of cashback cards: Small-to-nonexistent sign-up bonuses, the inability to transfer to airline and hotel partners to get even more value, and limited perks. What you see is what you get, so there isn't much aspirational upside to these programs, but they are consistent and deliver a currency accepted pretty much everywhere, and that can be used to buy travel or pay off debt.

Tip: Some banks such as Bank of America will give a bonus on cashback to those with a certain amount of assets at the bank. An example is the Bank of America Preferred Rewards program, where you can earn 25–75% on top of the base card earnings for having qualifying bank relationships (brokerage account, savings, and so on).

Co-Brand

A co-brand credit card is when a bank teams up with a partner, like an airline or a hotel, to offer a credit card that has rewards and perks with the partner. Technically, there are co-brand cards for retailers, universities, cruises, and beyond, but the most popular ones are airline or hotel options. For example, the United Explorer, the Delta SkyMiles Reserve, and the Marriott Bonvoy Brilliant are all co-brand cards. The base earning is usually 1 mile or point per dollar spent, with bonuses for spending on that partner or in other key categories. Most airline cards will offer 2–3 miles per dollar spent on that airline.

Pros: The real value of these cards tends to be in the perks that come along with them, such as free checked bags, discounted companion tickets, free hotel nights, lounge access, and priority boarding. These are also the cards that you want to have if you're hoping to earn elite status with the airlines or hotels, as credit toward status is now one of the most valuable perks that these cards offer. If you're comfortable earning just one type of airline mile or hotel point currency, and you're confident that you don't need to earn points or miles with other airlines, then you can get by using only the credit cards that are co-branded with your favorite airline or hotel.

Cons: Your rewards are restricted to a specific airline or hotel program, so you lose the flexibility of being able to transfer to numerous partners that transferable points cards offer. But just remember that these airline and hotel cards offer fewer options when it comes time to redeem your rewards (you're generally stuck with that currency and can't transfer to others), making these points and miles less valuable in the end. So by using these cards to earn rewards, you're making it easier to earn elite status and get valuable perks but forgoing the opportunity to earn more valuable transferable points and miles.

The way to value these cards is to do a calculation of points plus perks together to make sure you're earning more than if you were using a more valuable transferable points credit card, as explained in the next section.

Transferable Bank Rewards

These credit cards allow you to earn points with the credit card company's loyalty program, with multiple options for how to redeem them, such as transferring to their airline and hotel partners, redeeming for travel on almost any airline and hotel through their portal, or redeeming for experiences, gift cards, or even statement credits.

Every points expert that I know uses transferable points as the foundation for their points strategy, as they're the most valuable type of points in the travel world. In the next chapter, I will dive into how to redeem points to maximize value, but every loyalty program has its sweet spots and incredible redemptions, so instead of just accruing a single currency by having your points in a diversified transferable program, you increase your options, giving you a lot more flexibility.

These cards are popular and valuable because they offer the maximum flexibility and a lot of options for rich opportunities for both earning and redeeming travel rewards. I think everyone who wants to travel on points and miles should have at least one card that offers transferable rewards points. Of my 28 credit cards, 22 of them are transferable points cards, five are co-branded, and one is cashback.

The five major transferable credit card rewards programs are:

- American Express Membership Rewards
- Chase Ultimate Rewards
- Capital One Venture Miles
- Citi ThankYou Program
- Bilt Rewards

Pros: Versatile and valuable points that can be transferred to many partners, lucrative earning categories, promotions, and transfer bonuses that can increase the value of points and perks such as flight delay and cancellation coverage, lost baggage insurance, and responsive customer service.

Cons: You won't earn elite status with a particular airline for your credit card spend, and you won't get airline-specific perks like free checked bags, companion tickets, or hotel free nights. If elite status is important to you, you might want to split your spending between an airline card and one that offers you transferable points.

Best in Class: Chase Sapphire Reserve, American Express Gold, Capital One Venture, Bilt Rewards Mastercard

Some cards offer fixed bank rewards that you can't transfer to airlines or hotels. You can typically redeem these points to make travel reservations through the bank, which limits the flexibility of these points. The problem with these rewards is that the points you earn are generally worth just a penny each toward travel rewards booked through the bank's travel provider.

Bank rewards aren't as valuable as cashback or transferable bank programs, and there isn't one I would recommend unless you get a huge sign-up bonus. Even then, I would recommend getting a card that offers more valuable rewards (like transferable points) or flexible currencies (like cash). Why would you take 1 cent toward travel when you could have 1 cent in cash that can be used anywhere?

Personal Versus Small Business Credit Cards

Small business credit cards offer incredible opportunities to earn travel rewards. Before you dismiss this option, consider that most people in the US can qualify for small business credit cards even with a very small side hustle.

To apply for a business credit card you will probably have to provide an Employer Identification Number, or you can use your social security number if you apply as a sole proprietor (for smaller businesses or side gigs).

The pros of these small business credit cards are lucrative sign-up bonuses and perks. Also, once approved, the outstanding balances don't sit on your personal credit line; they sit on your business credit line, meaning the balances on them won't impact the utilization ratio aspect of your score. Business credit cards are secured by your personal line of credit, so if you default or pay bills late, your credit will suffer.

The downside of small business credit cards is higher interest rates, but that shouldn't matter since the golden rule of all cards is to pay off your bills in full every month to avoid interest.

And finally, don't confuse small business cards with corporate cards, which are issued to medium and large corporations, not individuals.

Tip: If your company doesn't mandate its corporate or small business card, then you should use your own credit cards and submit for reimbursement so you can personally earn points when you spend. And if your company gives you an American Express Corporate Card, then you might be able to pay $95 a year to earn points for your personal Membership Rewards account.

How to Supercharge Your Credit Card Strategy

- Take advantage of sign-up bonuses
- Maximize bonus category spending
- Maximize all other spending
- Buy gift cards
- Take advantage of credit card promotions

The Art of the Sign-Up Bonus

A sign-up bonus is a one-time bonus a credit card company will give you for opening up a new credit card. Usually, there is a spending requirement you'll need to meet to get the bonus, such as earning 60,000 bonus points when you spend $3,000 within the first three months.

The goal is to get you excited about spending on the card and get you in the habit of using it, even after you get your bonus. The bonus also helps you get to a point where you can redeem for a valuable award. Once you connect the value of credit card points with a reward that saved you money or allowed you to take a trip you didn't think you could, you'll continue filling up your account by spending on the card.

In 2010, when I started blogging, the standard sign-up bonus was about 25,000 points or miles, enough for a free round-trip domestic economy ticket. Nowadays, the standard is double that and often six figures. But as you'll learn in the next chapter, the cost of award tickets has increased, so the way to stay ahead of rising award ticket and hotel free night costs is to make sure you are earning as many points as possible, and getting numerous sign-up bonuses will help to keep your accounts padded.

You used to be able to get the same sign-up bonus multiple times (called churning), but most banks have clamped down on the rules to minimize how many sign-up bonuses they need to pay out.

On most credit card applications, you'll see an eligibility box for the sign-up bonus. Read this carefully to make sure you're eligible for the bonus (and call when you're not sure and have them note your account and be sure to get the rep's name in case there are any issues with the bonus posting down the line).

Note that you generally only get the sign-up bonus when you apply for a credit card as a new cardholder. So if you upgrade or downgrade an existing card to another product with that bank, you generally forgo any sign-up bonus (unless they specifically offer you an upgrade bonus).

When you start applying for credit cards, track the dates you sign up and spend. There are a variety of apps on the market that will do it, but if you don't want to share your data, just keep a spreadsheet with key information including the day you were approved, the spend requirement for the sign-up bonus, and any yearly perks you need to use by a certain date.

Be aware of the Chase 5/24 rule, which is an unofficial policy that prevents you from being approved for any Chase credit card if your credit report shows that you've opened five or more personal cards, from any issuer, within the past 24 months.

So, if you're new to credit cards, you'll want to plan your first five cards. I usually recommend starting with a Chase Sapphire Preferred or Reserve, a Chase Freedom, and a Chase Ink card (also known as the Chase Trifecta because they each have unique earning categories, which can supercharge your ongoing points earn). Then, only apply for another Chase card after 24 months from getting your fifth most recent card.

American Express takes the most extreme position by saying that you can't earn a sign-up bonus from any of their cards if you've received a bonus from that card at any point in your life. Before applying for a card that you've held in the past, you should always double-check that you're still eligible to make sure that you get the bonus.

In addition, American Express is now rolling out restrictions on getting a sign-up bonus for a lower fee card within the same "family." Amex groups the Green, Gold, and Platinum cards together; the same is true for the Delta Amex cards—the no-annual-fee Delta Blue, plus the Gold, Platinum, and Reserve cards. So, if you wanted all four sign-up bonuses, you'd have to start with Blue, then get Gold, Platinum, and Reserve.

Thankfully, American Express now notifies you if you don't qualify for a sign-up bonus before you can submit your application. I wish all credit card issuers had this nice feature.

To get the sign-up bonus, you have to make sure you hit that spending threshold or you won't earn the bonus (they often won't budge if you forget).

And be careful. You have to complete the minimum spending requirements within the time period, which begins on the day you're *approved* for the card, not when it's mailed, and not when you receive it, activate it, or first start using it. Track these dates with precision and spend early on to ensure you don't miss out on the bonus. Also note that cash advances, balance transfers, and the annual fee on the card don't count toward the spending requirement.

Some people will apply for multiple credit cards on the same day from different banks, but remember you will have multiple minimum spending requirements to track and meet, so make sure you can spend enough in the required time to get each sign-up bonus.

Don't expect credit card companies to be lenient if you miss spending the required amount for a bonus, even if you are $1 short or your statement closes earlier than you realized. In almost every case they'll deny your request for the bonus. It's your responsibility to make sure you hit the requirements and read the fine print on what does and doesn't qualify.

How to Find the Best Sign-Up Bonuses

Banks regularly offer large sign-up bonuses, just like retailers have regular sales. Card issuers frequently raise their sign-up bonuses by introducing so-called limited-time offers. So how do you know that you're getting the best sign-up offer? Research.

Take the credit card and type in the maximum bonus into a search engine, and you'll find decades' worth of posts so you can get a sense of what the norm is and if your offer is high, average, or low. At ThePoints Guy.com, there's a list of all current top public offers for most rewards credit cards, so make sure at a minimum you are getting the best publicly available offer you can find.

If you do see an exceptionally high offer, hop on it—don't always expect it to come back. The 100,000-point sign-up bonus offered when the Chase Sapphire Reserve Card first launched back in 2016 and has only resurfaced once or twice.

You should also check your email and even your postal mail for targeted offers (yes, credit card companies still send mail, and those are often the best offers). And there are online tools, too, such as Card-Match (https://thepointsguy.com/cardmatch/), which will check to see if you have any targeted offers from certain issuers.

Do your research before committing to a sign-up bonus, and don't get into debt when spending to meet the spend threshold. Beware of the trend that requires high spending thresholds for sign-up bonuses. New offers for the American Express Platinum and Business Platinum now typically require from $8,000 to $15,000 instead of $5,000, as in the past. The most extreme example of this trend may be the Capital One Venture X Business card, which once offered 300,000 bonus miles after spending $100,000 in the first six months! Offers come and go, but you should always comfortably be able to meet the card's minimum spend requirement without overspending.

How to Meet Your Card's Minimum Spend to Get the Bonus

To make sure that you get your sign-up bonus, I recommend spending 10% over the amount needed, just to be safe. If you happen to return something and they subtract that purchase from the required spending amount, some card issuers will take your bonus away.

· · · ·

Unsure if you're able to meet the minimum spending requirements necessary to earn a sign-up bonus? Here are some tips on how to spend on your card:

- **Consider prepaying some bills.** You can often do this with utilities, phone bills, and some insurance policies. When you overpay they'll use the credit toward the next bill.
- **Pay your taxes.** The three companies that are authorized to accept IRS payments will impose fees of between 1.82% and 1.98% (at the time of writing). But paying these fees is well worth it if it allows you to earn a valuable sign-up bonus. This strategy makes

sense even when you're earning 2X points or miles, such as with the Capital One Venture and Venture X cards. *TPG* values those miles at 1.8 cents each, so you're getting about 3.6% back while paying a fee of just 1.82%. So you're getting about twice the value of the fees paid. If your tax payment is greater than your minimum spending requirements, or you need to meet the minimum spending amounts for multiple cards, you can make up to two payments with each of the three companies authorized to accept payment on behalf of the IRS for a total of six payments.

- **Try to put every expense possible on your credit card.** Pay your local property taxes, private school tuition, charitable donations, and home improvement projects with a credit card. You can pay medical bills with your own credit card and get reimbursed rather than use the card offered by your Flexible Spending Account (FSA). One of the writers for *The Points Guy*, Jason Steele, convinced a car dealer to let him charge the entire $45,000 price of a new minivan to his credit card, without being charged an extra fee.

- **Do the calculations when it comes to fees.** While paying extra credit card fees often negates the value of the rewards you receive, it can be worth it to earn a valuable sign-up bonus. The American Express Business Platinum card often has a 120,000-point bonus after spending $15,000 within three months. Even in the worst-case scenario, if you incurred a 3% fee ($450), that would be well worth it to earn a total of at least 135,000 Membership Rewards points. I value this amount of Amex points at $2,700, and often much more when transferring points to airline partners.

- **Make a trusted family member an additional authorized user.** If you trust your relative to pay you back for their charges, you've got another way to meet the minimum spending requirements. An easier way can just be to pay someone else's big bills with your card and have them pay you back. Or, front the bill for a big group dinner and have everyone else pay you back. Small business owners can also make their employees authorized users so that their work expenses count toward your card's minimum spending requirements.

- **Buy gift cards instead of giving cash.** Instead of giving cash for weddings or other celebrations, use your credit card to buy a Visa or Mastercard gift card, especially when you can purchase it from a grocery store or an office supply store where you can earn large amounts of bonus points.

Bonus Category Spending

After sign-up bonuses, the next most important way to win at earning points and miles is by earning bonus points on purchases from certain categories. The credit card companies know that they need to work hard to earn and keep your business, so many will have bonus categories for certain types of spending. The goal is to get credit cards that offer bonus categories in the areas you spend the most. Choosing the right credit card for every purchase can more than double your total points earnings in a year, and that in itself could mean thousands of dollars in value, which can substantially increase your annual travel budget.

Here are the most common bonus spending categories and the cards that give you the most bonus points.

- **Airfare:** Most airlines offer co-brand cards where you can earn 2X or 3X miles per dollar spent on that particular airline. The upside is that most airline co-brand cards also count your spend on the card toward elite status, so in most cases, I only recommend using airline co-brand cards if you're chasing elite status or a specific perk that requires a specific spending level, such as a companion ticket. Otherwise, I put all airfare on a bank card with transferable points. Not only are the points more flexible, but often these cards have better protections if the airline loses your bag or delays or cancels your flight. Some bank cards offer rich earning when you book travel through their travel portal, but as we went over in chapter 4, when you don't book directly with an airline you open yourself up to headaches if you need to be rebooked. The Amex Platinum at 5X on all airfare is a category leader, but the travel protections on Amex are less lucrative than on the Chase Sapphire Reserve, which offers 3X points (plus Chase Points can be valuable when redeeming for airfare and hotel stays). So you need to decide which you prefer. When choosing what credit card to spend on, take into account how valuable the rewards are that you're earning and the other perks the card offers, like travel protections.

- **Hotel:** Most major hotel brands have co-brand cards where you can earn far more points than if you paid with a bank card, so if you frequently stay at a certain chain (like Marriott, Hilton, Hyatt, or IHG) I recommend using a hotel co-brand card because you'll often get valuable, additional perks. If you're not loyal to a specific hotel chain, then pay with a transferable rewards card that gives bonus points on all hotel stays, like the Chase Sapphire Reserve. This card offers 3X points per dollar spent on all travel purchases, including hotels (even those booked via travel agents or online travel agencies).
- **Rent:** The Bilt Rewards Mastercard is the only card that offers you rewards for paying rent. You earn one point per dollar, so long as you make five other transactions each statement period, up to $100,000 a year in rent, which is solid because there are no fees on the rent and no annual fee for the card, and the points transfer to many valuable partners.
- **All other travel, such as rideshares, cruises, car rentals:** The Sapphire Reserve offers you 3X on all travel purchases, and Chase has a broad definition that includes parking, tolls, public transit, and all travel agency purchases.
- **Dining:** Cards that also have dining credits mean you'll earn valuable points plus credits.
- **Gas**
- **Groceries:** Remember, you can buy so much more at grocery stores than just food, including pharmaceuticals, household supplies, and gift cards for added points.
- **Streaming**

- **Digital wallet purchases**
- **Online shopping**
- **Entertainment:** Eligible purchases include sports, theater, movies, aquariums, zoos, and dance venues.
- **Office supplies:** Maximize these bonuses by purchasing many things at office supply stores, including electronics, school supplies, and gift cards.
- **Telecommunications services:** Make sure you're getting cell phone protection coverage when paying for your cellular bills, which comes as a perk with some cards.
- **Drugstores**
- **Fitness**
- **Internet advertising**
- **Shipping**

Or, you can just note it on a Post-it and stick it to your card. No matter how you do it, just make sure you use the right card for each purchase.

Maximize All of Your Spend

You'll never be able to earn a bonus on all of your purchases. That's why it's essential that you also have a card that offers you the most valuable rewards for everything else. There are several cards that offer you better than one point per dollar spent on all purchases at the expense of having few, if any, bonus categories.

You can consider these purchases that don't qualify for any bonuses to be the base of your spending, like utility bills and insurance payments, car repairs, or just general retail spending.

Make sure the merchant codes the purchase correctly. Some small restaurants are miscoded as generic businesses, but you can always contact the credit card issuer and request the appropriate amount of points based on how the business should be categorized. Most credit card portals will allow you to see each purchase and how many rewards are earned for each.

Leverage Category Bonuses with Gift Cards

After earning sign-up bonuses and getting the most points per dollar spent on all of your purchases, you'll have to get creative to squeeze even more rewards from your credit cards. When it comes to earning points and miles, gift cards are magic.

Buying gift cards at a store that offers you a bonus is a great way to leverage these bonus categories and earn more points. An example might be if you have a $5,000 home improvement project where you can buy most of the materials at Home Depot. Most credit cards don't offer bonuses at home improvement stores, so you'd earn one point per dollar on almost all cards (though Discover has offered a quarterly rotating cashback bonus at home improvement stores). Instead, you can use a card that offers a category bonus on supermarket spending, such as Amex Gold 4X to buy Home Depot gift cards at a grocery store. You just moved $5,000 in home improvement spending into a lucrative 4X category earning you 20,000 points, conservatively worth about $400. Even if you did get 5% cashback, that's still only $250.

In addition to supermarkets, office supply stores often have gift cards. There are several lucrative cards that offer bonuses at office supply stores, so you can shift more spending into that category by getting gift cards—even Visa gift cards, which come with a small fee, are worth it for the number of points you get.

Tip: Give gift cards as birthday, graduation, and wedding presents. It's the thought (and points) that matter!

I asked *TPG* readers to share stories on how they maximize earning points for purchasing gift cards. Eleni's friend had her bridal registry at Macy's, but instead of buying something off of it, Eleni and her mom split the cost of a $500 Macy's gift card that they purchased from the Whole Foods website. They paid with Eleni's Amex Gold Card that gets 4X points per dollar on supermarket purchases—this would have earned her 2,000 points. However, that day, Whole Foods had an offer for 8X points per dollar, which netted her an additional 4,000 points. In total, she earned 6,000 Amex points (which I value at $120) for a $500 purchase, but since her mom split it with her, she only paid $250 out of pocket for points worth $120!

Pay Attention to Credit Card Promotions

Whenever you get a credit card, always opt in for communications from the issuer and, where possible, opt in to special offers. Credit card companies will often offer bonus points for adding authorized users or for trying out new features such as paying over time or international wires. You don't need to do much beyond activating the promotion and completing the required steps.

Referral Bonuses

One of the promotions offered by credit card issuers is for referring others to apply. You'll often see these offers when you log in to your account, and they can be lucrative. While a basic Amex EveryDay card may have a referral offer of 7,500 to 12,500 points, their Platinum card can have referral bonuses of up to 45,000 points. But before you get too excited and email everyone you know, you should note that card issuers put annual caps on what you can earn, and Amex limits most cardholders to earning 100,000 points per year per card.

Rakuten, which operates a shopping portal that can offer American Express Membership Rewards points, offers generous referral bonuses.

To get these bonuses, you'll have to generate a referral code, which you can do by logging into your account and clicking on the offer. Then, just send that offer to family and friends. Once they apply for the card and, here's the key part, are approved for a new account, you'll receive your referral bonus and the applicant will still be eligible for a sign-up bonus of his or her own.

Warning: Many credit card issuers will issue a 1099 for referral bonuses, as it can be considered income. Talk to your tax professional about how to handle this, as sometimes their valuations are high and you can point to the bank's public records to lower the valuation, closer to how banks value them for internal accounting.

Which Credit Card(s) Should You Get?

1. Understand how much money you spend per year and in what categories.
2. Make sure you get a credit card that offers bonus points on those categories.
3. Make sure your ideal redemption is a possibility with the currency you will accrue via that card. Read the next two chapters to understand redemption and perks before making final decisions. There are likely a number of cards you should get to maximize your return, and the order in which you apply for new credit cards matters, as you'll soon learn.

How Many Credit Cards Can You Get?

In short, there's no set limit. As I previously mentioned, I currently have 28 active credit cards. You might think that is crazy, but I'm on the more conservative side in the points world. However, I don't recommend starting off by getting a bunch of credit cards right now. Start slow and make sure you can pay off your bills on time and monitor your credit score. As long as you pay in full and on time, you'll see your score start to increase.

Once you're in the habit of avoiding interest by paying your balances in full and you're confident that you're not spending more money because you have more available credit, you can continue opening new cards. A conservative approach would be to open just two a year, and a more aggressive approach would be three to four.

If you're ever declined for any credit card, always call the reconsideration line (google that term and any credit card company's name for the number) to see if there's anything that can be done to get the card approved. Sometimes it's something as simple as confirming your updated income or shifting credit lines around. It never hurts to ask!

I recommend keeping the cards open for at least a year, and I'll get into when to close or downgrade a credit card later in the chapter.

Why pick just one? If your goal is to maximize cashback, I would get a 2% cashback card to use for most expenses and then one or two rotating category cards so you can maximize the bonus categories. In most cases, I recommend having at least one Visa, one Mastercard, one Amex, and two debit cards (in case one card ever gets locked and you need access to cash, especially when traveling).

I would then think about co-brand cards on airlines you fly, where you check bags, or where you pay for lounge access. When it comes to co-brand cards, get them with the airlines you fly and the hotels you stay at the most.

Remember, saving money from perks is just like earning cashback. Instead of giving that cash to the airline for checked bags or priority boarding, you keep it for yourself. As you'll read in chapter 8, the value you get from the perks on these cards generally outweighs the annual fee, so only spend on them when you're trying to get elite status or spend to get a specific perk.

For general spending, I almost always recommend putting it on transferable points cards. If your goal is to get valuable travel rewards, I recommend getting a mix of co-brand and transferable points cards. If you're working in "two-player" mode, you can refer your spouse or partner and maximize your net number of points earned.

The Second Tier: Partner Rewards
Shopping Portals

Most major airline, hotels, and credit cards have online shopping portals where you can earn extra miles and points for free, simply by registering, adding your loyalty number in the shopping portal, and then clicking through to your favorite online retailer. When shopping online always click through an online shopping portal for free rewards. These rewards are in addition to the points you'll get from using a rewards credit card. This is a prime example of double-dipping, as you can earn two types of points or rewards for the same purchase. Online shopping portals might be my favorite way to earn points for minimal effort and no cost. Even if you only have a debit card, you can earn free miles and points by clicking through to your retailers via an online shopping portal.

Online retailers know they need to lure new customers through as many channels as possible, so that's why you'll see your favorite influencers sharing their "links," which track your purchases and then kick back a bonus to the influencer.

But before influencer marketing, shopping portals were set up by the major airlines and hotel companies to encourage their loyal members to shop through "their links," and the shopping portals would share the commission in the form of miles and points—in the same way that cashback portals have been doing it.

Using these shopping portals is easy and free, and you can still use any discounts or coupon codes that you normally would when shopping online. Just know that there are some exceptions. Buying gift cards often won't trigger the earnings from the shopping portal, but sometimes it will, so it can't hurt to try. It's just one small extra step.

The earning rates of miles per dollar spent vary by retailer and portal, so it's best to always go to websites like Cashback Monitor or Evreward and enter a retailer's name so you can see the different options to earn via cashback, airline, hotel, and credit card portals. You can earn the most rewards when shopping for very-high-margin items, such as flower delivery and other gifts. It's common to see offers of 20X to 30X points or more for Valentine's Day or Mother's Day. Examples can include portal bonuses for booking Marriott hotels through Marriott .com or booking any hotel through the Rocketmiles site. Another great tool is the Rakuten Rewards browser extension.

Stacking Portals and Perks

You can also take this process a step further. Let's say you want to buy something at Saks Fifth Avenue using a points-earning credit. You can double-dip by using an Amex Platinum that gives you Saks credits every year as part of the card's benefits, as well as earning the points. Then, you can triple-dip by using an online shopping portal.

It's not just retail stores on shopping portals. There are many travel brands as well, such as Hotels.com and Vrbo. I once spent $20,000 on a villa in Mykonos with friends and we all split it. I was able to book it via the United Airlines shopping portal, earning 3X United miles per dollar, plus the 3X Ultimate Rewards points I got for using my Chase Sapphire Reserve Card. My friends reimbursed me for their portion of the villa, and I kept all of the credit card and shopping portal points. (And no, I didn't feel bad about it—that's my commission for doing all the planning!)

Dining Rewards

Most people don't realize that you can enroll all of your credit cards in something called Rewards Network (www.RewardsNetwork.com), which partners with the world's biggest loyalty programs. These programs allow you to earn extra miles anytime you visit a restaurant that participates, without the need to carry around any coupons or tell your server to apply a specific offer.

So, not only am I earning Rewards Network points when I use my Amex Gold card to pay the bill, but I'm also getting 4X Membership Rewards points for the meal thanks to the card's bonus points.

Let's say I take some friends out to eat, and we rack up a $400 bill. As a VIP member with United MileagePlus Dining (someone who's already completed 11 transactions within a year), I'll earn 5X United miles, on top of the 4X from my Amex Gold card, for a total of 9X points per dollar spent on the bill. Multiply that by the cost of my dinner, and now I just earned 2,000 United miles and 1,600 Amex points, worth a combined total of about $62. By double-dipping between the credit card rewards and the dining rewards program, I just earned rewards worth over 15% of my dinner bill.

Another valuable dining program is Bilt Neighborhood Dining, which offers you extra Bilt points at featured restaurants. Even if you don't have a Bilt Rewards Mastercard, you can participate in the program. For example, if you registered your Amex Gold in the Bilt Neighborhood Dining program, you'd double-dip and earn 4X points per dollar spent at that restaurant in addition to the Bilt Reward points, for eating at a participating restaurant. If the restaurant is bookable via OpenTable, you can even triple-dip and earn OpenTable points.

If you live in a large city with lots of restaurants, it's easy to choose one in these rewards networks and accumulate a lot of points. When I hosted a lot of work dinners at my previous job, I raked in hundreds of thousands of miles from dining every year—in addition to the credit card points for the actual bill.

Partnerships

Partnerships are another smart way to earn points. Two companies will team up to offer points or miles with one when you make a purchase from the other. It's free and easy to sign up for. Some of the major companies offering rewards-earning partnerships are:

- **Uber and Marriott.** With the partnership between Uber and Marriott, you can earn Marriott points for your everyday Uber and Uber Eats activities. I use Uber enough that this partnership has become one of the main ways that I earn Marriott Bonvoy points.
- **Delta and Starbucks.** Delta and Starbucks customers enrolled in both Delta SkyMiles and Starbucks Rewards loyalty programs can link their accounts by visiting either DeltaStarbucks.com or StarbucksDelta.com. You just have to register your loyalty numbers in both programs and when you spend with either partner, you earn rewards in both.
- **Delta and Instacart.** The Delta SkyMiles program also has a partnership with the grocery delivery service Instacart. You earn one SkyMile per dollar spent with Instacart, and those with the $99 Express membership earn 1.5 miles per dollar.
- **Lyft and Hilton.** The partnership between Lyft and Hilton allows you to link your accounts to earn 3X Hilton points per dollar spent on individual Lyft rides and 2X on shared Lyft rides. You can also redeem your Hilton Honors points for Lyft credits—but at a mere 0.22 cents in value, you'll be getting about half of what these points are normally worth.

- **American Airlines and Hyatt.** Hyatt elites can earn one World of Hyatt Bonus Point for every dollar spent on qualifying American Airlines flights, on top of the AAdvantage miles you would have earned. And if you have elite status in both programs, then you earn an American Airlines AAdvantage mile for each dollar spent at Hyatt.

Promotions tend to require a onetime registration, so don't forget to register. And just like with credit cards, expect frequent promotions from airline and hotel programs offering bonus points and miles—keep an eye on your accounts for these and sign up.

The Third Tier: Travel
Air Travel

It used to be that you earned one frequent flyer mile for each mile traveled, but that formula is rarely used anymore in the US, where most frequent flyer programs are now revenue-based. Instead, most airlines now award a number of miles per dollar spent, and that number is determined by your status in their frequent flyer program and how much you spend on airfare. With American, Delta, and United, you'll earn between 5X and 11X miles, depending on your status. I'd argue these programs are now more frequent buyer—than frequent flyer—programs.

You don't have to bank miles from your flight to the airline you're flying. Most airlines have partnerships with other carriers or airline alliances such as OneWorld, SkyTeam, and the Star Alliance. If you are chasing elite status, you must bank the miles to that carrier. However, if you don't care about elite status and want to earn the most valuable miles possible, sometimes it makes sense to bank the miles from your flight to a partner airline that has a more valuable mileage currency (or where you're trying to get your balance up so you can redeem for an award). To find the best program to credit your flight to, there's a helpful website called WhereToCredit.com.

I don't care for JetBlue miles since they're pegged at around 1.3 cents apiece, and they make it hard to redeem on partners. So when I fly Jet-

Blue I'll instead bank the miles to Qatar Airways, which has a much more valuable and flexible program. I can transfer Qatar Avios to my British Airways Avios account and transfer in credit card points to get my account to a level where I can redeem for rich rewards on OneWorld partners.

Hotel Stays

Most hotels use a revenue-based earning system, where you earn based on how much you spend, but some chains will allow you to earn airline miles or even cashback rewards rather than hotel points. I generally like to earn hotel points, as you can redeem them for aspirational hotel stays that have outsize value (like at luxury resorts in the Maldives).

Beware of booking through OTAs. Hotels will generally only give you points if you book through them or through a corporate travel platform. If you book via an online travel agency, they generally won't award you any points.

Double-Dipping with Small Business Frequent Flyer Programs

Most major airlines have separate loyalty programs for small businesses. The premise is that the owner of the small business can get credit for their employees' flights, and the employees will still earn their frequent flyer miles—a win-win. So, if you have a small business (even a tiny one!), I would recommend signing up for these programs, as they're free. The miles earned in the small business program are separate currencies from the normal loyalty and generally aren't as valuable, but if you're booking flights anyway, all you need to do is add the small business frequent flyer number.

Buying Miles

At a high level, it only makes sense to buy frequent flyer miles or hotel points when you can purchase them at a price that is lower than what you can redeem them for. I only recommend buying a points currency if you know how to redeem that specific currency and are aware of the risks involved, like the currency could change its rules or your award could disappear. So have a specific redemption in mind, or even put an award ticket on hold while you purchase the points so you know for a fact you'll be able to redeem them for your intended purpose.

For example, you need to go New York to Paris in business class, and the cheapest flights are $5,000 round trip. This is a route the airlines rarely discount because they know that passengers will pay a premium.

But Air France Flying Blue often sells miles at bonuses that bring the cost anywhere from 1.5 to 1.8 cents a point. At 1.8 cents, 100,000 miles would cost you $1,800. Air France Flying Blue has a lot of award seats between JFK and CDG (I book it all the time, and often there are more than five seats available) at the 100,000 miles round trip, plus $541 in taxes/fees. So would you rather pay $5,000 buying directly or $2,341 by purchasing miles? As a cherry on top, when you redeem miles for a flight, you can usually cancel for a small fee to get your miles back. In my opinion, this is a better option than buying that ticket in cash and getting a voucher if you need to cancel, which can expire.

I know a lot of people, especially those who don't live in the US (where it's so easy to earn points), who buy points cheaply via promotions and then maximize them on redemptions. While those in the US have access to really lucrative credit card offers, those abroad can get in on these buying promotions, which can be beneficial if you know how to use the points or miles.

When to Buy Miles

Ideally, you'll buy miles when you have a redemption in mind, but sometimes good deals come up. This is why you may want to buy in advance, even if you don't have a redemption in mind today.

The airlines/hotels can change redemptions on a moment's notice, so if you bought thinking you might only need 50,000 for an award, that number could increase, so understand the risk involved when buying currencies controlled and regulated by a corporation. If you don't have a need and are not 100% sure of the best way to redeem the miles, you might prefer to steer clear until you have a plan in place.

Also, beware that when you redeem miles on most airlines you won't earn elite miles and you may have limited options to upgrade. If the price to buy is not hugely discounted from the outright price, I would probably just buy the ticket.

What Credit Card to Use for Purchasing Miles?

It would be ideal if the airlines sold miles themselves and coded the purchases as airfare or travel, but most airlines process the mileage purchase through a third-party vendor, such as Points.com, which means you'll only earn 1 point per dollar spent. A notable exception is American Airlines, so use one of its co-brand cards or a general airfare card like Amex Platinum for 5X points on the purchase.

I usually only buy miles in foreign frequent flyer programs for less than 2 cents apiece and when I know I can redeem them for much more in value.

Buying Miles for Sweet Spot Redemptions

I've purchased Virgin Atlantic miles for 1.1 to 1.3 cents each, depending on the sale. Virgin Atlantic has insane fees on its own award tickets to and from London, but it has a number of partners that charge little in taxes and fees, making those redemptions a much better value. The holy grail of the Virgin Atlantic partners is an All Nippon Airways (ANA) award in business class for 90,000 miles round trip from the West Coast. You can buy the miles required for a $7,000 flight for roughly $1,200, which is incredible. And if you can find its first-class award seats, it will cost you 145,000 miles, or about $1,600 to $2,000, a small fraction of the $20,000 first-class fare ANA charges. You might be saying "I can never find these great deals," but in the next chapter I'll clue you in to the expert tools I use to "hunt" for them.

Other Times It Can Make Sense to Buy Miles

You might want to top up your account when you're close to a redemption. Say you're 2,000 American Airlines miles away from a business-class award and no credit card transfer programs transfer to American, and you need to get miles quickly. Buying them, even when there isn't a sale, may be worth it because it allows you to get your mileage level to the amount needed to get an actual valuable reward ticket—remember, miles aren't worth anything *until you actually redeem them.*

Key Tips for Buying Points and Miles

1. Buy miles and points when you know you'll be able to redeem them for more than what you paid for them.
2. Wait for promotions to get a discount—avoid buying them when asked while checking in or at a kiosk.
3. Understand the expiration rules of the miles and make sure you know how to keep them active. While many loyalty programs have done away with expiration policies, some have tricky expiration rules that require flight activity to keep miles from expiring.

Chapter 7

How to Win at Redeeming Rewards

*Now that you're earning those points, be smart
and savvy about redeeming them.*

Think of being smart about points not as a frivolous coupon-clipping activity but as more of a financial tip that can allow you to reallocate your cash for other things, such as a down payment on a home or investing in the stock market while still being able to travel and enrich your soul.

As thrilling as booking an amazing award may be, it's not always a slam dunk. Sometimes you'll be left with a nagging feeling, wondering if you got the best deal possible. When redeeming points, you want to feel good about the redemption, but you need to also let go of the need for perfection. Perfection in the points world is a moving target. Even I don't redeem my miles for the absolute maximum in some instances.

Hoarding your points for an unknown future use is an unwise strategy, as miles generally lose value as soon as you earn them. It's much more likely a loyalty program will devalue points (making redemptions more expensive) than make them even more valuable.

Just like in the real world, we've seen inflation balloon in recent years—triple that for the loyalty world. Redemptions that five years ago cost 100,000 miles now cost 300,000 miles (or more). But the opportunities to supercharge how many miles you *earn* have also increased, so as long as you are focused on earning and redeeming, you can stay ahead of the curve.

The Unique Challenges of Maximizing Miles and Points

The most challenging part of miles and points is that there isn't one unified system that tells you the best way to redeem them.

Unlike buying flights and hotel stays, which airlines and hotels distribute on shared platforms such as Google Flights or an OTA, each airline and hotel has its own loyalty platform on its own site. Airlines and hotels are much more guarded around their loyalty pricing—they might not even show all the available options on their website, or they might have the best options buried deep in results while more expensive options are at the top of the results.

Airlines and hotels make a lot of money when they bring consumers into their ecosystem, where they can be sold credit cards and other ancillary services, so they don't want anyone coming in the way of their loyalty members. They don't want you to comparison shop for mileage tickets, because they don't want you leaving their ecosystem or realizing how high their award rates are compared to other loyalty programs' rates.

This fragmented system benefits the airlines and hotels but not the consumer, who's left to have one-on-one relationships with all of their loyalty programs, making it overwhelming to know where to begin when searching for a trip. Historically, the process for searching for the best rewards has been manual and time-consuming, with many consumers giving up and redeeming their points for whatever is easiest, even if it's a terrible value.

The "how to use points" conundrum compounds when you factor in credit cards that have transferable currencies, which give you a lot of options when it comes time to redeem them. That level of choice can induce decision paralysis. You can transfer points from Amex, Chase, Citi, Capital One, and Bilt. Each transfer partner has numerous alliance partners and other partners, so the math can be impossible for any human to do when it comes to the question of "So where do I transfer my points to book the flight/hotel that I want?" And most important, is there availability so I can book what I want today? Do I transfer points or book directly via the credit card travel portal?

The decision should be based on a number of factors including paid pricing, award availability, and how many points you have. The goal of this chapter is to teach you the basic math to know when you're getting a good deal and give you the expert strategies that I use to make good redemptions.

Keeping Track of Your Points and Miles

The first part of getting maximum value from your points is knowing how many you have. While apps exist, none are perfect and sharing your login credentials with third parties always puts you at an elevated risk of a security breach.

The safest way to track your balances and perks is by creating a spreadsheet with multiple tabs: one for your current balances, one tab for credit cards, one tab with notes for any special spending requirements or perks you need to use and by which dates, and a final tab for all redemptions so you can keep track over time and remember how much value you got from each redemption.

As you enroll in more programs and get more credit cards, manual tracking can become time-consuming, so you can use apps that will help. These apps can tabulate how many miles you have and alert you to better ways to spend your money, help you take advantage of credit card perks, and more.

I recommend utilizing a password management system like 1Password that will allow you to easily manage unique credentials for all of your loyalty programs. If one is breached, the likelihood of those credentials being used for other accounts decreases if you have different unique and secure passwords for all of your accounts. Loyalty fraud is becoming more and more common, so you should be changing passwords often and also have alerts set so you can see when miles and points are debited from your accounts. The sooner you know about fraudulent activity, the better.

The Best Tracker: Award Wallet

The most extensive miles and points tracker is AwardWallet, which currently features tracking for more than 638 loyalty programs. It provides info on when your miles expire, keeps track of your rewards earnings, and helps you manage your itineraries and reservations.

Never Let Points Expire

While many loyalty programs have gotten rid of expiration dates, plenty still have them. Be mindful of the rules of any program you participate in, but note that most will allow any activity, like a single online shopping portal or co-brand credit card purchase, to reset the clock, while some have much more draconian rules (e.g., you must fly to keep the miles active and some will expire them after a certain date, no matter what).

Keep an eye out or set alerts for programs with expiration dates and make sure your email address is up-to-date (and add that airline as a permitted sender to your main inbox) so you can get expiration reminders. And for credit cards, points generally don't expire as long as your account is in good standing, but if your account is ever closed, be sure to use or transfer your points out before you close the account. If your points are going to expire, at least donate them, which most programs will allow you to do for free, to an organization such as Make-A-Wish or Rainbow Railroad that depends on mileage donations to fund their important work.

How to Redeem Your Airline Miles

If you're a beginner, this chapter may get confusing. Don't panic, and give yourself the time to learn. This book is a high-level overview into the world of loyalty (points and miles) and not necessarily a master class in expert points sorcery (though even advanced participants may learn something).

Consider this your map to find treasure, but not all of the exact instructions are dotted out. You'll see the treasure chests to seek but will likely have to do your own research after reading this book.

Strategy One: Leverage Technology to Find the Best Airline Awards

Most airlines have their own proprietary technology systems and websites that power their loyalty programs. This is different from paid airfares, where most airlines distribute paid fares on shared distribution systems so consumers shopping online, or corporate travelers booking through their company portal, can all shop and see the most available fares on a given route on any date.

The hunt for award tickets is much more fragmented and manual, as you historically have had to search route by route, airline by airline, unless you know how to use tools that have been largely made by experts, for experts. If you search for award tickets at one singular moment in time on a single airline website, there is a low chance you'll find what you need at a great value. Leaving the average consumer to fend for themself in a system of complicated and glitchy websites is bound to lead to people getting fed up and thinking that points and miles are useless.

You need to adopt a better, more clever mindset to get the best deal. My best tip is to forget about figuring out the millions of possibilities and partners. Instead, let technology do the work.

There are a handful of free and paid tools on the marketplace, but there are two that have saved me so much time and money. I'll still teach you the basics of evaluating loyalty program types and how to best redeem your points, but I need to lead with tools because they'll continue to change the way consumers book award travel. These tools will take you from beginner to intermediate, and I would recommend paying for at least one premium tool if you plan on redeeming for more than one trip a year.

Warning: No tool is 100% accurate. Many airlines offer more award availability and at discounted pricing for their elite or co-brand credit cardholders, which these tools don't always take into account, so it's always beneficial to search on the airline's website where you have elite status or a co-brand credit card to see if there are better deals than what you see on the tool. These tools will help you sniff out some of the best deals, but they all have flaws and sometimes have outages where they won't show every single possible option.

A Free Place to Start

Points Path is a free Google Flights plug-in that shows you how many miles the airlines are charging for flights on the airlines in the search results. For the limited airlines it supports, you can pull up paid flights and see how many miles it costs for that flight. The problem is that it's only supported by a few airlines so far and won't pull in other options on other carriers that could be a much better deal.

This tool can be helpful when searching so you can get a sense of how many miles are needed for flights, which is especially useful when deciding whether to buy a flight, redeem via a credit card portal, or transfer points to the loyalty program to book. Once installed, you don't have to do anything else—every time you search for flights on Google Flights, it'll populate how many miles supported airlines want for their flights.

AwardHacker.com is a free tool that I often use to start my search, entering the route I want to fly to see what the cheapest options are. It doesn't search for availability but tells you the best loyalty programs for that route.

For example, the site found the best redemption option for the JFK to Malé, Maldives, route is using 70,000 AAdvantage miles to fly on Qatar. It also shows me Alaska Airlines charges 70,000 miles to fly on British Airways, but I would avoid this option, as BA charges huge fees and American doesn't charge fees on Qatar Airways awards. AwardHacker will basically give you the goal (but not show you if it's available), which is the ideal starting place.

If you can get the rates listed there, you're winning at your award. Now the hard part comes trying to find flights that have award availability that will price out at that low benchmark. That's where I turn to paid technology options that will help me find that coveted award availability.

The Paid Tools I Can't Live Without

For searching one route on a specific date across a wide variety of loyalty programs and credit cards, I use Point.me. It's $129 for a yearly unlimited membership at the time of writing, but free for Bilt and American Express Membership Rewards cardholders. However, the Point.me versions for those credit card partnerships will only pull in options for transfer partners of Bilt or Amex, respectively, so you're not seeing the bigger picture unless you use the paid tool.

This user-friendly award tool searches a specific route and date extensively, pulling most options, including transfer partners. It has 99% accuracy, so if you see something you like, it's almost certainly bookable (many other tools have cached data that can be old, so you may not be able to book what you see).

Imagine you have a lot of different points and want to fly JFK to Paris on a certain date. Point.me will pull in a list of options including how much it would cost in taxes/fees for each flight. You can filter by credit card currency, number of stops, duration, and how many points. I filtered nonstop flights and Point.me sorted the following options, from least to most expensive:

- AA: 113,500 miles and $5.60
- Air France: 135,000 miles and $225
- Delta: 350,000 miles and $5.60

While you might think the AA one is the no-brainer, I would probably use Air France miles for several reasons. They're one of the easiest currencies to get (you can transfer them in from Amex, Chase, Citi, Capital One, and Bilt, and often at more than 25% in bonuses) and the Air France business-class product is nicer than AA's, with sliding doors and fancier food. If I were flexible on dates I would search to see if I could get Air France down to as low as 50,000 miles one way, which I often am able to get, but if I were set on this date I would likely go that route and save my AA miles for a better redemption, since AA miles are much harder to come by (you can only transfer Marriott Bonvoy to AA and at a not-great ratio).

If your situation is different, and you're sitting on an excess of AA miles, then by all means go with the AA option. My point is that sometimes you don't want to go with the fewest number of miles if it's a currency that's hard to get or could be better used on a different redemption.

For a faster and broader search capability, AwardTool.com (the pro version is $131 per year, though you can often find discounts) has similar functionality as Point.me. It lets you select your origin, date(s), destination, number of passengers, one way or round trip, and class of service. This tool is helpful because you can pull in a number of different departure airports from which you'd be willing to leave. So if you live in New York and don't mind traveling to Philadelphia, DC, or Boston to find a great deal, it will pull in a lot of options to choose from. It supports

20 major airlines, including the main US programs: American, Alaska, United, and Delta.

For finding sweet spot awards on a specific carrier, I love Seats.aero (the pro version is $9.99 per month), which allows you to search a route (as generic as North America to Asia, for example) up to a year at a time over a single program. You can quickly search for United Mileage-Plus awards from Newark to anywhere in Asia in seconds and then sort them all by economy, premium economy, business, and first class. Then, you can filter down results by seasons, dates, and departure and arrival airports.

Seats.aero is a tool I use when my dates are flexible and I want to search a specific airline program. Where Point.me goes far and wide on a certain date, Seats.aero can search far and wide on dates with a single loyalty program. I often use this website when I want to fly a certain airline, say Emirates first class between JFK and Dubai. For example, I searched JFK to DXB and first class was available on 98/365 days over the next year.

You can look as far as a year out to find availability and then plan your trip around it. If you're looking to see the best deal on a certain date across all of your points, Point.me is the way to go. Even if you can't find what you want, the tool lets you set alerts so that if award inventory opens up you can get an email or text.

This tool does have its downsides. You can only search one program at a time, so if you have credit card points that you can transfer to numerous programs, it can take awhile to search all options. It also only supports a handful of airlines and doesn't pull in airlines like Singapore and Cathay Pacific, which open up a lot of award space to their members. Sometimes you can't see how many seats are available, so if you need two or more, you have to go to the airline website to see if there are more.

There are also a few paid newsletters I subscribe to where the editors hunt for new releases of award seat inventory and email their members to book great deals as they come up.

Often, airlines will add new routes or upgrade to larger planes, which will result in a new award inventory hitting the market. As a consumer, you'd only find this if you just so happen to be searching for it, but these newsletters notify me when these rare releases happen. I have booked numerous trips because of the emails I get, so if you're lazy and want to get deals without putting in the work, it might make sense to pay a relatively cheap amount to get deals delivered to you.

Thrifty Traveler Premium ($99 annually) sends information on award seats and premium fare deals from your home airport. You also get access to a private Facebook group and free rewards card consulting.

I also subscribe to *Straight to the Points* ($99 annually), which features award deals with two or more seats. You could also opt for a concierge-style booking ($200 per ticket) with Point.me's concierge service. If you don't have the time to search for yourself, pay the professionals who search for you, building an itinerary that meets your needs and can save you thousands of dollars versus buying it outright.

I also recommend following these Instagram accounts that post award seat deals for free: @thriftytraveler, @straighttothepoints, @roame.travel, @thepointsanalyst, @findflightsforme, and @thepremiumpassport.

Strategy Two: Understand the Different Types of Airline Programs and Use the Ones with Rewards That Fit Your Needs

There are four main airline loyalty program flavors (and most programs are now a hybrid of multiple flavors):

1. **Zone-based**, where the price of an award is calculated based on the zone from where you leave and where you land. Domestic awards were 25,000 miles round trip in economy and 50,000 in first class, and US to Europe was 50,000 miles round trip in economy and 80,000–100,000 miles in business class. Most airlines have zone-based charts for partner flights. Partner awards are crucial, as they are often the cheapest way to fly and avoid exorbitant pricing.
2. **Distance-based**, where the price in miles of your award depends on total flight miles flown, so the more you fly within certain bands, the more miles you need to redeem.

3. **Fixed value**, where the number of miles you need is directly correlated to the cash price of the ticket. A $500 flight is the same if it is 500 or 2,000 miles.
4. **Dynamic pricing**, where the number of miles needed is determined based on a proprietary formula but is generally tracked to the price and demand of a flight, although not exactly.

Zone-Based Awards

Historically, most frequent flyer programs were created with zone-based award charts and then evolved from there. These programs are ideal for flyers who want to fly expensive flights over long distances, as the value of the ticket isn't tied to the number of miles needed, so it can be a fun game to get as expensive of a ticket as possible for as few miles required. These programs provide consistency in pricing, which makes it easier when planning a dream trip: You need to accrue a certain number of miles to fly between two destinations, as long as there is availability on that airline or any of its partners. These programs allow you to maximize the value of your points and routing rules, so you can squeeze in a lot of flights for one low price.

A zone-based award chart often features sweet spots, meaning there are ways to take advantage of how the airline groups the zones. The Turkish Airlines Miles and Smiles program includes Hawaii as just another part of North America, allowing you to book an economy-class ticket from Newark to Honolulu for a mere 10,000 miles each in economy or 15,000 in business class one way—the same price as Newark to Boston.

The downside is that the airlines are often stingy with award inventory in these programs, and they can be feast or famine: You either find amazing options, or you have nothing at all. This system works when award seats are filling the margins (the seats that might go out empty), so the opportunity cost is low for the airline.

These programs are also known for blackout dates over premium periods, which led to enough outcry from consumers to create a new model that allowed more flexibility in redemptions. Hawaiian Airlines, Avianca

LifeMiles, and Turkish Miles and Smiles have zone-based awards, and most programs have these charts for pricing their partner awards.

Distance-Based Awards

The longer the distance you fly, the more miles you pay, but usually within groups (called bands) so it isn't directly correlated to exact mileage. You can maximize these types of awards when airfare pricing isn't exactly related to the distance of the flight. British Airways charges one rate for flights that are under 650 miles, another for flights that are 651 to 1,151 miles, and so on. These awards can be fantastic when you are crossing zones or squeaking in just under the limit, where the distance is short but fares are high.

British Airways has great pricing on short-haul flights; they charge far fewer miles than American does for its own flights on short-haul segments, like Miami to the Caribbean. Even for West Coast to Hawaii it is cheaper to redeem via British Airways than it is American for its own flights. LAX to HNL is 25,000 one way in economy on AA but only 16,000 Avios and $5.60 with British Airways. The airline often has transfer bonuses from the major credit card companies, making it even cheaper.

Fixed-Price Awards

These programs are simple, with a fixed value for each point or mile redeemed. Southwest points are worth about 1.4 cents each when you redeem for flights, and JetBlue's points tend to be about 1.1 to 1.3 cents each. With these programs, the price you pay in points tracks the price you'd pay in dollars, and there are as many awards as there are seats. This arrangement is ideal for families and other large groups, as fixed-value programs have the most available seats for redemption. It also makes sense when your travel plans are inflexible and when low-priced awards are hard to find, like over the holidays.

The downside is that when the ticket is extremely expensive, so is the cost in miles. Looking to redeem miles for a last-minute economy JetBlue flight to London that costs $1,000? You'll probably end up having to redeem around 80,000 points. But if award space is available on its partner Qatar Airways, you'll pay just 25,000 miles no matter what the cash price is.

Using a fixed-value award chart means that you'll never get extreme value from these kinds of programs. That's okay. Not everyone needs to be a points maximizer all the time. Some people may just want to take their family on vacation during Christmas or spring break when they wouldn't find extreme value with distance or zone-based charts. Just be sure to book these awards in advance, as the cash price of tickets increases within 60 days of departure and often again two weeks (or less) prior to departure.

Dynamic Pricing

Dynamic pricing means that the cost of a flight redemption using miles fluctuates based on a number of factors, but primarily demand, just like paid cash tickets. On the plus side, you'll find more seats are available for redemption. On the downside, these kinds of frequent flyer programs will often charge more miles than those that use the traditional distance or chart-based ways of calculating the miles required. And, you'll never know what to expect when searching, which can lead to disappointment when you see the number of miles required for a flight.

Over the last 10 years, American, United, and Delta have all been evolving toward dynamic programs for pricing their own flights but then use charts to price partner awards. The upside to these programs is that you can redeem for nearly every flight, so if you don't have a lot of flexibility but do have lots of miles, these programs can work for you, as long as you maximize how many you're earning by getting elite status and credit cards with category bonuses. Some dynamic programs like Delta are moving toward a fixed-value proposition, where every mile is worth around 1 cent for extras like upgrades and premium seat assignments.

Strategy Three: Book with Airline Partners for Fewer Miles

Dynamic pricing shows no signs of stopping in the industry, and while it's tough to see the inflation in terms of how much flights cost in miles, you need to balance that with how much you can earn these days. Historically, some of the best-value redemptions of any airline loyalty program would be on their partner airlines.

Why? While the major US airlines have been inflating the cost of their own awards via their "dynamic pricing" models, a lot of partner awards have been left untouched at much more reasonable redemption rates. And many foreign carriers (especially Asian and Middle Eastern flag carriers) have much better in-flight experiences than the US airlines. So not only are you redeeming fewer miles, but you're getting a better experience than on a US carrier, which is key for higher-value redemptions.

Alaska, American, Delta, and United still price most of their partner awards using a zone-based formula, even though it's not published. The reason is that the airlines strike agreements on how to charge each other for awards, so in many cases airlines have agreed on a set pricing structure.

Stick to these partner awards, and you'll usually get the best pricing, both in terms of miles and taxes and fees. Avoid flying British Airways using American Airlines miles, as British Airways imposes fuel surcharges (now rebranded as "carrier-imposed surcharges") that can be higher than the cost of an economy-class ticket.

Alliance Partners

Over the years, the airlines have inked partnerships that allow them to expand their route networks through regional partners versus actual expansion. Most of the major airlines in the world are split up into three alliances: Star Alliance, OneWorld, and SkyTeam. Alliance partners have integrated systems that allow for streamlined experiences, meaning you can earn and redeem miles with other airlines in the same alliance as well as check bags and book connecting flights all on the same ticket.

A United Airlines flyer can earn United miles when flying Singapore Airlines since they're Star Alliance partners. And, vice versa, a Singapore Airlines customer who flies Singapore to Newark on Singapore Airlines and then connects Newark to Boston on United can earn Singapore Kris-Flyer miles for their entire itinerary.

Most important, alliance partners generally make award seats available to all other members in the alliance, with some exclusions. A big trend with airlines is to make more availability for their own members versus those of alliance partners. This is largely to encourage members to accrue miles into their own program and to get a co-brand credit card to accrue miles and get access to a special trove of awards.

If airlines released all of their best availability to their partners, those partners' customers would potentially use up all of the awards, making the airlines' own elite members upset. Air France does this for their top-tier Platinum members, making their incredible La Premiere first class only bookable for those with Flying Blue. I bank all of my SkyTeam flying to Air France to maintain my Platinum status year over year so I can access these awards (plus, there are other easy ways to get elite qualifying miles on Air France, which I'll cover later).

Lufthansa Group (this includes airlines like Lufthansa, Swiss, and Austrian) gatekeeps far more business and first-class awards for their own members than other alliance partners. They only release Lufthansa first-class awards to partners starting 14 days prior to departure. Singapore Airlines has significantly more premium award space for KrisFlyer members; so does Cathay Pacific. You see the trend here, so don't assume that the same space is available to all members because sometimes United will block certain Star Alliance member award space, even though you can book it on other Star Alliance carrier Air Canada's Aeroplan website.

Other Airline Partners

Not every airline is in an alliance. Carriers such as Southwest, JetBlue, Etihad, Aer Lingus, and Emirates remain free agents but have partnerships with many airlines, including those in the major alliances. Leveraging these partner airlines is key to maximizing the value of your miles. Often these airlines won't show up in online search results (or they'll be buried), but understanding which airlines you can redeem with is an important step to realizing the value of any mileage currency.

Ideally, every airline would release the same seats to its partners as it does to members of its own frequent flyer program. But in practice, many programs only release some of their space to their partners, and some release none at all.

Singapore won't release any of its highly coveted first-class awards to its partners. Likewise, Swiss and Air France will only let members with elite status book their international first-class awards. And you can't use Delta SkyMiles to book international first-class awards on any of their SkyTeam partners, such as Air France, China Airlines, Korean Air, and Saudia. I'll often see Lufthansa flights available on Aeroplan but not on United, which is another Star Alliance partner.

Every loyalty program is trying to manage its profit and loss, and sometimes it's more profitable to block off access to certain partner awards, which veers their members to higher-priced awards on their own flights. While this is annoying, it's yet another reason why you should focus on earning points in transferable credit card currencies so you have as many options as possible when it comes time to redeem. If you put all of your miles in one airline, you are held to that airline's rules, which may not be favorable when it's time to redeem.

The best example of an airline with many partners is Air Canada. They're a member of Star Alliance (which has the most members) and have inked more other airline partners than anyone, bringing their total partners to 48. Its website pulls in most of those partners. So when I'm deciding on going to a destination, I'll often use an Aeroplan .com search to pull in both Star Alliance and other partners as a first step to seeing what availability is out there.

Aeroplan prices most partner awards at the same rate, except for Emirates, for which they have a separate award chart (which is reasonable in economy and business but has outrageous pricing for first class).

Strategy Four: Opt for Loyalty Program Sweet Spots, Avoid the Landmines, and Consider Upgrades

Becoming an expert will require time and trial and error, but with the resources available on the internet, just know that any question you might have has already been answered by experts. I recommend starting with the top currencies where you have the largest points balances and doing Google searches for "How to maximize [insert loyalty/credit card name here] miles/points" and also the same for "X loyalty program sweet spots." That is a great starting point to understand the strengths of a particular loyalty program and where to begin.

Choose the Sweet Spots

Award travelers are always looking to stumble upon ways to redeem their miles for extreme value. Redeeming your rewards for these so-called sweet spot awards can make collecting points and miles really fun. Sometimes these deals exist due to the unusual ways that airlines classify different regions.

Most airlines will carve out Hawaii as a separate region, making awards to Hawaii no more expensive than those to any other state. When pricing award flights, the Flying Blue program of Air France and KLM includes Israel as part of Europe, while nearly all other airlines place it in their Middle East region and charge additional miles to fly there.

Another example is the LifeMiles program run by Avianca, which is part of the Star Alliance. You can sometimes find gems like JFK to Lisbon, Portugal (on TAP or United), for just 35,000 miles each way in business class. Newark, just a few miles away, to Lisbon costs 63,000 miles (as do most other routes from the East Coast), so the JFK to Lisbon is more of an anomaly than a one-off sweet spot of the chart.

Finding sweet spot awards can be a bit like a game of cat-and-mouse, as airlines and hotels realize that they're undervaluing these awards. You can count on the loopholes being closed or the prices being raised, but sometimes these awards stick around for years.

Avoid Landmines: Exorbitant Fuel Surcharges, Phantom Award Availability, and Strict Program Rules

Fuel surcharges and change fees are two terms you should be familiar with for any program. You may find an amazing deal that ends up being a bust thanks to fees and surcharges. Virgin Atlantic has round-trip business-class awards from the US to London for just 95,000 miles but then charges $2,300 in taxes and fees!

Since JetBlue started flying to London, business-class fares have come down and are often in the $2,500 range, so using 95,000 miles to save $200 would be an abysmal value—less than one-tenth of a cent per point, plus you forgo earning valuable miles and elite miles if you just bought a ticket outright.

That model changes when the flights are more than $5,000, which they can be last minute. Fuel charges can put a damper on good redemptions, so be mindful of the programs that are most notorious for charging them (British Airways, Virgin Atlantic, Emirates, ANA, and Air France). Sometimes fuel surcharges are unavoidable and can still net you a good redemption, but always check the math on what a paid ticket costs, as it might make more sense to book the ticket using points through a credit card portal instead of transferring to a loyalty program.

When transferring your credit card points to a partner to book an award, ideally you want to put the award on hold so you know that it is 100% bookable and nothing will happen while you transfer your credit card points to the currency. Not all programs allow this, but if you can, I recommend it. Usually you need to call and ask for an agent to put an award reservation on hold. If they won't allow a hold, I recommend calling to double-check that award space exists, as often airline websites will show phantom availability, which is a glitch that makes it seem as if award space is available, but it isn't when you go through to book.

Once you transfer your credit card points to an airline, they are generally there for good. It's difficult to reverse a transfer, so make sure the space exists before transferring points.

In the same vein as phantom availability, be mindful of mixed cabin itineraries. Some airline websites will make it look as if you are about to book a business-class award, but the business class is only on a small portion of the trip. An example could be a flight from Chicago to Rio de Janeiro via Sao Paulo, but the only leg that is in business class is the one-hour Sao Paulo to Rio de Janeiro flight.

Be aware of inflexible and strict rules that some programs have. I transferred a massive number of miles to Japan Airlines and tried to book a business-class award ticket for my nanny and the JAL rep said that she didn't qualify as a household member, so I couldn't use my miles to book for her. Sure enough, its website has a strict interpretation of who you can use your miles for, but I hung up and did the reliable method of calling again and hoping for an agent who could help me resolve the issue. Luckily, a second agent booked the ticket, no questions asked, and I never had an issue.

Other programs such as Cathay Pacific Asia Miles have complicated and time-consuming processes for canceling and getting your miles redeposited. I recently had to send an email, fill out a form, and pay a fee to have them redeposited, and the process took several weeks. When possible, cancel your award on chat or with a live agent and ask for the miles to be redeposited right away. When you do it online, it can often take much longer, which can be harrowing when trying to book another award ticket using those miles without losing availability. And some airlines like Etihad charge punitive amounts to change awards.

The Truth About Mileage Upgrades

If you want to upgrade on an airline, you should book a paid ticket with that airline (and not on a codeshare), and ideally directly with the airline. Confirm that the fare you plan to buy is upgrade-eligible before you buy it, and ask if there is confirmable upgrade space available. I don't expect to get upgraded unless I can confirm it at the time of booking.

You're playing a risky game if you buy a ticket and hope to upgrade and waitlist, as many airlines won't clear your upgrade in advance. Some airlines will let you upgrade on partners (like using United miles or Plus-Points on Lufthansa), but often there are expensive copays and additional taxes and fees.

You can search for upgrade space with United Expert Mode for United. For Delta and American, it shows for elites, and if not, you can call.

Booking ANA Business and First Class to Japan with Virgin Atlantic Miles

Let's put these concepts to practice by booking a sweet spot award.

One of my favorite destinations to visit is Japan. The service on Japan Airlines and All Nippon Airways is phenomenal, and I recommend flying Japanese carriers when flying to Japan (or even when flying to Europe). Both airlines have gorgeous new business- and first-class products, but finding space can be tough. You need to be flexible and if you're lucky enough, you can get incredible deals on them by redeeming through partners.

ANA is a Star Alliance airline, but it has a partnership with Virgin Atlantic with amazing redemption rates. From the US to Japan, one-way flights in business class cost 45,000 to 47,500 miles (West Coast departures are 45,000 and East Coast are 47,500). First-class seats are 72,500 to 85,000 one way, depending on if you depart from the East or West Coast.

Those rates alone are way lower than what any US airline will charge for their subpar products, but it gets better. Virgin Atlantic miles are among the easiest currencies to get and they often have transfer bonuses from the main credit card currencies. At the time of this writing, both American Express and Chase have 30% transfer bonuses to Virgin Atlantic, meaning a one-way business-class ticket from the West Coast to Tokyo would only cost 45,000 miles/1.3 = 35,000 points. 35,000 Amex points redeemed for airfare is $350, but instead you can transfer and take advantage of a sweet spot redemption and fly business class.

To confirm it's not phantom availability, I would search Seats.aero for United MileagePlus, which is an ANA partner. North America to Asia. Then select Chicago, DC, NYC, and Boston as departure airports and Narita and Haneda (the two main airports in Tokyo) as the arrival airports, then select "All Nippon" to filter out all other airlines, and then "direct flights" so you can scan all of the availability for an entire year. There are only six options when leaving within the next three weeks, as ANA can be stingy with award space, but they do release seats within three weeks of departure. You'll see in Seats.aero that United charges 110,000 miles one way for Chicago to Haneda on ANA, but we aren't booking via United. We're just using them to find and confirm the availability (if ANA makes an award seat available to United, it generally means it is available to all other partners, including Virgin Atlantic). So disregard the pricing, because that only applies if you are using that currency to book. In this case we'll book via Virgin Atlantic to get a much better rate.

Bingo! On May 6, I see business-class flights available from Chicago O'Hare to Narita, Tokyo, and Chicago O'Hare to Haneda, Tokyo. Normally, I would fly into Haneda as it is much closer to Tokyo. But in this case I would want to make sure the plane I am flying on has ANA's incredible business-class suite called The Room. Two-thirds of their 777s have The Room, and you can always double-check to see if a flight has The Room by searching the ANA website: It'll display "The Room" next to business class on results.

Unfortunately, the Haneda flight uses a plane with its old business class, so I would choose Narita instead. While I'm on ANA's site I'll check the price to buy this ticket outright so we can get a 1 cent per mile valuation on this redemption. It's $8,091 one way to buy this ticket, but all I would need to do is transfer 35,000 Amex points to Virgin at the 30% bonus. Then, I would have 45,500 Virgin Atlantic miles, which is enough for the one-way business-class ticket, plus a reasonable $315 in taxes/fees that comes out to a whopping 22.2 cents per point in value.

Booking Iberia Business Class between Spain and the US with Iberia Avios Leveraging Off-Peak Pricing and Low Fees

The key to Avios is avoiding redemptions on British Airways and partners via London Heathrow by flying on Iberia or Aer Lingus off-peak for low miles and fees (and to stack transfer bonuses to make it even cheaper!).

International Airlines Group (IAG) is the parent company of British Airways, Iberia, Aer Lingus, and several other smaller subsidiaries. These airlines all have their own loyalty programs under the Avios name and one of the unique features is that you can transfer Avios between programs like British Airways and Iberia. Iberia often has far fewer fees and surcharges than British Airways and you can book the same flights via Iberia Avios and save hundreds or even thousands of dollars.

Let's hunt for Iberia flights from Miami to Madrid. I would start by opening up Seats.aero, and even though British Airways and Iberia aren't supported, their OneWorld partner American is, so we can find the award space on American and then price it out on Iberia and British Airways to see the difference in pricing.

Start by applying these filters (note that you'll need an upgraded membership to do this search): Seats.aero ⟶American AAdvantage ⟶ North America ⟶Europe. Then select Full year ⟶Miami as departure city and Madrid as arrival, nonstop only, Iberia airlines, and then sort for business class. There are only 16 dates available nine-plus months away.

It shows 57,500 miles using AA, but when searching on Iberia, it's 42,500 miles and $128 in taxes and fees. Note that Iberia's award chart has a sweet spot thanks to those aforementioned "bands." This is the Chicago ORD to Madrid flight, which is priced the same as the New York and Boston flights, at just 34,000 Avios one way in business, off-peak, with just $150 in taxes and fees.

Strategy Five: Take Advantage of Promotional and Off-Peak Awards

The beauty of increased competition in the loyalty space is that programs are vying for our attention and to do so, they run special promotions that can vary from average to incredible. The key is understanding how special a promotion is and if it can work for your redemption needs.

American, Delta, and United have all had award sales, and the Flying Blue program of Air France and KLM regularly publish award sales that they call Promo Awards. These awards, which have been released every quarter for many years, list various city pairs that you can fly out with, along with a featured class of service, with discounts of 25 to 50%. To get notified about these promotions, I recommend signing up for *The Points Guy* daily newsletter, where staff recap all relevant deals in the industry and do the math if they're worth it or not. You can also sign up for the weekly newsletter I write, which has firsthand tips and advice.

Also opt in to marketing emails from all of your loyalty programs.

Sometimes promotions are targeted, so always log in to your frequent flyer account. United regularly has Mile Play, which is a targeted offer to earn more miles for flights—you just have to opt in. We all like to avoid spam emails, but in the mileage world, you want to make sure you opt in to marketing emails because they can contain super-valuable deals.

You might be able to fly from Detroit to Paris in premium economy for 26,250 miles or in economy class for 15,000 miles each way. And if you're lucky enough to combine a promo award with a transfer bonus, then you could come away with an overseas trip for just a few thousand miles.

Delta is also known for having award sales, although these are much more likely to feature routes that already have highly discounted airfare when purchased in dollars. Even American and United have occasional fare sales.

Airlines will often have promotions with their partners that can be enticing. Recently, Virgin Atlantic offered the ability to redeem miles on its sister company Virgin Voyages. A $3,000 weeklong Mediterranean cruise in peak summer for 160,000 miles, or about 1.9 cents per point, is pretty solid.

But it was even sweeter for those with Amex or Chase points, because at the time of the promotion there was a 30% transfer bonus to Virgin Atlantic, meaning that weeklong cruise for two only required 124,000 points transferred, bringing that redemption value to 2.4 cents per point, which is excellent for a non-air redemption from an airline loyalty program.

Strategy Six: Use Award Holds Before You Book

When you find award availability it can be exciting, but you may not have the dates off work or have enough miles in your account, so you need to transfer from a credit card or buy miles. Before you do any of that, if the program allows, put the award on hold so you know that they are available (and not phantom award space), and it will give you breathing room to make clear decisions on how to get the required miles to ticket the awards. We often make rash decisions when in a panic or rush, so award holds allow you to think clearly and not stress about losing the space.

Here are the loyalty programs that allow award holds (accurate at the time of writing). If you can't do it online, a phone agent should be able to do it easily as long as you provide them with the flight numbers, dates, and class of service of the flight you want:

- Air France/Flying Blue: Three-day holds, $25 phone fee
- American Airlines: Five-day holds for travel beyond 14 days (otherwise, it offers one-day holds). Available online, but $35 if done over the phone
- Cathay Pacific: Three-day hold, $39 for partner ticket phone reservations
- Lufthansa: Five-day hold, $20
- Singapore Airlines: At phone agent's discretion, $25
- Turkish: Two-day hold
- Virgin Atlantic: Two-day hold

Strategy Seven: Understand Routing Rules and Using Them to Add More Flights to Your Awards

One of the most overlooked ways you can juice more value out of your airline miles is by understanding the routing rules and then taking advantage of them. Routing rules are the set of rules that can allow you to add in extra flights for free or a small additional cost. Most people think you can only redeem for one-way or round-trip flights, but many popular airline programs will let you add on extra flights or stopovers in cities at no extra cost.

If you want to visit more places and spend less on flights, I highly encourage you to educate yourself on airline routing rules. It would take an entire book to do a master class on this, but I want to show you the concepts, and you can do the extra research to take your award flights to the next level.

Layovers and Stopovers

A layover is a period of time at a transitional airport between your original and final destination that is less than four hours for domestic flights or less than 24 hours for international flights. If you book a flight from JFK to Budapest with 12 hours between flights at London Heathrow, your time in London is considered a layover, even if you leave the airport and go into London to explore.

If you stayed over 24 hours from the time your flight landed, your time in London would be considered a stopover. Or, if you fly LAX to Dubai and then spend three nights in Dubai and continue on to Malé, Maldives, your three-stay stay in Dubai is a stopover, not a layover. This distinction seems trivial, but you'll soon realize these details matter when maximizing award routing rules. In general, layovers are permitted without penalty, but stopovers can trigger more miles and higher fees.

There are some frequent flyer programs that allow stopovers of greater than 24 hours without increasing the price in miles. An award with the Flying Blue program of Air France and KLM would allow you to fly from New York to Paris, stop over for a week, and then continue on to Istanbul, and it would price out the same as it would with only a two-hour change of planes in Paris.

In practice, you'd have to find both legs at the lowest mileage rate, but this free stopover allows you to add on that Paris to Istanbul leg for a nominal number of miles. I know so many people who book flights to Europe and then "figure out the rest of the flights later" when they could be getting extra flights free as part of the award ticket that got them to Europe.

If you decide you want to visit your friend in Switzerland for a week on the way to Thailand, instead of paying for two business-class awards, 60,000 miles one way from New York to Zurich and 80,000 miles from Zurich to Bangkok, Aeroplan would price that as a single New York to Bangkok flight, which costs 87,500 miles in business class, plus a 5,000-mile stopover fee, bringing the cost of both legs to just 92,500 miles total in business class, one way. This saves you a whopping 47,500 miles by booking a stopover instead of two separate award tickets.

Alaska Airlines offers one free stopover on one-way international awards and two free stopovers with round-trip awards. I suggest an itinerary like flying from the US to Australia with a stopover in Fiji, which would cost the same as an award from the US to Australia.

Cathay Pacific Asia Miles allows free stopovers on round-trip awards and also has a complicated but generous multicarrier award that allows up to a massive five stopovers, which is ideal if you want to take an extended round-the-world-type trip.

These stopover awards are helpful for expats who may want to visit several stops in the US on their way home. It takes some time to learn the rules, but you can extract incredible value from these awards. You can book most of them on Aeroplan.com, so start playing around with the multicity search/stopover feature and see how creative you can get.

Open Jaw

This is a kind of itinerary where you return to a different city than the one from which you departed, like if you flew from New York to London but returned to Chicago. Alternatively, an open-jaw itinerary could have you flying into one city and out of another. For instance, you could fly from New York to London, then take the Eurostar train to Paris before flying home (a great strategy that allows you to save hundreds of dollars' worth of UK departure taxes and fees). A double open jaw would have you departing from and arriving at unique cities on both legs of your trip. These open-jaw award itineraries are essential for those who take cruises that start and end at different ports.

One Way

A one-way flight is simply one that doesn't have a return ticket. Some frequent flyer programs only allow round-trip awards, although most permit you to book one-way tickets. All Nippon Airways of Japan doesn't permit one-way award tickets with its Star Alliance partners. The ability to book one-way tickets is great for mixing and matching award tickets booked with miles from different airlines. You can also use one-way tickets to put together three-legged trips.

United's Excursionist Perk

There's one type of stopover award that deserves its own description. Years ago, United's MileagePlus frequent flyer program eliminated stopovers on its award tickets, replacing them with a unique type of routing rule that it calls the Excursionist Perk.

United describes this offering as "a free one-way award within select multi-city itineraries." When you book a round-trip ticket from one region to another, you can get a free one-way ticket within the same class of service. Let's say that you are flying from the US to Perth, Australia, and then back home from Auckland, New Zealand, which is considered to be in the same region as Australia. If you book your award as a multicity itinerary, it shouldn't charge you any additional miles for the one-way flight between Perth and Auckland.

Strategy Eight: It Never Hurts to Ask

Award booking may be as much of an art as it is a science, and even with all the tools in the world, you can spend hours hunting for the elusive international awards in business and first class. But before you've wasted an entire afternoon and pulled all of your hair out, you may want to resort to something simple: just asking.

One of the best tricks for redeeming points is also one of the oldest and most basic. Simply be nice and ask for what you need. Airline employees are people, too, and most want to help their customers. If you politely explain your situation and ask for their help, you may be surprised to find someone willing to go out of their way, especially if you have elite status.

I've had agents call the revenue management division to open up award space when it didn't exist. While this is rare these days as airlines have opened up more seats for redemption (albeit at higher prices), you can always try asking. This can work over the phone, but you could try requesting a better route when you check in at the airport.

Strategy Nine: Book Placeholder Awards and Keep Up the Search

It can be nerve-racking to wait and see if a good flight deal materializes before you travel, because airfare can start to climb astronomically as the flight date approaches. It's normal to want to have tickets booked.

However, as airfare climbs last minute, so does the lowest level award availability. Airlines try to do whatever possible to fill every last seat, whether with a person paying astronomically to get on a last-minute flight or an industrious travel hacker who knows that airlines release the best seats last minute.

The key strategy here is that even if you have an award booked on a less-than-ideal itinerary on an airline you don't like or that has a long layover, keep monitoring to see what opens up and when something better (whether that's the nonstop or in a higher class of service) comes along, change your old reservation to the better one. This used to cost $150 to $200 per change/cancellation and was only waived for top-tier elite members, but a by-product of the pandemic is that most major airlines started waiving these fees, making it easy to keep checking for something better.

You can keep checking manually to see if saver (the lowest level, most affordable awards on many airlines) or cheaper awards open up or you can set alerts with Seats.aero to notify you if saver-level inventory opens up on a certain route and date. Once you get an alert, book it ASAP, as there's a chance others might be eyeing the same flight.

I was booked to Guatemala on a 65,000-mile United reservation (a $1,200 flight, so I still felt decent about the redemption), but a day prior to leaving, it dropped to 35,000 miles round trip, so I went online, changed it, and got miles refunded back into my account—for free.

Imagine you redeemed your United miles to book an award flight home from Cape Town, South Africa, to Washington Dulles. When you booked it, all that was available was an award flight on their partner, Ethiopian Airlines, via Addis Ababa (a mediocre carrier and a long itinerary). You can wait for a better award to open up or if there's a schedule change, meaning the operating carrier changes times of the flights, sometimes the issuing airline, in this case United, might make an exception and book you onto their own flight nonstop.

I always recommend checking your reservations online, as often it will indicate if there's a schedule change and many airlines allow self-service where they will auto-populate change options. If there's a better option, take it. If not, call and ask if the agent can switch you to the nonstop or a better option that you've researched.

Your best bet is to do the work for them, ask kindly, and you might get what you need. If they don't go for it, it's okay—politely hang up and call again and maybe you'll get lucky with another agent. If that doesn't work, keep waiting for other award inventory to open up so you can change the award when it does.

Strategy Ten: Use Timing to Your Advantage

Loyalty programs usually start releasing award seats anywhere from 331 to 360 days in advance. You may be able to grab multiple seats if you're first to book on the release day. What's interesting is that you can get a leg up on other people by booking via programs that allow you to book the furthest out.

One of the best perks of the Avianca LifeMiles program is that it lets you book 360 days in advance. Let's assume their Star Alliance partner All Nippon Airways releases one business-class seat per route when their schedule opens 355 days out from departure at 12:01 Tokyo time. A LifeMiles member can book it when it opens, whereas United MileagePlus members would have to wait 18 more days to be able to book that seat.

Airlines with a shorter booking window disadvantage their own members from getting the best award space when it releases, so you might want to have miles ready in Aeroplan or LifeMiles to book Star Alliance awards. Or, have British Airways Avios for OneWorld or Air France for SkyTeam, as those programs have a head start on their US counterparts.

Frequent Flyer Program	Days in Advance Award Space Releases
Air Canada Aeroplan	355
American AAdvantage	331
Alaska Mileage Plan	330
United MileagePlus	337
Delta SkyMiles	331
Air France-KLM Flying Blue	359
JetBlue TrueBlue	331
Virgin Atlantic Flying Club	331
Avianca LifeMiles	360
British Airways Executive Club	355

However, certain airlines will start releasing unsold seats within two weeks of departure. One of my favorites is Lufthansa, which is famous for waiting until two weeks before departure before offering most of their unsold business- and first-class seats as awards to its Star Alliance partners like United, Avianca, and Air Canada. Delta, American, and United now allow you to change your award tickets for free, as do many others (some charge a minimal fee).

Strategy Eleven: Split the Team

Traveling as a group can be fun, but your ability to find low-priced international award tickets gets harder as the group size increases. Finding one or two award seats is relatively easy, but three or four on the same flight can be difficult to find.

This is especially challenging for families with small children, but if your group is comfortable with it you can split into smaller groups and reunite at the final destination. If you can find award availability for part of the group on one flight and part on another, and then before departure see if space opens up on one flight or worst case on the day of departure ask at the airport if they'll put the group together.

Especially helpful lounge agents can sometimes bend the rules if there are available seats, and airlines have gotten more flexible with same-day changes on flights. Just because you split the group at booking doesn't mean you'll all fly separately.

If the airline changes the schedule or there is a cancellation, you might all be able to fly together. Flexibility is key and while some families may not want to split up, I did it on our first family points redemption to Grand Cayman in 1996 and it was a fun bonding experience for my mom and me (my dad and brothers went separately) that I still think about today.

Strategy Twelve: Book Positioning Flights

By now you probably realize that airline technology for searching award seats is not great. And when you make it work even harder by trying to find connections, the chances of it returning something good drop precipitously. So, if you live in a non-hub city and always have to connect and you can't find space, I recommend starting with the longest flight you need and then working your way back. If you live in Kansas City and want to go to Buenos Aires, I would try to search from Dallas, Houston, Atlanta, and Miami, and if you can find something from those hubs, work your way back. If you can add in a leg to your home city or a city close by, great. If not, maybe you want to book the expensive long flight and then book what is called a positioning flight, which is a separate flight to get you to the city where your award ticket leaves from.

Someone who lives in Nashville might be unable to find a low-priced award to Europe, complete with connecting flights from their home airport. However, after a quick search it becomes clear that Air France has low-priced 50,000-mile awards from Washington Dulles and Chicago O'Hare to Paris. In this case, the best solution might be to book the available award from the major international airport and then book a positioning flight to the international gateway. That flight could be paid for with points or miles, but you can even pay cash for a short flight and still save plenty of money on the entire trip.

The big risk here is that when you book separate flights, if your first flight is delayed and you miss your connecting flight, you're out of luck.

In this case, since you used miles for that second flight you could always cancel it at the last minute and get the miles back, usually for free or a nominal fee. You'd then still have to get yourself to Europe, which might be a challenge last minute.

To avoid this scenario, try to position yourself the night before a flight, if possible, or at least six hours ahead of the flight to pad for any delays. When possible, book your positioning flight with a partner of the airline with which you redeemed an award. In the case of Air France, you'd want to book a SkyTeam partner. Since there aren't any SkyTeam partners that fly nonstop Nashville to Dulles, you'd probably just want to buy a ticket on United and collect your bags (if checking) and recheck them with Air France at Dulles.

You can also use this strategy in reverse by booking your flight into a major international gateway overseas and then continuing to your destination on a separate ticket. This strategy can work brilliantly when you're able to connect to an ultra-low-cost carrier in Europe. Always tackle the big flight first and then work your way back, and remember the placeholder strategy I mentioned earlier—if something better opens up that is all on one ticket, change to that.

How to Tell If the Redemption's Solid

Apart from fixed-value programs, where you're going to get a set amount of value per point/mile redemption, trying to figure out how much you're getting from your redemption requires some simple math. Here's how I get a sense of whether I'm getting good value for my airline miles.

I take the cash price of the ticket I'm redeeming for and subtract it from the taxes and fees I'm paying on my award flight. For example, I want to fly from New York to London round trip in business class. The cash price of the ticket is $3,566 and to redeem it would cost 189,500 AA miles and $326 in taxes and fees.

I first subtract the taxes and fees from the cash price: $3,566 − 326 = $3,240. Then, I divide the updated cash price by the number of miles: $3,240/189,500, which gets me a value of 1.7 cents per point. This would be a decent redemption for AA miles. I can get higher when I redeem for their partners, like Qatar Airways and Cathay Pacific long-haul business-class awards, but I wouldn't feel bad about getting 1.7 cents.

US airlines give around 1 to 1.4 cents per point with their dynamic redemptions. Here's a cheat sheet to see if you're getting a good value on your redemption. In most airline programs:

- Less than 1 cent per point = bad redemption
- 1–1.4 cents per point = average
- 1.5–1.9 cents = good
- 2–3 cents = great
- 3–4 cents = excellent
- 5+ cents = quit your job and become a points blogger

You're generally not going to accrue elite miles with most programs, so if you're unsure and are aiming for elite status that will give you a lot of value, you might want to buy the ticket outright. Or, you could consider redeeming flexible rewards in a portal like Chase or Amex Travel. While you may not get those excellent valuations, they'll be average to good, and you'll still earn points on your ticket.

On the flipside, when you redeem miles, it's like getting a refundable fare, since most airlines will let you cancel free of charge (or for a nominal fee) and get your miles back. So don't necessarily compare your economy award redemption to the cheapest basic economy flight because that has way more restrictions than an award ticket. I would do your cent-per-point analysis on a refundable fare, or on one with similar change fees to the loyalty program you're redeeming with.

The same goes for hotel stays—if you redeem points for a flexible rate, you can cancel up until the day before arrival and compare the room cost to a rate with similar flexibility, not the absolute cheapest, nonrefundable rate. There is value in flexibility, so don't shortchange your redemption value by comparing it to a much less flexible paid option.

When deciding your valuation, comparing the price of the flight or hotel can be the easiest way. But especially when you're redeeming for expensive business- and first-class flights, it can appear that you're getting up to 12+ cents in value. That's great, but if you weren't actually about to shell out $10,000 for those tickets, can you actually say you "saved" $10,000? Or is the true value closer to what you would have realistically paid for that flight? But the flaw with that valuation is that we don't get to choose the price we pay for flights, so it's a little disingenuous to say the value received is some random number you think the flight is worth when you could have never purchased it for that amount.

I wouldn't get so hung up on the semantics of "how amazing" a redemption it is. If you're happy and you know you got a good deal, you're winning! If you feel like you're not getting the best value or you're letting miles and points expire, those are the scenarios when you need to focus on making sure you know the best ways to redeem, and if you're not satisfied with the options that your credit cards or loyalty programs are giving you, you can always change.

How to Redeem Hotel Points

Redeeming hotel points is much simpler than redeeming airline miles, although the airline loyalty world has many more sweet spots and ways to get extraordinary value than the hotel world. But being smart about your hotel strategy can save you money and get you valuable perks like free breakfast, suites upgrades, and early check-in and late checkout, which can be priceless on long travel days or when stressful travel situations crop up.

While there are many similarities between the airline and hotel industries, they are different business models and it's important to understand the differences as you engage with each. While airlines own or lease their planes (for the most part) and control the customer experience from ticketing, to check-in, to the actual flight, the hotel industry is fundamentally different in that hotel chains are marketing platforms for independently owned hotels. It might shock you to know that Marriott only owns a small percentage of the hotels in its portfolio; for the others, it leases its name, brand, and marketing to individual hotel owners who pay handsomely for the prestige and marketing that comes with being associated with that chain.

Hotel owners pay management fees, and it's up to hotel management companies to market and fill their hotels with guests. Most real estate developers aren't marketing experts who know how to convince customers to fill their hotels, so they need to partner with companies that do—enter the major hotel brands. Not only do they know how to design hotels and rooms to suit customer needs, but they also advertise the chains and fill rooms by offering customers loyalty points and enhanced recognition. The loyalty programs and customer information is what makes hotel chains valuable. In the words of former Marriott and Hilton VP of revenue management Jeff Borman, "Hotels own customers, not real estate."

Every time you stay at a chain hotel like Marriott, Hyatt, or Hilton, the hotel is paying a portion of your stay to pay for the points you receive as part of that stay. This is why you don't earn points on stays booked through online travel agencies, because the hotels have to pay them a hefty fee for bringing you in as a client.

Hotels know that the promise of loyalty points and recognition is enough to make you book directly, so instead of paying around 15% to an OTA, they'd gladly pay 5% to Marriott in the form of rewards. Marriott then pools that money into the Bonvoy program, and when members redeem points to stay at properties, the properties get reimbursed based on a formula related to the average daily rate during your stay and occupancy. The higher the occupancy of the hotel, the more money they make, so in a way many hotels want as many bookings as possible, because they get reimbursed more with higher occupancy.

The reason this matters is because to win at hotels, you need to engage not only with the loyalty program but with the hotel management itself, as they're two distinct entities with differing interests.

As a general rule, the best way to redeem hotel points is on hotel stays. And similar to airlines that used to have award charts based on zones, hotels used to have category-based free nights, meaning all hotels would be assigned a category and if a standard free night was available, it would be priced at the category it was in. Over time, hotels added in peak and off-peak pricing ranges, and the latest trend has been to shift to fully dynamic programs that price based on demand. There are still some hotels that have category-based redemptions, though most of the industry is shifting to dynamic pricing.

Use Technology: Hotel Award Booking Tools Can Help

Similar to airlines, there's no one platform to comparison shop multiple hotel award rates. Luckily, there are startups that will help you search across wide swaths of dates quickly, which can be very useful when booking in-demand hotels, as the average consumer only knows how to use hotel websites, which give a very narrow window.

But just like the airline tools, these tools aren't perfect and often cache data for quick processing, but that means what you see may not be bookable since it could be old data. Verify the availability on the hotel website before transferring any points.

One of my favorites is Awayz.com ($12.50/month). It shows you cash and hotel award pricing for a particular trip from all of the major hotel chains, allowing you to filter by the points you have (even transferable points) as well as by hotels that will accept free night certificates from co-brand credit cards. Additionally, you can search by calendar for hard-to-book hotels and set alerts if award inventory does open up for certain properties.

Some other tools I like that have free versions with paid options are:

- AwardTool $131.88/year
- MaxMyPoint $95.88/year
- Rooms.aero $99.99/year
- StayWithPoints $129.99/year

Let's discuss the top major hotel loyalty programs along with their sweet spots and drawbacks.

Marriott Bonvoy

Marriott Bonvoy is the loyalty program for over 30 hotel brands like Marriott, Ritz-Carlton, Sheraton, Westin, St. Regis, W Hotels, Edition Hotels, Aloft, and Courtyard by Marriott, with more than 8,800 properties globally. Marriott is the largest and most popular US program with a huge footprint of hotels from budget to luxury, but with a large portion of aspirational hotels and resorts.

The Marriott Bonvoy program prices awards dynamically, so the price you pay in points will depend on supply and demand, largely mirroring its cash prices, even though Marriott doesn't officially designate peak and off-peak periods.

Marriott has an incredible array of properties, from budget hotels to luxury resorts, making it a top loyalty program for travelers who want choice but also a lot of high-end options. Marriott offers a fifth night free when you book four consecutive award nights, and the cheapest of the five nights will be the free night. And if you redeem for an upgraded room category, you'll only get the free night for a base room at that property, so the value of that award diminishes when booking higher-priced suites.

Marriott Bonvoy also allows you to use cash and points to pay for stays of two nights or more, and you can decide to use points for the most expensive nights of a stay. It shows the paid rate alongside points, and you can pick and choose where to pay and where to use points. Just note the cash rates don't include taxes and fees, so using points is even more valuable as you don't pay taxes on award stays (only resort fees where applicable; more on that below).

It's easy to book premium rooms using points or a combination of cash and points with Marriott. It's also simple to search by month for availability, which is helpful when booking high-demand properties with limited availability.

Marriott also has a large number of co-brand cards that come with valuable perks like free nights and elite credits, making it relatively easy to requalify for status and get much more in value than the annual fees on those cards just from the free nights alone.

In general, I'm able to get about 1 cent or more per point in value when redeeming at high-end properties like the W South Beach, especially when I get the fifth night free. For mid-tier and budget properties,

I generally see about 0.7 cents per point in value, meaning a 20,000/night hotel would have a cash rate of about $140.

One of the useful things about the Marriott Bonvoy program is that you can transfer your points to miles with 39 airlines, a feature it inherited when it took over the old Starwood Preferred Guest program. Points transfer at a 3:1 ratio, in 5,000-point increments—you'll need to transfer 30,000 Marriott points to receive 10,000 airline miles. However, you get 5,000 bonus miles (or 10,000 United miles) for every 60,000 Marriott points transferred. These transfers can make sense when you find fantastic awards on one of United's partner airlines or need to top up an account that isn't a transfer partner of any of the major credit card programs, like American Airlines AAdvantage, Lufthansa, and Japan Airlines.

Just note that many transfer times aren't instant, so look into having the airline hold your award. When this works, it works well, as you have access to miles with airlines that aren't part of any credit card transfer programs, like Japan Airlines (JAL). I've been able to transfer Marriott points to JAL and use them to upgrade from business to their incredible first class, an excellent value.

Marriott offers many ways to redeem points, and the value varies depending on the reward. You can redeem points to sail with the Ritz-Carlton Yacht Collection at a rate of 90,000 points, for a $500 savings (minimum 180,000 points total), making your points worth 0.55 cents each toward this option, which isn't great. It will only take a small amount off an expensive cruise. Another option is Marriott Homes and Villas, but you'll only receive 0.6 cents in value per point redeemed.

You can also use Marriott Bonvoy points to redeem for experiences, like Formula 1 and box seats at concerts, which can often be complicated to get otherwise.

You can transfer points to Marriott from Amex or Chase. But at just a 1:1 ratio, you won't be getting a reasonable value, as these points are worth less than 1 cent each. But when you need to top off an account, or if there's an attractive transfer bonus, then it could make sense.

On the downside, Marriott imposes costly "resort fees" on awards at a number of their properties, which can increase the cost of your stay. I once paid over $100/night in resort fees at the St. Regis Bahia Beach in Puerto Rico.

Marriott also has limited blackout dates, which some other hotel chains have gotten rid of, though generally I find Marriott properties to be honest with the room inventory they show on the websites. Some hotels will play games to discourage award bookings, but Marriott properties get reimbursed a good amount, so many, like the Ritz-Carlton Maldives, encourage points bookings, and Bonvoy members are often the ones who fill the resort when paid bookings are low.

World of Hyatt: The Underdog and Expert Favorite

Despite its modest number of properties, this program is a favorite of many in the miles and points world because their points are worth the most, and they still have categories for their hotels and reasonably priced awards along with valuable perks from their elite status program.

I value Hyatt points at about 2 cents apiece, as I redeem for higher-end properties, often booking the 45,000-point awards for stays that are generally over $1,000/night. Award nights are priced out on a semi-dynamic award chart, with slightly higher prices at peak times and occasionally lower prices for award night stays during off-peak times as well as what it calls standard pricing the rest of the time. Hyatt doesn't explicitly designate which nights at each property are priced as peak, standard, and off-peak, so the only way to know is to price it out. But unlike Marriott, Hyatt does publish an award chart for its standard rooms.

You can expect prices of 3,500 to 15,000 for Category 1–3 hotels, which are typically mid-tier brands like Hyatt Place and Hyatt House in small and midsize cities. More upscale brands and properties in larger markets tend to be Category 4–6, which price in the 12,000-to-29,000 point range, with high-end hotels in major cities reaching as high as 45,000 points per night. Hyatt offers cash and points rates, with the price you pay per point varying widely between just over 1 cent each to as much as several cents each.

Hyatt doesn't impose resort fees on award stays, which can be incredibly valuable at a time when the price of these questionable fees is soaring— often in the $50 to $100 per night range. Hyatt also offers plenty of perks to its top-tier Globalist members, including free breakfast, 4 p.m. late check-out, and free parking on award stays, but unfortunately, it doesn't offer a fifth night free of awards.

Hyatt offers points plus cash awards as part of its Pay My Way program. When available, the points plus cash option will offer the night for 50% of the cash and 50% of the points. So if the night is $250 or 18,000, then it could be available for $125, plus 9,000 points. So whether you redeem points for part or all of that night's stay, you'll receive the same value per point. But, as with Marriott's option, you can choose to pay with points for some nights and with dollars for the others. And once again, you'll find the most value in paying cash for the least expensive nights, while redeeming your points for the more expensive ones.

Hyatt Homes and Hideaways is its foray into the vacation rental market. While this seems attractive, you only receive about 1.2 cents per point, less than you can usually expect from redeeming your points for award night stays. You can transfer Chase Ultimate Rewards and Bilt Rewards points to Hyatt, both at a 1:1 ratio, which makes Hyatt the most lucrative points transfer hotel program out there and generally a better option than redeeming for Hyatt stays through those travel portals, though not always.

Hilton Honors

Hilton is a larger chain than Hyatt, but not quite as big as Marriott. Points in its Honors program are worth about half a cent each, or less depending on how you use them. Like Hyatt, Hilton doesn't impose resort fees on award stays, which makes it a great choice, and Hilton is popular with mid-tier elites as it offers limited free breakfast for Gold and Diamond elites. And as with Marriott, it offers a fifth night free to award stays of four or more nights.

Hilton operates on a dynamic pricing model, though there is somewhat of a base level for hotels related to standard room availability, though no published chart of categories. As with the airlines, you can find good deals when awards are available at the lowest fixed rates. But when those rooms are booked (if they were ever available), then the prices rise in a fully dynamic way. Want a superior room or a suite? It can end up costing several hundred thousand points per night.

Hilton does have peak and off-peak pricing. As with Hyatt, it doesn't publish which hotels and which nights are peak versus off-peak—you just have to search to find the price. And when standard rooms are unavailable, or you're looking to book any kind of upgraded room or suite, then the pricing becomes very dynamic—often several times the price of a standard room.

When you do find a standard room award at the lowest level of points, award nights in mid-range hotels in small markets can often be about 40,000 points per night, which can feel high when room prices are low. But when booking awards at luxury hotels in large markets, the lowest rates for awards can be around 80,000 points. Even the Waldorf Astoria and Conrad brands top out at 150,000 points per night. This can feel like a bargain, as these properties might sell for five times the price of the lesser hotels in dollars but cost half or a third as much in points. You'll get stronger value from your Hilton Honors points when you use them for luxury stays and when you redeem points for five-night stays.

Hilton also offers Points and Money awards that allow you to pay for any portion of your stay with points, in 1,000-point increments, and your points are typically worth about 0.5 cents each toward this option, which is just below its average valuation.

IHG One Rewards

IHG stands for Intercontinental Hotels Group, which includes Intercontinental Hotels, Holiday Inn, Crowne Plaza, Kimpton, and other brands. Unfortunately, it imposes resort fees on award stays and has a fully dynamic award chart, with no predefined peak and off-peak periods.

Their best sweet spot is that you get your fourth night free when you book three consecutive award nights, but only if you have one of their co-brand credit cards. IHG offers cash and points rates that tend to come out to 0.75 to 1 cent per point. You could transfer your points from Chase to IHG at a 1:1 ratio, but you shouldn't, as their value is almost always below 1 cent each. Because of this, you're better off booking IHG hotel stays through Chase Travel at 1.25 to 1.5 cents a point, depending on which Sapphire card you have.

Wyndham Rewards

Wyndham has many budget brand properties like Ramada, Days Inn, and Super 8; mid-tier brands like Wyndham and Tryp; as well as vacation rental properties through Vacasa, which can be a great value redemption. The program is simple with three categories. All of the nicest properties are 30,000 points per night, but there are some decent ones at 15,000 points per night, with most budget properties priced at 7,500 a night.

The Wyndham Rewards program doesn't have any peak or off-peak pricing, so the best use of these points is during the high season and special events, when room prices in dollars can soar but award prices in points remain low.

In addition to free night stays, which it calls "Go Free" awards, it also offers a cash and points option, which it calls "Go Fast." With Go Fast awards, instead of paying 15,000 points per night, you'll typically redeem 3,000 points and pay about $90 to $120 per night. And if the Go Free award is 30,000 points per night, you'll redeem 6,000 points and pay $200 to $280 per night. Ultimately, this is like buying Wyndham points for about a penny each, or slightly less. Most people would be better off with the Go Free awards and holding on to their cash.

Another wild card here is Vacasa, which is a vacation rental management company owned by Wyndham. You can redeem 15,000 points for one-bedroom units that cost up to $250 per night, including taxes and fees, and 30,000 points for two-bedroom units or one-bedroom units that cost up to $500 per night. These price caps increase the cost of many but not all vacation rental properties. But when you can find a good vacation rental property that slips underneath this cap, you could get nearly 2 cents in value per point.

You can transfer points from Capital One and Citi to Wyndham at a 1:1 ratio. One trick to win with Wyndham is to have its Rewards Earner business card, which gives you Diamond status and allows you to redeem 15% fewer points for awards.

Choice Privileges

Like Wyndham, Choice brands fall mostly into the budget category, like Comfort Inn and Econo Lodge. But don't count them out, as their awards can provide plenty of value, especially at some of their nicer properties in Europe. They have lots of sweet spots at pricey locations in Scandinavia, which you can book for very few points. Choice also lets you use your points to book rooms at the Preferred Hotels and Resorts collection, which includes many high-end properties.

Choice also offers a Points Plus Cash option, which amounts to purchasing points for 0.85 cents each. This is more than the 0.6 cents that these points are normally valued at, but as with all points plus cash options, it can make sense for those who don't have all the points necessary for the award nights that they need.

Unlike most other hotel programs, Choice doesn't impose higher prices during peak travel periods, so you can potentially find great value in its awards. However, one quirk with this program is that you can only book award stays 100 days in advance, so this rules out many peak-period redemptions. But when you do find a great award stay available, it's nice to know that you can transfer Citi ThankYou points and Wells Fargo points to Choice at a 1:2 ratio. American Express Membership Rewards points also transfer to Choice, but only at a 1:1 ratio, which isn't usually worth doing.

Tips for Getting Value Out of Hotel Points

Leverage Sweet Spots: Fifth Night Free

Hotel brands such as Marriott and Hilton offer the fifth night free and IHG offers the fourth night free (to co-brand credit cardholders) on award stays. This can be a great way to save your points while having a longer vacation.

Build a Relationship with the Hotel

If you stay at a hotel and know that you'll want to return, make sure you meet the head of guest services and the general manager. The GM has incredible control over reservations and can allow the rooms department to not only release award space for you but also make sure you get assigned to the best rooms, or get you a room even if the hotel is technically sold out (many hotels will still have some extra rooms available even if it shows as sold out online).

If a hotel treats you well and you want to continue a good relationship with them, make sure you publicly rate them well on Tripadvisor and any other consumer platforms. They notice and appreciate it greatly. I can't underscore enough how creating relationships with the management at the hotels you frequent the most can be the most valuable move you make and will increase the chances of an elevated experience or stay.

Use Points for High Season Stays

Some hotel programs allow you to book award stays in any unsold, standard room. These programs include Hyatt, Wyndham, and Choice (although you have to wait until 100 days before your arrival). When you book your award stays far in advance, you can lock in your free rooms during peak seasons, when prices soar. Even with Choice, you might be surprised to find that rooms are still available 100 days out, as properties can increase their cash prices to match demand.

Watch Out for Hotels Playing Inventory Games

Hyatt claims to make any unsold standard room available for awards, but independently owned properties have become skilled at skirting those rules. It's not uncommon to find most rooms designated as nonstandard, such as a "high floor" room in a three-story hotel, or a property that classifies nearly all of its rooms in its downtown location as having a "city view." You can always ask the hotel to release a room as a standard award—it never hurts to ask.

Work Around Minimum Stay Requirements

Some hotels will block one-night stays, hoping to keep rooms available for those who book longer stays, especially over weekends. If they block availability, try increasing the length of your reservation and if it magically appears, book it as long as it's refundable. You can then try to change it online to the originally intended one-night stay and get the points back for the nights you didn't want.

. . . .

Search for one or two guests, not more. Sometimes hotels will block three or more guests in a room, so search for two and book it, then add a third guest later. Just make sure to eventually add that third guest to the reservation.

Wait Until 30 Days Before Arrival

Sometimes, a hotel won't have any rooms available as awards because it has a very large group booking. But most groups will release any unneeded space 30 days before their event. If this happens, you should be able to book an award night stay at a property that was previously unavailable. Set alerts so you'll know if any award nights become available, as people are always canceling reservations.

Don't Become a Points Hoarder!

Since prehistoric times, humans have hoarded food to prepare for the next famine (remember those toilet paper shortages during the pandemic?). And while it's good financial advice to save money, hoarding points and miles (either airline or hotel) isn't a great strategy.

It makes sense to keep some points and miles around, just in case you need to travel in an emergency or you just want to be spontaneous—especially flexible rewards points. But hoarding points long-term isn't an optimal strategy because you can't earn interest on your points (Bilt is an exception, as it lets members with elite status earn a little bit of interest on their points).

But the main reason you shouldn't hoard points is because airlines and hotels are notorious for devaluing their programs, and often with no notice. I frequently meet travelers who are angry that the airline wanted 160,000 miles for the business-class award flight to Europe that used to cost just 120,000 miles when they first started saving up for their trip a year or two ago. Even once you've accepted this inflation, airlines, in particular, make finding the lowest-priced awards near impossible.

How to Redeem Credit Card Points

If you have a transferable points currency like Chase Ultimate Rewards or American Express Membership Rewards you will have four main ways to redeem, which I'll rank most valuable to least:

1. Transferring to loyalty partners
2. Redeeming for travel through issuers' travel portals
3. Gift cards
4. Cashback/statement credit

Win by Transferring

It is routinely possible to get more than 2 cents per point in value when transferring credit card points to travel partners. In general airline miles can get you the most bang for your point, but there can be ways to get great value out of hotel transfers, too, especially when there are transfer bonuses.

You can also win big at redeeming points when you transfer them to hotel programs such as Hyatt, Wyndham, and Choice, ideally for expensive rooms during the peak season. But beware, you'll almost never want to transfer credit card points at a 1:1 ratio to Marriott, Hilton, or IHG. The points for these three programs are usually worth less than 1 cent each.

There are exceptions, like one of my stays at the Ritz-Carlton Maldives. At the time of writing, you can stay December 29 to January 4, over the peak New Year's holiday, for 656,000 points for six nights. The cash rate of that overwater villa is $6,370 per night, for a total of $38,220. $38,220/656,000 points is a fantastic redemption at 5.8 cents per point in value.

Take Advantage of Transfer Bonuses

You can win big when a rewards program is offering a transfer bonus, and these are becoming increasingly popular. It's not uncommon for Amex,

Chase, Citi, and Capital One to offer bonuses of 20 to 30% to certain airlines or hotels for weeks at a time.

Bilt has had one-day transfer bonuses of up to 150% for its elite members to celebrate Rent Day—I've personally taken advantage of them to transfer to both Flying Blue and Virgin Atlantic. It can be difficult to speculatively transfer points to a currency if you don't know how to use the points, so only transfer if you're comfortable with the program and will know how to get a great redemption in the future. In general I recommend keeping points with the credit card company until you have a great redemption in mind. If you transfer them all out and then a better bonus comes along, you can't transfer them back.

Redeem Through Credit Card Issuers' Travel Portals

Many credit card portals have their own travel sites where you can spend your points. This is one of the better options for redeeming credit card reward points and is relatively easy for beginners. Chase, Capital One, and Amex all have their own travel portals.

The Chase Sapphire Preferred and the Ink Business Preferred cards offer 1.25 cents in value per point redeemed for anything booked through Chase Travel, including flights, hotels, rental cars, activities, and cruises, so 100,000 Chase points redeemed through the portal would be worth 125,000 points. That's not as bad as getting a penny a point or less, but it isn't stellar. But those who have the Sapphire Reserve receive a substantially better 1.5 cents per point, so 100,000 Chase points redeemed through the portal would be worth 150,000 points.

And when you consider how easy it is to just book a trip with points, compared to hunting for scarce, low-priced award seats, it's an attractive option. It's an even better option when you realize that you'll earn miles on the flights redeemed through Chase or other credit card issuers' travel portals. When airlines are having a big sale on business-class flights that earn even more miles, booking through Chase Travel can be a winning choice for Sapphire Reserve cardholders.

The same is true for those who have an Amex Business Platinum card. This card offers a 35% points rebate for select flights booked through Amex Travel. That means you'll receive a net value of 1.54 cents per point redeemed. To be eligible, the flights must be booked with the carrier that you chose for your annual $200 fee credit, or any reservation booked in business or first class.

	Cashback	Gift Cards	Travel Reservations	PayPal Purchases	Amazon Purchases
Amex Membership Rewards	0.5	1.0	0.7 for hotels, 1.0 for airfare	0.7	0.7
Amex Business Platinum 35% Rebate			1.54*		
Chase Sapphire Preferred	1.0	1.0	1.25	0.8	0.8
Chase Sapphire Reserve	1.0	1.0	1.5	0.8	0.8
Capital One Miles	0.5	1.0	1.0	0.8	0.8
Citi ThankYou Points	1.0	1.0	1.0	0.8	0.8
Bilt Rewards	N/A	N/A	1.25	N/A	0.7
Wells Fargo Rewards	1.0	1.0	1.0	1.0	N/A

* (Business- and first-class airfare booked through Amex Travel or flights booked with carrier chosen for $200 annual airline fee credit)

If You Want Cashback or Gift Cards, Get a Cashback Credit Card
If you have a travel rewards card, you should redeem it for travel—transfer to travel partners or redeem via the portal. You significantly lose the value of your points when you redeem for less than 1 cent a point.

The American Express Membership Rewards program offers a terrible 0.5 cents per point redeemed as cash in the form of statement credits. So, $100,000 spent on a Platinum card would be 100,000 points. Those points redeemed for statement credit would be a measly $500. If you had used a Citi Double Cash at 2% back for that same $100,000 in spend, you'd have $2,000 cashback to use as you see fit (and the Double Cash card doesn't have an annual fee!).

Chase Ultimate Rewards offers a more respectable 1 cent per point toward statement credits, but you'll still get much more value redeeming those points for travel at up to 1.5 cents apiece or transferring to airline and hotel partners for 2-plus cents a point in value.

Another poor redemption is purchases through retailers such as Amazon, or credits on PayPal. Chase, Capital One, and Citi all allow you to redeem points for purchases from Amazon.com, but at a terrible value of 0.8 cents each. Citi and Chase offer redemptions through PayPal for 0.8 cents each, while Amex only offers 0.7.

Don't Redeem Points for Gift Cards

When you redeem travel reward points for gift cards, you are losing much of the value you could get from travel redemptions. If you have points that you are redeeming for gift cards, consider getting a cashback card for 2% back on your purchases, which is better than redeeming travel points for less than 1 cent each.

How to Check to See If You're Getting a Good Deal

Can't decide whether to book an award flight or hotel through your credit card travel portal or to transfer your points? Here's how you can do the math. Once you find your best flight or hotel option using point transfers, check how many points you'll need with your credit card travel portal.

Let's say you found an economy-class award flight to Europe for 80,000 miles round trip on a partner airline. Then, you price out that itinerary, or a similar one, for $1,200 on a credit card travel portal. Using Citi, Capital One, or Amex Travel, that's going to price out at 120,000 points. So transferring points is the obvious choice. If you have a Sapphire

Preferred, you'll get 1.25 cents per point, so it will be just 100,000 points. Better, but not good enough to make you go that route over transferring your points.

But if you have a Sapphire Reserve, you're getting 1.5 cents per point through Chase Travel, making the award 80,000 points, the same as the point transfer option. Plus, when you book via the travel portal, it's like a paid ticket so you earn miles and elite miles, so in this case, it would be better to book through the portal.

With flights, when the price in points is close, you'll usually want to choose the credit card travel portal option, as you can still earn frequent flyer miles and credit toward elite status when you book the reservation through a travel agency such as Chase Travel.

However, generally the tickets are not refundable like award tickets are, so there's a trade-off—if you think you might cancel or change your flight I would go with transferring and booking an award because its much cheaper and easier to change awards than it is most paid tickets, where you're stuck with that airline (or potentially a voucher) if you want to cancel.

For hotel reservations, you'll want to transfer your points and book your room through the hotel. When you book your hotel stay through a travel agency, you usually won't receive any of the perks of having elite status or credit toward earning or renewing elite status. And many hotels will give the worst rooms to guests who book their stays through travel agencies.

Chapter 8

How to Win at Perks

Points may open up a world of travel possibilities, but perks can make travel way more enjoyable—and save the day when travel goes awry.

While I stand by my statement that we are in the Platinum Age of Travel, I will admit I'm biased because I know how to work the system. I see firsthand how novice travelers are treated like cattle. They are forced to line up during every part of the journey—when waiting in line to speak to an agent, checking a bag, going through security, and boarding the plane.

. . . .

You can turn down the friction of travel several notches by taking advantage of the perks offered on many credit cards. And before you look at the annual fees on some of these cards and say you could never justify spending that much "on a piece of plastic," what if I told you the value you could squeeze out of the card could save you twice as much as the annual fee every single year or even more?

You might rethink your credit card strategy, *which is the entire point of this chapter.* If you learn one thing, it'll be one of the most salient lessons my dad taught me when I was starting to buy clothes: "Cheap is expensive."

Buy cheap clothes, and you'll have to replace them and spend more than if you just bought high-quality items that are built to last. The same goes for credit cards. Many no-annual-fee cards don't offer a very good value, since cards with nominal fees have perks that far exceed the fee and can save you precious time. But the first step is understanding how to get the most value from them, so let's get started.

How to Win at Airport Lounge Access

As the post-pandemic travel boom continues, each new year sees a new record number of air travelers, but one of the biggest pain points in the US travel ecosystem continues to be our overcrowded and outdated airports. In many of the largest airports, our infrastructure is painfully inadequate. I'm talking about facilities that were built over 30 years ago, which were designed for a time with far fewer flights and passengers and far less stringent security requirements. While many airports have undergone fancy facelifts, there isn't enough space to expand in most major metropolitan areas, so terminals will continue to be crowded.

More severe weather patterns overwhelm our already understaffed and outdated air traffic control system, with little additional slack to handle disruptions. As air travel continues to break records and shows no signs of slowing down, airport crowding will continue and we'll all likely be spending more time inside airports as weather and our outdated infrastructure continue to wreak havoc on aviation.

The airport experience doesn't have to be terrible, and having access to a lounge can sometimes make it downright enjoyable. And unlike the "old" days, you no longer have to be an ultrafrequent flyer to enjoy airport lounge access. Today, many credit cards offer airport lounge access, but not all of these memberships are the same, and the rules for access have been changing rapidly in recent years.

Credit cards with lounge access aren't cheap, but they are cheaper than buying access from the airline, and they come with a ton of other perks and benefits, so if you want lounge access consistently, the best way is to get a credit card that gets you into the lounges you want to visit.

The Three Types of Airport Lounges
Airline Lounges

In the US, lounge access is much different than in most of the world, where lounges are primarily for business- and first-class travelers and top-tier elite flyers. In the US, generally, a first-class domestic ticket isn't going to get you access to the lounge. You need to pay—either via membership, by getting access through a credit card, or by flying internationally in a premium cabin or with qualifying elite status.

The major US airlines have two tiers of lounges: general and premium, the latter usually being in core hubs and only granting access to premium-class flyers on international itineraries or very select elite members. The United Club is the general lounge, and the Polaris lounges are only for passengers on premium international flights in business class. No exceptions.

The Lounge Experience

Airline lounges in the US offer complimentary beer/wine and limited spirits, plus an extensive list of premium drinks that are an upcharge. Food is usually large spreads with salads and soups and sandwiches, though increasingly lounges are adding hot buffet items such as pasta and meat/fish options, usually around mealtimes. Often lounges will have quiet workspaces and showers, which can come in handy when returning from an international trip.

One of the most overlooked benefits of airline lounges is that they are staffed with highly skilled customer service agents who can fix your flight delay and cancellation troubles. This can be a lifesaver when there's a mile-long line to speak with a customer service agent in the terminal—those lucky to have lounge access can go straight to the VIP customer service desk and be taken care of in a fraction of the time that it takes those who have to wait in the general lines. If your flight is experiencing a rolling delay (when it keeps getting delayed and delayed), the airline lounge agents can usually call down to your gate to find out when the plane will *actually* board.

While the pricing of airline lounge memberships varies, the biggest differentiator is the guest policy, which is critical for couples and family travelers. As its Sky Club lounges have become more and more crowded, Delta's guest policy has become the most restrictive, with no complimentary guest access for cardholders and standard members (those with a $1,495 Executive membership are allowed two complimentary guests).

In contrast, the American Airlines Admirals Club and the United Club memberships are much more generous.

Pro Tip: Foreign Partner Elite Status: A Shortcut Airline Lounge Access

An interesting way to gain airline lounge access is through having elite status with a foreign partner carrier. For example, travelers who reach the "Silver" tier in the British Airways Executive Club program are given the "Sapphire" benefits when flying with OneWorld Alliance airlines, such as American, Qantas, Japan Airlines, and Cathay Pacific. These benefits include access to the standard lounges for domestic flights *as well as the fancy premium lounges*, even when traveling in economy class.

You can reach British Airways Silver status with just four flights that accumulate 600 Tier Points, which can be as little as two round-trip business-class flights. You may also be able to request a status match from one frequent flyer program to another, granting you valuable foreign partner status that you can use to enter premium lounges for free. Often these foreign airlines will match your status from a US competitor, so always google the airline and "status match" to see if there are any fast-track ways to get status.

Credit Card–Branded Lounges

In 2013, American Express opened its first Centurion Lounge in Las Vegas, setting off on an ambitious journey to open its own branded lounges in key airports across the country. Centurion Lounges were incredibly well received by cardholders, as they were several notches above what you could expect from a typical airline lounge. Since then, both Capital One and Chase have begun the long process of opening up their own premium airport lounges.

American Express Centurion Lounges

Centurion Lounges originally offered free access to their Platinum (and ultra-premium Centurion, aka Black Card) cardholders, plus two guests. But due to overcrowding, they now restrict access to cardmembers only, and they charge for guests, unless you've spent $75,000 on your card.

Once inside the lounge, you'll enjoy buffets of locally inspired, complimentary cuisine with no upcharges and premium beverages, unlike typical airline lounges. The Centurion Lounges expanded rapidly over the last decade and have far more locations than the Capital One and Chase Sapphire lounges, which only started appearing in recent years.

Capital One Lounges

Capital One has been working aggressively to join the ranks of premium travel reward credit card issuers, and its burgeoning network of Capital One airport lounges is part of that effort. Its lounges feature ready-to-eat food stations, grab-and-go snacks, and full bars with complimentary premium beverages. They even go so far as to include wellness options such as Peloton bikes, yoga facilities, family areas, showers, and relaxation rooms. But what might set these lounges apart is their focus on service, with friendly attendants regularly offering to see how they can meet your needs.

Chase Sapphire Lounges

While Chase has long been a major player when it comes to travel rewards credit cards, it only started opening lounges recently. The brand opened its first Sapphire Lounge in Hong Kong in 2022, followed by several in the US, and more on the horizon. So far, these lounges are on par with both the American Express Centurion and the Capital One lounges.

Third-Party Lounges and Lounge Networks

There are several worldwide airport lounge networks, such as Priority Pass, Escape, and Plaza Premium. With over 1,500 lounges and experiences around the world, the Priority Pass network is the largest of these networks by far.

These lounges vary wildly in quality, and usually the best ones are outside of the United States. Some are gorgeous, like the Punta Cana International Airport (PUJ) VIP Lounge, which offers a spectacular pool with a view of the airfield. Others (mainly domestic) are overcrowded with poor-quality food and overrun buffets. Many facilities can be better than waiting in the gate area if they aren't too packed, but not by much.

Having access to these lounges is nice but not something I depend on. On the other hand, if you're lucky enough to enjoy a high-quality, third-party lounge at your home airport, at your destination, or during a long layover, then it can be a lifesaver.

Obtaining a Priority Pass Membership

A Priority Pass membership can be purchased by anyone for $99 a year, and each visit is $35. The Standard Plus membership is $329 and includes 10 free visits, and are subsequently $35 each, while the Prestige membership is $469 a year and includes unlimited visits, and guests pay $35 each.

It's not the best value to purchase a membership directly from Priority Pass. That's because so many US credit cards offer Priority Pass Select, which usually provides unlimited free visits for the cardholder, with either two free guests or guests for $35. The annual fee of the card may actually be less than the membership cost itself, which makes it well worth it to get a credit card instead of just paying for Priority Pass Select separately.

If you have multiple credit cards with Priority Pass Select, make sure you use the membership from the card with the best guest access.

You can't just show your credit card—you have to enroll to activate your membership. Some issuers will allow you to enroll online, but when in doubt, call the number on the back of your card and ask them to enroll you.

How to Value Lounge Access

Valuations are very personal, but as you make more money and realize how precious your time is, you'll start to value these perks more, especially when it comes to fixing problems when they happen. In my 20s, I would often take $200 to be bumped to a flight two hours later. Now, there is no way I would do that (unless the plane two hours later was much nicer and I was in no rush!).

Even if you are tight on cash, I urge you to take a fresh approach to the credit cards you have because sticking to no-annual-fee cards is likely costing you serious money. Here are the key ways I would evaluate whether it's worth it to pay for a card with lounge access:

Food and Beverage Value

The easiest way to start valuing lounge access is to estimate how much food and beverage value you can get per visit. At many lounges these days, you can now get a full meal and unlimited free drinks. And considering that airports have overpriced concessions, I'd value a meal with a glass of wine at about $50, conservatively. Even a brief lounge visit for water and snacks could easily save you more than $20 in the terminal.

Troubleshooting During Delays and Cancellations

Airline lounges are often home to the most skilled agents—ones who can work their magic to get you home when others can't. This is one of the biggest pros to airline lounges, as it means you can deal with knowledgeable and helpful reps who can fix situations as they arise without long lines and waits. They can do things like process upgrades, assign seats that may not be available on the app, and let you know when a delayed flight is actually starting to board.

Sanity (and Hygiene)

Finally, there's the general convenience value of having access to a lounge. As a new father, I've come to value lounges especially when traveling with my child, as many lounges have family rooms, lactation rooms, and clean facilities to change diapers. It's hard to put a numerical value on this, but having this option in a crowded airport can give you the dose of sanity (or cocktail) you need when traveling with little ones.

Best Credit Cards for Lounge Access

The best card for you is what gets you into the lounges you want to visit the most and will depend on what airline you fly and which airports you fly out of the most. If you're an American Airlines flyer, you'll be hard-pressed to find a better card for lounge access than the Citi Executive card. United flyers will appreciate the United Club Infinite.

The American Express Platinum card has the most lounge access of the bank cards, with access to Centurion Lounges, Delta Sky Clubs, and lounges in the Priority Pass Select network. The Chase Sapphire Reserve offers access to Sapphire and Priority Pass Lounges. Capital One Venture X Rewards is another good option, as it allows you to add up to four additional cardholders for free. Each cardholder gets full access to Capital One Lounges plus guests and a Priority Pass Select membership. Capital One Lounges are some of the newest and most comfortable. Currently, their footprint is small with just a few lounges in Dallas, DC, and Denver, but more are on the way.

If you visit a lounge just five times a year, I think the cost of having a premium co-brand credit card that offers lounge access is justified, so long as you're able to use some of its other perks (which we'll get into later in this chapter).

How to Win at Credit Card Statement Credits

The easiest and fastest way to get value from your travel reward card's annual fee is by leveraging the travel credits and other statement credits offered by it. Growing up, I remember selling Entertainment Books for school fundraisers, which would have provided potentially much more value back—as long as you used the discounts at the participating retailers.

Many premium credit cards have evolved into similar coupon books, each with a litany of credits and offers that can provide value. Card issuers have chosen this model to encourage their customers to keep their cards on "top of their wallet," becoming the card they use for all purchases. But just as with the big coupon books I sold as a child, it can take a lot of effort to realize the most value from cards with numerous statement credits, and quite often, I lose out on value because I simply don't have the time to monitor which credits from which cards I need to use and in which cadence.

My favorite kind of statement credits are for travel purchases since they're generally easy to use, and most people applying for a travel credit card will easily be able to get the full value back. But not all travel credits are the same. The key things you should consider are:

- **What does the card issuer classify as travel?** The American Express Platinum cards offer a $200 annual travel credit, but only for airline fees purchased from a chosen carrier. In contrast, the Chase Sapphire Reserve offers a $300 annual travel credit that applies to nearly every conceivable travel expense, including airfare, hotels, and car rentals, as well as parking and tolls.

- **Is the credit automatic, or do I need to opt in or submit for reimbursement?** The best travel credits on the market are those that are automatically reimbursed when you make a travel purchase. For example, you must opt in and choose an airline to receive the $200 American Express airline fee credit, but there are no steps necessary to receive the Chase Sapphire Reserve's $300 annual travel credit.

- **On what basis does the credit reset—the calendar year or the account year based on when I opened the card?** Every card is different, so make sure to understand these terms. In fact, I recommend double-checking your card's statement credits twice a year just to make sure that you're using them.

Other Statement Credits

One of the most common credits is the $120 credit toward the application fee for TSA PreCheck or Global Entry (which includes PreCheck). This credit is now available on dozens of cards, and it's helpful to realize that you can still receive the credit when you offer to pay for someone else's application (the card issuer has no way of knowing who the applicant is). Sharing these credits is a great way to make sure they don't go to waste while ensuring that your travel companions don't have to wait in line. Some cards are now starting to offer credits toward the CLEAR service, which can help you shortcut the TSA lines.

Statement credit offers can include general reimbursements for travel purchases, airline fees, and hotel stays. Others are offers that only apply to purchases from specific merchants, like the $50 credit that American Express Platinum cardholders receive twice a year for purchases from Saks Fifth Avenue stores.

The key to winning here is just calculating the value. Statement credits can range from streaming credits to Instacart memberships to shopping credits. Would you have shopped there before you got the card? How valuable are these credits, really? Evaluating the price of the annual fee to the value of the statement credits is key.

Free and Discounted Flights and Nights

Many airline cards offer companion tickets that can easily justify the cost of their annual fees and more. Consider the following when evaluating if a companion ticket is worth it: the cost to use the ticket (often there are taxes and fees attached to it, so it is rarely "free"), whether it can be used for first- or business-class tickets, and if the companion ticket can be upgraded. It's also helpful to know if you can transfer the companion ticket to someone else, so your spouse and child can use it, or if it is more restrictive and requires you to use it.

A big winner is the pass you can earn with the Delta SkyMiles Reserve card, which you can use for an economy- or first-class companion ticket. Although it can only be used in the lower 48 states, you can still receive well over $2,000 in value by adding a companion to your first-class, transcontinental ticket or to a trip to Aspen during ski season.

Alaska also offers its credit card users a companion fare, but it's good for only an economy-class round trip on an Alaska flight (not partners), and it costs $99 plus taxes and fees. So there's the chance to save several hundred dollars on a longer, more expensive flight.

And no discussion of companion tickets is complete without a mention of the Southwest Airlines Companion Pass. It offers *unlimited* companion tickets whenever you buy a flight—even if you use points. You have to earn this companion by spending $125,000 on their co-brand credit cards to earn 125,000 points. If that still sounds out of reach, note that the points earned from flying, as well as the new account bonuses, also count toward the Companion Pass, and those are generally 50,000 points or more, so if you get a personal and business card, you've nearly achieved the status from the sign-up bonuses alone.

Once you qualify for the status, you have it for the rest of the year you qualify, plus the entire next year. The goal is to qualify as early in the year as possible so you have nearly two years of a companion flying for free (just paying the small $5.60 or so in fees per segment).

My top pick for the best companion ticket is the Delta Reserve, though if you can score a Southwest Companion Pass and fly Southwest a lot with a companion, you can get thousands of dollars out of the status if you time it correctly.

Award Discounts from Co-brand Cards

Another perk that airline co-brand cards offer is a discount on any award ticket purchases. Delta offers a 15% award discount on all miles redeemed. If you redeem 100,000 miles a year, that is 15,000 miles you saved, worth roughly $200, which is more than the annual fee on their lower cards. The more you redeem, the more you save, so this perk can actually save hundreds of dollars a year for big spenders.

Valuable Perks You Hope to Never Have to Use: Travel and Purchase Protections

- Flight delay and cancellation coverage
- Trip cancellation coverage
- Purchase protection
- Cell phone coverage
- Concierge/reservations

While these aren't always the most lucrative or fanciest perks, they can come in handy. For example, you might pay $11 to $14 per month for an AppleCare plan that covers losses from theft or damage. Many credit cards now come with a similar mobile phone protection plan at no cost as long as you pay for your service with your card, an easy way to save about $150 per year for each phone on your plan.

One of the lesser-known perks of having certain cards is the ability to call the concierge to help you with things like travel booking and dining reservations. Cards such as the Amex Platinum offer a concierge service, but one of the most valuable concierge services is offered by the invite-only Amex Centurion card.

How to Win at Airline Elite Status: The Newest Credit Card Perk

Everyone likes special treatment, and getting it during travel can make all the difference. Having elite status can make travel more enjoyable, with perks like the ability to choose the best seats, board early, and sometimes even scoring free lounge access or upgrades.

The Elite Status Basics: What It Is and What It Gives You

Today, you earn airline elite status by some combination of money spent on airline tickets, the number of flights taken, and/or the amount spent on the airline's co-brand credit cards.

With hotels, elite status is earned by the nights stayed, although many hotel credit cards offer additional night–stay credits. To make it easier, many hotel cards offer elite status just for being a cardholder, and upgrades to higher levels of status just for reaching a spending threshold.

What does having elite status do for you? It all depends on the airline or hotel program, as well as your level of status. At the entry-level airline status, you can expect a free checked bag, as well as access to extra legroom seats, but only what's left over by the time you check in. You also get a higher group for priority boarding, so that you can be sure there will be room for your carry-on suitcase in the overhead bins. And while entry-level elites are eligible for upgrades to first class, don't count on it. These upgrades have the lowest priority behind all other elites, not to mention everyone who originally purchased a first-class ticket or paid to upgrade later. Other benefits include priority service over the phone and at the check-in counters.

As you rise through the ranks, you can expect up to three additional free checked bags as well as higher priority for the extra legroom seats and first-class upgrades. You'll also receive more redeemable miles per flight, and even valuable certificates for confirmed upgrades.

When it comes to hotels, the basic status will often get you a better room, perhaps on a higher floor or one with a view. At the very least, it should keep you out of the least desirable rooms that are in loud places, have poor views, or haven't been renovated recently. You'll also receive priority check-in, which is valuable when there's a big line at the time of peak arrivals. Mid-tier status should get you better priority for nicer rooms, and perhaps a late checkout. And with most hotel programs, there's a big jump up to top-tier status that usually offers complimentary suite upgrades based on availability, lounge access, free breakfast, and an even later checkout option.

The Elite Status Backstory

Up until fairly recently, the only way that you could earn that status was to fly frequently, which is why they were called frequent flyer programs, while hotels had frequent guest programs. When you took a flight, you used to receive one frequent flyer mile for every mile the airplane actually flew.

The airline and travel industry in the US is unique in the culture of lavish upgrades just for being a VIP. Most foreign airlines never got in on the complimentary domestic upgrade game and even today are stingy for top-tier elites when it comes to upgrading. You generally pay for upgrades in cash or miles on most airlines—they couldn't care less if seats went out empty; in fact, it makes the experience better for those paying.

Frequent flyer programs used to focus on enticing and retaining business travelers. A majority of first-class seats were given out as upgrades as few people would pay the outrageous fares that airlines were charging. Airline pricing models were based on fleecing the 1% of passengers who would pay exorbitantly (mostly last-minute business travelers) and then rewarding their elite members with seats that otherwise would have gone out empty.

My first taste of elite status was in 2004. I somehow qualified for US Airways Gold status after flying two transatlantic coach tickets and a handful of super-cheap $89 round-trip flights between Pittsburgh and Philadelphia. Southwest had just entered the route and fares were cheaper than taking Greyhound.

With Gold status, I was upgraded on nearly every flight—as a broke college student with a negative net worth. The system seemed too good to be true! It was then that I stumbled upon FlyerTalk and realized there was a global community of "points people" who had been doing what I inadvertently did: qualify as cheap as possible for airline status and then maximize the hell out of the perks.

In addition to upgrades, I was treated like a king by the airline. Then I graduated and moved to Manhattan, living paycheck to paycheck for years, so elite status moved further down on the list of needs. But I would never forget that year of airline royalty and promised to return to it when I stabilized my finances and could think about affording travel again.

The Shift from Frequent Flyer to Frequent Buyer Programs

Twenty years later, the landscape has changed. No longer do airlines hand out valuable status to cheap college kids mileage running between Pittsburgh and Philadelphia a handful of times. Spending requirements are continually increasing—and cost upward of $30,000 for top-tier status.

In 2023, Delta announced staggering changes to its elite program that would require $35,000 a year in spending on the airline (though they later lowered this to $28,000 after public outcry, which is where it stands today) or $250,000-plus on its co-brand credit cards. The airlines are now competing with bank loyalty programs, which you read about in the last chapter, that offer more value to the consumer in the form of more flexible points. The airlines and hotels have realized their key advantage to winning in credit cards is by winning on perks that you can't get anywhere else, like fast tracks to elite status, companion tickets, upgrades, and more. When analyzing any credit card, you have to look at the value of earning, redeeming, and the perks.

Is Elite Status Worth It?

In many ways, elite status is like a drug. Once you have it, you have to keep it, and the process of weaning off of it can be painful, especially to the ego. I'm not going to tell you whether you should keep qualifying for elite status, but now that status (and how you get it) has changed so much, I'm going to help you to analyze if it still works for you. The opportunity cost of elite status (which now requires an enormous amount of spending on the airline and/or on its co-brand credit cards) has never been higher.

How to Create Your Airline Elite Status Strategy

Elite status still very well may be valuable, but you need to ask yourself: What value am I actually getting out of it? Airline elite status used to be an easy choice to chase when free upgrades were aplenty and the cost to attain the status was minimal. Airlines now sell first-class tickets for much cheaper and offer more paid upgrades at the expense of giving them away free to elites, so the value of elite status is murkier.

When you are deciding whether to allocate your spending to a co-brand card to get elite status, just ask yourself: Will I fly enough and get enough future value to justify putting spend on an airline card, forgoing the opportunity to earn more valuable points on another, transferable points credit card? Just remember the opportunity cost of accruing one singular airline currency versus being able to earn more flexible, transferable points.

Instead of begging for upgrades or trying to get complicated companion certificates with annoying blackout dates, just book flights for free using points and book first- and business-class tickets with them so you won't need to be worried about upgrades. The key to success is becoming a points pro and maximizing your earnings, which gives you so many redemption options. It's not about putting all your money with one airline and getting status and hoping it works out. Take control, know the currencies, and you'll win at points and perks.

My Airline Elite Status History

Let's start with a closer look at my situation. Over the last 15 years, I have been top tier on American (2012–2019), Delta (2010–2012), and United (2019–February 2024). The year 2024 is my first without holding top-tier status on an American carrier. Here are the reasons why top-tier status isn't worth the hassle for me (though it may be for you—this is just my personal experience, so it's important to evaluate your own situation):

1. I'm able to earn so many valuable points by maximizing my spend on flexible rewards that I can accrue enough points to redeem for any flight I want on various airlines, not just with one specific carrier.

2. I generally don't like flying US airlines internationally, as their business class pales in comparison to the competition, and I try to fly international first class, which US airlines no longer offer (American technically does but its Flagship First is on very limited routes and is more like a business-class product).

3. The value I get from top-tier status used to be in upgrades for international flights, though for many years I would end up with expired upgrades because I could never use them. Airlines have gotten stingy with clearing upgrades in advance and the stress of not knowing whether I'm in business class isn't worth the hassle when I can just use miles to confirm myself in business or first class at the time of booking versus spending time checking to see if upgrade space has opened and stressing out.

4. One of the perks I loved most about top-tier status was being able to cancel and redeposit award tickets because I am a master award changer. I'll often change an award multiple times before departure as better options open up. However, during COVID this was a perk most major loyalty programs had given to all members, thus decreasing the value of elite status.

5. During flight delays/cancellations mid-tier status is usually as effective as top-tier status. Plus, I usually book flights via Amex Travel and have found that the experienced agents on the Centurion line can handle any issue. Or, I'll go to the lounge and have the top agents there rebook me in less time than it would take to wait on the phone for an agent.

6. Instead of spending indiscriminately to get super-top-tier Global Services/Delta 360° and then hoping they'll treat you well, pick you up at the plane in a Porsche, I just buy that service when I need it, like when traveling with my son and on a tight connection or coming off an international trip. It's way cheaper than putting thousands on a co-brand airline credit card.

7. For me, time and comfort are paramount, so I'll always choose the best plane and time for my schedule. Being a free agent allows me to choose the best option. When flying from New York to San Diego, I had the choice of a United 737-Max with tight recliner seats for the six-hour flight or JetBlue Mint with lie-flat seats and amazing food. If I were chasing elite status, I would feel pressure to book the inferior flight just for the miles. Nowadays, I pick what the best experience is and what gets me home to my son quicker.

What do I miss about top-tier elite status? Nothing.

I love having as many options as possible when I travel and can focus on the best experience and what saves me the most time. I understand my situation is unique, but I tell this story to encourage everyone to think clearly about elite status to evaluate if it's worth it for you. It can make sense for many people based on where you live and the type of tickets you buy (if your company only buys economy and you fly routes where you consistently get upgrades, then by all means it could be worth it to dedicate your valuable credit card spend toward a co-brand), but I just want everyone to understand the opportunity cost of forgoing extremely valuable points when you're chasing a status that may or may not deliver the desired benefits.

How to Win at Hotel Elite Status

Almost all major hotel chains have loyalty programs, and it's relatively simple (and affordable) to obtain some form of status with many of them, especially if you tap into credit cards.

Hotel co-brand cards offer a lot of perks, including elite status, which can offer you room upgrades, late checkouts, and even free breakfast. But the most valuable perks offered by hotel cards are generally the free nights you get after renewing your card. You'll generally get a sign-up bonus that is worth several free nights, and then every year you renew and pay the annual fee, you get a free night and some offer second free nights when you spend a certain amount during a calendar year. The goal with credit card free nights is to use them for the most expensive night possible.

When it comes to offering elite status as a perk, hotel co-brand cards are far more generous than airline cards, with many offering entry-level status, credits toward higher tiers, or even top-tier status from day one. And I'd argue that hotel status is at least as valuable as airline status, as it can offer you confirmed room upgrades, access to lounges, free breakfast, and late checkouts. You'll also receive bonus points on your paid stays and priority service at check-in and over the phone.

Many hotel credit cards will offer between five- and 15-night-stay credits each year toward elite status, and some brands allow you to earn nights from both a consumer card and a small business card.

How to Create Your Hotel Elite Status Strategy

Many travelers fixate on airfare and focus too much on airline cards. We often forget that hotels and lodging can be a huge piece of the travel budget and I've seen greater inflation in the price of hotel rooms than I have overall in airfare. Remember, a flight is just a few hours compared to a week you might spend in a hotel.

Compared to locating scarce airline award seats, it's easy to redeem hotel points, as most chains offer free nights in any unsold standard room. So, to win at perks, don't overlook hotel credit cards, since they often come with free nights that are easy to use and almost instantly negate the annual fee—and then some.

With hotel elite status, the choices are simple. Hotel programs such as Hilton and Wyndham will offer top-tier status to holders of their premium credit cards and mid-tier or entry-level status to those who have their lower-priced cards. With Marriott and Hyatt, you can gain mid-tier status easily through their credit cards and earn additional credits to achieve top-tier status without too much effort. It's not uncommon for frequent travelers to hold top-tier status in multiple hotel programs and mid-tier status in others. The American Express Platinum even grants cardholders mid-tier Gold status with both Marriott and Hilton, as long as you remember to take a moment to request it.

On one extreme, some Hilton credit cards offer a free night certificate that can be worth well over $1,000 at Waldorf Astoria properties in a destination like New York. But even though the free night certificate offered by the World of Hyatt card is only valid at the lower-priced half of their properties, you can still see $300 to $500 in value when you redeem it. Not bad for a card with a $95 annual fee.

When choosing a hotel rewards credit card, you have to do the math. Add up all of the value of all of the perks: If it's more than the annual fee, it's easy to justify keeping the card, which is why I hold so many hotel cards. But if the perks don't justify the fee, it may be time to move on.

Chapter 9

Hate the Wait: How to Win at Lines

Why wait in lines when you can be relaxing at the airport lounge?

No one likes waiting in line or waiting at all, especially in today's culture of instant gratification. Yet, every time I head to an airport, I just see lines of annoyed people. I always wonder, don't these people know there are quicker and easier options for streamlining their travel experience?

What if I told you could trim those waits? There are so many ways to minimize how long you're in line. I've learned several travel shortcuts over the years, and a smooth travel experience starts before even leaving the home.

IDs and Passports

Have proper, up-to-date identification documents with you every time you travel so there aren't any surprises when you get to the airport.

Have the Right ID (You Don't Have to Have a License to Fly Domestically)

Start off by making sure you have the right ID. The TSA.gov website lists out what you need to show to get through security—and surprisingly, there are many options on there that aren't a driver's license or passport, such as a permanent resident card or DHS trusted traveler card (Global Entry, NEXUS, SENTRI, FAST).

Do note that starting May 7, 2025, your driver's license will need to be REAL ID–compliant for you to fly domestically.

Passport Best Practices

If you don't already have a passport cover, I recommend getting one now. It doesn't have to be fancy, but you should have it protected at all times. Many passports these days have chips inside, and if the passport gets too worn, it can be rendered useless and you'll have to spend time and money getting a new one. Not only that, but some countries will outright reject you from entering if your passport is in bad condition. I used to always keep mine in my pocket and once was yelled at by an immigration officer at JFK, "Treat that thing with more respect!"

Even if you don't have a trip planned, I always recommend everyone have a valid passport. You never know what might come up and I can assure you it is not fun praying your passport arrives in time to take a trip. I'll never forget the week before a friend's destination wedding in Italy, the best man called me in a panic. He'd known about the trip for a year but simply forgot to check the expiration on the passport. He was luckily able to snag a last-minute appointment in Puerto Rico at the passport office there, but he had to eat $400 in unnecessary flights to get the passport in time.

Everyone right now should take note of when their passport expires, and if it is approaching six months of validity, I would recommend renewing it as some countries will require six months of validity to enter.

Go a step further and set a calendar alert nine months before your passport expires (and if you have children, do this for them, too. Remember, kids' passports are only valid for five years, not 10).

It's also a good idea to always have a few blank pages in your passport, as some countries, like South Africa, require this for entry. When getting or renewing a passport, always get the large one that has extra pages—this way, you won't run out. You used to be able to add additional pages to a passport, but not anymore. So, the best plan is to get the larger book from the start.

You can also get a passport card, which only works to enter the US. The card is for US citizens who travel by land and sea from Canada, Mexico, Bermuda, and select Caribbean countries.

If you do need to get a visa or fill out any forms upon arrival, make sure to research this information in advance so you can get it handled before you leave. Always ask flight attendants if there are customs forms available on board that you can fill out ahead to save time upon arrival in foreign countries, and even when they don't have forms, do a quick Google search to double-check as I have been told no forms were needed on more than one occasion, except to be told they were upon arrival. And by the time I was able to fill out the form, the lines had formed, and I had to wait.

Rush Passport Renewal

Most people can use the standard, eight-week renewal service. However, if you need to rush it, use the expedited service ($60) to get it renewed in two or three weeks (note that this doesn't include mail time). If you're traveling sooner than that, you have two options: the Life-or-Death Emergency Service and Urgent Travel Service. Those traveling within three business days due to a qualified life-or-death emergency get priority appointments. Qualifying events include having an immediate family member who has died, is dying, or has a life-threatening illness or injury.

But if you're making a last-minute trip (or you've procrastinated), you can still make an appointment online within 14 calendar days of your international travel date. If your travel is within three days, you'll need an emergency appointment rather than an urgent appointment.

Make an emergency passport appointment at one of two dozen passport agencies around the US. If you don't live in one of those cities, you'll have to travel to one and bring proof of your international travel. For appointments, call 877-487-2778 between 8:00 a.m. and 8:00 p.m. Eastern Time from Monday to Friday and 202-647-4000 after hours, on weekends, and during federal holidays.

If your passport is out for renewal and you need it sooner than expected, call your local congressperson's office—they can put in a request to the Department of State to expedite your processing.

A Word of Caution About Passport Expediting Services

When the need to urgently renew or replace your US passport happens, travelers become desperate and are vulnerable to fraud. There are many companies out there that are eager to prey. The US State Department is the only entity that can issue a US passport, and its website lists this advice: "If you use a courier company, you will not receive your passport faster than applying at one of our passport agencies. Courier companies charge extra fees for their services. We do not charge a fee to make an appointment. If you are asked to pay, consider the request to be fraudulent."

How to Get a Second Passport (and Why You May Want To)

Unless you're a dual citizen, you probably never considered getting a second passport. However, there are several reasons why you may want to get two US passports. For example, you could have stamps from a country that would cause you to be denied entry into another country.

More likely, you could have multiple international trips coming up, and sending one passport out for a visa may prevent you from traveling in the meantime.

Request a second passport by sending in your original passport, along with the DS-82 form used for renewals, and two additional passport photos that are different from the first one. You'll also need a letter clearly explaining why you need the second passport, along with proof such as your flight itineraries or problematic passport stamp and the fee.

If you can't send in your current passport, you can go through a similar process to the one you did when you first applied, including your birth certificate or other proof of citizenship. Then, you'll need to make an in-person appointment at a local passport application acceptance facility, like a post office.

How to Minimize Waiting in Line at the Airport

Check-In

If you're only carrying on luggage, check in online and avoid the check-in counters altogether. If you are checking a bag and flying in first or business class or have elite status, you can use priority access lanes to avoid waiting in long lines.

Many carriers also allow you to enter your passport information or even scan a picture of it in their app, so even when traveling internationally with just carry-on luggage, you can also skip the check-in desks, though you will likely have to validate your passport at the gate. I'd recommend doing this prior to boarding so you don't hold up the boarding line when they ask to verify your passport. This allows you to check in online, skip the counter, and show your passport at boarding.

If you are checking a bag, many airlines have curbside check-in. Just be prepared to leave a tip—$5 a bag is customary, but feel free to give more if the service is above and beyond. If this isn't an option, many airlines let you check in and print your bag tags via an automated kiosk and then wait in a shorter line to drop your bags. Some airports even have a remote bag check option, where you can check bags on train platforms, in parking lots, or at rental car centers.

Holding elite status with an airline usually awards you the right to wait in a priority (read: shorter, in most cases) line. Or, sometimes, you can get this benefit by holding a certain credit card. Of course, holding a large stash of points can help you avoid lines because you can use points for upgrades or to buy business- or first-class tickets, which means you'll be able to queue up in a shorter priority line.

Security Lines

Going through long lines and unpleasant screenings at airport security are some of the worst parts of travel.

TSA PreCheck

The easiest way to make this process less arduous is to get TSA PreCheck, a service that costs $78 for five years and $70 to renew. However, there are nearly 40 credit cards out there that offer statement credits for TSA PreCheck (or Global Entry, which includes PreCheck, as I'll discuss below). And if you have more than one of these cards, you can use your credit to pay for a friend, client, or family member—it doesn't have to be used by the person the card was issued to.

Having PreCheck means that you'll nearly always wait in a shorter line that moves faster than the standard one. It also means that you can leave your shoes on, leave your belt on, and leave your liquids and laptops in your carry-on suitcase. You also go through a plain old metal detector rather than having to endure a slow, intrusive full-body scanner. For those of you old enough to remember, just think of PreCheck as pre-9/11 security.

Signing up online is simple, and then you complete the process at any TSA PreCheck enrollment center. This used to mean a trip to the airport, but there are now enrollment centers located in many areas. Even many Staples office supply stores have enrollment centers. Once there, expect a 10-minute process that includes fingerprinting, document and photo capture, and payment.

If you have an American Express Platinum or Business Platinum card, you can also receive a credit for up to $120 on PreCheck or Global Entry for each authorized user. Platinum cardholders can request additional Gold cards, each of which includes the fee credit, for no additional annual fee.

CLEAR Plus

Another potential way to save time going through security is a private service called CLEAR Plus. This service is available in over 50 airports in the US, and it means you'll skip the initial ID check performed by the TSA. Instead, you're asked to confirm your identity by showing your boarding pass and having a fingerprint or retinal scan. You're then escorted past the TSA identity checker to the actual security screening, which can still be TSA PreCheck if your boarding pass indicates that you qualify.

The standard price for CLEAR Plus is currently $189 for an individual plus $99 for each family member. Some credit cards offer a $189 annual statement credit toward a CLEAR Plus membership, and it's also a benefit of some top-tier elite status programs, while discounts are offered to members of certain airline loyalty programs.

CLEAR Plus is most useful for those who frequently travel out of airports that have this service available. To see if it's a good fit for you and saves you time, consider signing up for a trial first. And always double-check to see if the PreCheck line is shorter.

Other Ways to Bypass Security Lines

- **CLEAR Reserve.** The same company that offers CLEAR Plus also has a free service called CLEAR Reserve at over a dozen airports in the US and Canada and a few in Europe at the time of this writing. As the name implies, this program allows you to reserve a spot in line for security; however, it doesn't work with TSA PreCheck. So I skip it here at home, but I use it in Europe, where PreCheck isn't offered.
- **Priority security.** Long before PreCheck, the airlines convinced the TSA to create a separate lane for passengers traveling in business or first class and those with elite status. While most frequent travelers will skip this line and go straight to PreCheck, it's usually so empty that it can save the day when even the PreCheck lines are long. When outside of the United States, traveling in business or first class is often the only way to enjoy priority service at security.
- **Travelers with disabilities and small children.** Most TSA checkpoints will allow those in wheelchairs and parents with children in strollers to cut the standard lines or go through special lines.
- **TSA PreCheck: Touchless Identity Solution.** This is the latest generation of TSA checkpoints that rely 100% on facial recognition. At the time of writing, it's only in the demonstration phase. Delta passengers at a few select airports and United passengers at some airports have access.
- **Find an alternate security checkpoint.** Even with access to every priority service mentioned above, you can still arrive at the airport at peak travel times, only to find that all of the security lines are severely backed up. But sometimes, you can find a different checkpoint with shorter lines. If the security checkpoint you arrive at is a mess, take a look at the airport map and see if an alternate checkpoint is available that will still allow you to access your gate. For example, Monday mornings at Atlanta's Hartsfield-Jackson International Airport can

be a zoo as business travelers converge on the main terminal at the world's busiest airport. But at the airport's international terminal, two miles to the east, it's a ghost town, as nearly all overseas flights depart in the afternoon and evening. And here's the thing that most travelers don't realize: All of the airport's gates are connected to both terminals, and you don't have to be traveling internationally to use the international one. The same trick works in Los Angeles now that all terminals are connected behind security. And in Miami, Terminal D doesn't have CLEAR, but just a short walk away, Terminal E does. Use the MyTSA app to look up TSA wait times.

- **VIP ONE from Priority Pass.** This service started in 2023, but it's only available at New York (JFK) Terminal 1. It starts in a private screening area where you remove the items from your pockets before being escorted to the front of the TSA line, allowing you to clear security in seconds. And while anyone can purchase this service for $45, the beauty is that it's available for free to Priority Pass members.

- **Fast-track security in Europe.** Several airports in Europe offer fast-track security services for a fee. In Greece, Aegean Airlines sells passengers fast-track service for €6 or less, and in Dublin, Ireland, that fee can be as little as €7.99. Other airlines and airports charge more, but it's always worth a look to avoid having to get to the airport hours early, just in case.

- **Access to fast-track security with the American Express Platinum Card.** Cardholders can show their card and their boarding pass to receive priority security at some airports in Europe and Canada.

Immigration

Global Entry

Sign up for Global Entry, which is a service offered by the US Customs and Border Protection (CBP). Global Entry costs $120 for a five-year membership, but it also includes TSA PreCheck. Global Entry for applicants under the age of 18 is free (as long as they apply with a parent, but more on this in the family travel chapter). However, many credit cards will give you a credit for Global Entry as long as you pay for it using your qualifying card.

Having Global Entry means that I usually clear immigration in less than five minutes on average. Not only can it save me tremendous time waiting in lines, but it also allows me to schedule shorter connections when arriving in the US. Once you have it, you can skip the lines and visit a kiosk that takes your photo. In a few moments, you go see an officer who will usually ask you if you have anything to declare and if not, you're on your way.

The biggest downside to Global Entry is the time it takes to get it. First, you have to apply online. Then, you'll have to wait for conditional approval, which can be anywhere from two days to a year (but usually around one to two weeks). Note, if you are stuck waiting for approval, traveling internationally will trigger the system to process your conditional approval and then you will be eligible to do your interview on arrival when you come back into the US. This process isn't foolproof but many people have reported success.

Finally, you'll have to schedule an "interview" with a CBP representative at an enrollment facility, which is most major airports and a few off-site locations, like Bowling Green in Manhattan. Appointments are often booked for months, but CBP now offers interviews on arrival and even some interviews on departure that don't require an appointment, as well as virtual interviews in some cases.

If you're really struggling to get an appointment, the Appointment Scanner app will help you find last-minute available interview slots (for a $29 fee). If you're conditionally approved and choose to do an interview on arrival from an international flight, you can't use the Global Entry lane until you are approved, so if possible, it's best to do your interview *before* an international trip so you can use the lane when you arrive.

Also, all children and babies need to have their own Global Entry. Even infants need to do an "interview," though it is more to take their photo so they can use the kiosks (yes, I need to hold my infant son so the facial recognition can recognize him—and it does!).

NEXUS

One alternative to Global Entry is the NEXUS program. This service is primarily designed for those frequently crossing the border between the

US and Canada, but it also includes the benefits of Global Entry and a TSA PreCheck membership. It's available to US, Mexican, and Canadian citizens and costs $120, which is reimbursable by some credit cards. The downside is that you need to enroll at a US/Canadian border facility, so if you don't live near one, it might not make sense to get it unless you're crossing the Canadian border often.

Mobile Passport Control

Without Global Entry or NEXUS, your only other option to skip the lines is to use the Mobile Passport Control (MPC) app, which the CBP offers at no cost. To use it, download the app and spend a few minutes scanning your passports before your flight. You can use it for everyone you're traveling with, and it's even available to foreign nationals from countries that are part of the Visa Waiver Program with approved ESTA (Electronic System for Travel Authorization).

Upon arrival, you open up the app, enter your flight information, and fill out a few standard arrival questions. Once you submit the form, you'll receive a barcode that you show to the CBP officers at immigration, just like Global Entry users.

So it's simple, quick, and free. What's the catch? For reasons known only to the CBP, they don't open the Mobile Passport Control lines at all times. So unless you have Global Entry or NEXUS, using MPC is like having an unreliable parachute: It's great when it works but terrible when it doesn't.

Traveling Abroad for Work? Join the US APEC Business Travel Card Program

Verified businesspeople and US government officials who are US citizens and existing members of a trusted traveler program can apply for this program, which fast-tracks entry for 20 countries. A "verified business person" is considered to be someone who is engaged in the trade of goods, the provision of services, or the conduct of investment activities in the covered countries (athletes, entertainers, and media don't count).

Getting Into the Lounge

You've made it through security in record time, and now you're making a beeline toward the lounge—but there's a line.

Sadly, there's not a whole lot you can do to skip the line into a lounge. At major international airports like LAX and JFK, you might find that you have access to multiple lounges. For example, Priority Pass offers three different lounges at JFK airport's Terminal 1 and another three at Terminal 5. And if you have a business- or first-class ticket, you can access the lounge of the airline you're flying but also the lounges of their alliance partners. For example, someone flying EGYPTAIR in business class out of JFK Terminal 1 has access to both the Turkish Airlines Lounge and the Lufthansa Business Lounge.

American Express lets you check in to its Centurion Lounges in advance, but it only saves a few moments when checking in—you don't actually get to skip the lines. Thankfully, Capital One's new lounge network allows you to check in online in its app and saves a place for you in line. Let's hope that Amex and others take a cue from Capital One going forward.

VIP Lounges and Service Packages

The newest trend is for airlines and other parties to offer even more exclusive lounges and packages of services. For example, American offers its Five Star Service that includes access to Flagship First Check-In and the Admirals Club lounge, as well as priority boarding. And if your flight is delayed or canceled, you even receive priority status for re-accommodation. You'll also enjoy personalized service through the airport and car service coordination upon arrival. However, you must have a ticket in business or first class, and the cost is an extra $350 for the first person, plus $100 per additional adult and $50 per child aged 17 and under.

If you want more, you can book the Five Star Select service, which also includes Flagship First Dining and American Airlines vehicle or cart transfer inside the airport. The cost here is $650 for the first person, plus $150 per additional adult and $75 per child aged 17 and under.

Delta offers its VIP Select service that includes being met by a Delta representative at the curb, as well as an escort through security and into the Sky Club with a reserved table. You'll then be brought to your gate upon departure. It doesn't guarantee a tarmac transfer in a Porsche, but some passengers receive it. The cost is $500 for the first passenger and $100 for each additional traveler, up to four, and you can be traveling in any class of service. It's available at Delta's nine largest hubs and focus cities.

Then, there's the PS services available at LAX and Atlanta, which are both major destinations for those in the entertainment industry. They offer access to a private luxury terminal with a tarmac transfer to your flight. The cost is $1,095 for the "Salon" and $4,850 for the Private Suite, with discounts available to those who purchase an annual membership ($1,250 for the Salon membership or $4,850 for the All Access Membership). Amex Centurion cardholders currently get two free visits a year.

Bypass Boarding Lines

Lines to board an airplane aren't the worst, but being toward the end of the line often means that by the time you board, the overhead bins are full, and you may have to check your carry-on. Many gate agents will force you to check your carry-on, even when there's actually plenty of space in the overhead bins. They just want to get the flight out on time, even if it unnecessarily inconveniences passengers.

Having elite status or being seated in business or first class will offer you a better boarding position. Some airlines will also give preference for those traveling with disabilities, as well as families and active duty members of the military. If you have an extenuating circumstance like an injury and would like to board early, always ask the gate agent nicely, and they will more than likely let you board early.

After that, holding certain airline co-brand credit cards means you'll be able to experience priority boarding. It may only be group 2, or somewhere behind everyone in business or first class and those with elite status, but it's enough to avoid waiting in a long line or being forced to check a bag.

If you're with someone who has priority boarding (or who's seated in a different class), you can try boarding together—but it likely won't be allowed. In the end, it's at the gate agent's discretion, so it might be permitted or overlooked, especially if one person needs assistance.

Minimize Wait Times When Calling Airlines

Wait times can be long (up to hours) to speak to an agent on the phone, especially during weather events when everyone is trying to get in touch with the airline. I always try doing what I need to do online, as many airlines will now let you rebook yourself online. Try the chat feature in the app or on the website, as those agents are empowered to change your itinerary and you may get through sooner than you would on the phone. Some airlines also have social media customer service teams.

One tip is to call one of the airline's foreign offices, as most airlines will have English-speaking agents. Or, call the US airline's number and choose the Spanish-speaking option. These centers often have shorter wait times and their representatives are usually bilingual and also speak English.

Minimize Waiting to Check In at Hotels

Hold Elite Status

Most hotels have dedicated lines for those with elite status in their loyalty programs. Nearly all hotel cards come with entry-level status that's enough to give you access to a priority check-in line. The American Express Platinum card offers entry-level status with both Hilton and Marriott—you just have to request it.

Check In Online

The hotel industry is increasingly upgrading its properties to allow online check-ins with mobile keys. To be eligible for this, make sure to sign up for the hotel's loyalty program. Note that you may still have to visit the front desk to show your ID the first time you attempt to use online check-in and mobile keys.

Look for a Kiosk

You'd be surprised how often I see a long line of weary travelers waiting to check in to a hotel, completely ignoring a lonely kiosk that would allow them to quickly check in and receive their keys. So before you resign yourself to the hotel's long line, take a quick look around and see if you can do it electronically.

Minimize Waits for Rental Cars

For many travelers, the last stop before departing the airport is often the rental car counter. And sometimes, these lines can be long.

But rental car lines may be the easiest ones to skip. All you have to do is sign up for the company's frequent renter program. This allows you to enter your credit card and driver's license into your profile. In many cases, this lets you skip the counter and go directly to your car. With most companies, you'll see a message board at the entrance to the lot, telling you which car is yours. However, some rental car companies are offering customers the ability to simply select the car of their choice from an available section or choose their car in advance online.

Minimize Waits at Tourist Attractions

You've made it to your destination, and you're excited to see the Parthenon, the Louvre, the Pyramids, or the Taj Mahal. Once again, long lines can conspire to ruin your experience at major tourist attractions all over the world. Here's how you can limit that from happening.

Plan in Advance

Most major tourist attractions now sell tickets online, in advance, and many require reservations. When it comes to the busiest ones in the world during peak season, you can't just walk up and buy a ticket like you can for your local museum. So unless you're visiting during the off-season, you need to buy your tickets in advance (some even have timed entries) for major attractions in European capitals. Just be careful to buy your tickets from the official source, as there are many copycat websites that will gladly sell you tickets with a huge markup, and what you get may not even be valid.

Consider Attraction Packages

There are companies that offer packages that include tickets to many attractions, along with "skip the line" privileges. Companies like this include CityPASS and Hop-On Hop-Off sightseeing tours. This can be an effective way to skip *a line* even if you don't skip all the lines. While you might not have to wait in line to purchase the ticket, you may have to contend with a line to enter the attraction. Still, it's better than nothing.

Book a Tour

In many countries, tour guides get priority access to major attractions. This can either be an official policy or an informal financial arrangement between local guides and those who staff the entrances. Either way, you'll find that a guide will quickly escort you past the lines and into the attractions in places like Mexico, Egypt, and India with a few friendly words in the local language. Thankfully, these are also countries where you can often book a car, driver, and guide for the day for a very reasonable price, at least by American standards.

Disney: The Happiest Place on Earth (If You Can Skip the Lines)

Children's love of Disney theme parks may only be matched by a parent's hatred of their long lines. Entire books have been written about how best to experience Disney parks, but if you're looking to breeze past lines, you should purchase a Lightning Lane Multi Pass or a single-use Lightning Lane Pass up to three days in advance. Guests at Disney properties can book seven days out.

Multi Pass starts at $30 per person at Disneyland and between $15 and $35 at Disney World. The cost of Individual Lightning Lane Passes vary by ride and demand. There is also the Lightning Lane Premier Pass, which is still in its pilot stage with limited availability. This daily pass ranges from $129 to $400 (not including regular admission) and offers one-time access to every Lighting Lane ride in your chosen park, meaning you'll get to skip those long lines and enjoy rides at the times you want.

Those with bigger budgets can purchase VIP tours that include prearrival planning, Lightning Lane access, and a tour guide. These tours cost

$450 to $900 an hour for groups of up to 10 guests, depending on the season. There's a minimum of seven hours, and park admission isn't even included, so get ready to spend for these privileges.

There are also private VIP tours of attractions like Disney World and Universal Studios. These services are also pricey but could represent some savings compared to the official services.

If all of these options are out of your budget, you can still use Disney's free Genie service, a planning tool that's part of its app that attempts to predict crowd levels to best plan your day.

Chapter 10

How to Win at Traveling with a Family

*Traveling with children is a skill that will
improve over time and with practice.*

Starting to travel early on with your children will help them become savvy and seasoned travelers from the beginning, but that isn't always an option, so don't stress—whenever you decide you're comfortable traveling with your family will be the right time to start.

I thought I was a true travel expert before having a child, but I had no idea that I would have to learn yet another convoluted system, especially when traveling internationally. Understanding the system and family travel infrastructure (or lack thereof, in some cases) will make travel much easier. This chapter outlines the basics of what you should know when traveling with babies, kids, and teens, including some mistakes I've made and successes I've had, airline rules and regulations, key things to understand, and more.

Said T. Daneshmand, MD, a board-certified OB-GYN and IVF expert who helped me start my own family, gave me advice and tips on family travel as a medical professional and father of three.

Consult your physician before traveling while pregnant. If you are traveling with a child who requires a car seat, you may consider speaking to a Child Passenger Safety Technician to determine what best practice will be for your specific trip itinerary.

How to Win at Traveling When Pregnant
Travel starts to change even before your child is born.

Basics of Travel When Pregnant

- Check with your airline for rules on up until when you can fly
- Consult with your doctor before flying
- Get travel insurance when traveling internationally, as US health insurance generally does not apply internationally
- Travel to destinations with accessible healthcare and have a list of reputable facilities in the case of an emergency

When to Fly

In most cases, if you have a healthy pregnancy, understand possible risks, and feel well enough, experts say it's safe to fly until around 36 weeks. Certain doctors may also advise against air travel in the first trimester, especially before your first ultrasound. ACOG, the American College of Obstetricians and Gynecologists, says that most women with "normal" pregnancies can travel safely up until their due dates, though you may be uncomfortable as your due date approaches.

"Medical studies have shown that in the absence of any underlying medical conditions complicating pregnancy (such as diabetes, high blood pressure, growth restriction, conditions requiring rest and frequent monitoring, among others), air travel is deemed safe during pregnancy," according to Dr. Daneshmand. "It's also important to note that the most common obstetric emergencies occur in the first and third trimesters. Check with your doctor before planning any travel to decide what's right for you."

Flying when pregnant is largely a personal choice that depends on many factors, but the most important thing is to check airline policies before booking travel. Some airlines require a doctor's note for travel after a certain number of weeks while others have no requirements. You may have a doctor's note but find the airline never asks you for it; other airlines may require you to upload the note online before travel.

Planning a Babymoon

A babymoon is a fantastic idea for many reasons. Adults need one final trip before being parents, and it's a great time to recharge and focus on the final stretch of pregnancy. Many people opt to take this trip sometime during the second trimester, when hopefully most morning sickness subsides and also before they have to think about delivering or worry about running into airline policies requiring doctor's notes.

If you're planning a babymoon, you may want to consider the duration of air travel when selecting your destination. "During pregnancy, physiological changes occur which may increase the risk of blood clots. In addition, low cabin humidity, changes in cabin pressure, and restrictions on aerobic activity can lead to changes in heart rate and blood pressure with possible increased risks of venous thrombosis. Fortunately, these risks are low, and there are preventive steps that can be taken to minimize them," says Dr. Daneshmand. These steps include walking around and moving your lower extremities, wearing compression socks, drinking water, and wearing loose, comfortable clothing.

When selecting a destination, avoid areas with extreme temperatures or poor air quality. "The CDC recommends pregnant travelers avoid areas with a Zika outbreak for the duration of the pregnancy," Dr. Daneshmand notes. The CDC website has more information on which areas of the world have high risks of Zika (Central and South America) and malaria (Africa). You may also want to avoid flying anywhere that requires intensive vaccines (like yellow fever) or where you have a higher risk of contracting serious infectious diseases.

Pregnant travelers should make sure to plan ahead. It's always a good idea to pre-research a nearby hospital or doctor you can visit in your destination should you have any issues. Dr. Daneshmand advises looking for "facilities that are capable of managing complications of pregnancy or newborn/pediatric problems."

When traveling internationally, you might want to consider both booking your trip on a credit card that offers medical evacuation and purchasing travel insurance since US health insurance policies often won't cover you when traveling outside the US. Just note that most travel insurance policies will only cover unexpected pregnancy-related costs, not a normal delivery if you are traveling near your due date. As with all insurance, the devil is in the details, so I recommend comparison shopping on

InsureMyTrip.com and choosing the policy that best suits your situation and destination.

Where to Sit and Other Tips

When flying while pregnant, aisle seats are usually a good choice so you can get up and move around and use the lavatory as needed. Bulkheads are good options, as they can be closer to the lavatory, and you won't have people reclining into your space. Just know that bulkheads often don't have moveable armrests, so if the seat next to you is empty, you won't be able to take advantage of the space.

While most airlines allow pregnant women to sit in an exit row, you must be willing and physically able to assist in case of an emergency, so keep that in mind when choosing a seat, depending on how far along you are. Airlines can deny someone from sitting in an exit row if they feel the person can't complete the procedures in case of an emergency or might impede the emergency exit process so just know if you pick that actual seat, you may be asked to move.

Have plenty of water and snacks, especially if you're battling any nausea, and avoid foods or liquids that encourage gas.

Although turbulence injury risks are rare, the Federal Aviation Administration encourages all passengers to wear their seat belt whenever they are in their seat, even if the seat belt sign is off. Dr. Daneshmand especially encourages proper seat belt use for pregnant passengers. "The seat belt should be belted low on the hip bones, between the protuberant abdomen and pelvis," he said.

And don't forget to pack useful OTC medications in your carry-on. Dr. Daneshmand suggests, "In addition to travel health kits, pregnant travelers should pack antacids, antiemetics, graduated compression stockings, hemorrhoid cream, and medication for vaginitis and yeast infections."

Partners and Fellow Passengers: Be Ready to Assist

Partners, if you're traveling with someone pregnant, be ready to do all the heavy lifting, both figuratively and literally. Your partner is dealing with (and actually carrying) a heavy load, so taking charge of some of the organization, packing, and logistics is something they'll appreciate. And fellow passengers, if you see a pregnant person struggling with, well, anything—a suitcase, a child, or even to stand up, offer a hand, especially if they're traveling on their own.

Giving Birth on a Plane

If you're pregnant and worried about giving birth on a plane, it's highly unlikely—though not impossible.

It's extremely rare for babies to be born in the air, aka skyborns—only 76 babies are known to have been born on planes. In 2021, a woman flying Delta from Salt Lake City to Honolulu gave birth unexpectedly at 29 weeks. Luckily, there was a doctor and several NICU nurses who delivered the baby using what they could, even using shoelaces to cut the umbilical cord!

Babies born in the sky face unique citizenship challenges. If a baby is born over US airspace or in US waters, they receive US citizenship, but the same is not true in the UK. If the baby is born in international airspace, sometimes the citizenship or place of birth is where the aircraft is registered. In a few cases (reportedly on airlines like EGYPTAIR and AirAsia), these babies have been given free flights on that airline for life. However, this is a drastic way to get a freebie—learning the points and miles game is a much safer and more enjoyable way to travel inexpensively for the rest of your days.

How to Win at Traveling with an Infant

How early can babies fly? My son, Dean, flew at three days old, so I understand how daunting it can be to fly with a baby so young when your instinct is to protect them at all costs. But if you do have to fly with a newborn, as many parents who adopt or have surrogates do, here's what you should know.

Newborn Age and Health to Fly

Always consult your pediatrician before flying with a newborn. Mayo Clinic suggests that babies should be at least a week old before flying, and

Dr. Daneshmand offers the same recommendation. Meanwhile, some healthcare professionals suggest waiting until your baby is a few months old (or has had their first round of vaccines, especially if you're traveling abroad). This depends on various factors, such as your baby's general health and your own, especially if you've just given birth, as jet lag, general exhaustion, and postpartum can be a challenging combination.

All airlines have different rules, with some stricter than others regarding newborns flying. United Airlines is firm with its seven-day rule, while American Airlines allows babies just two days old to fly (though they'll need a doctor's note if younger than a week old). Delta says that newborns under seven days old need a doctor's note, and Southwest's ruling is 14 days, but fewer with a medical release.

Most international airlines have similar rules. British Airways allows 48 hours (but recommends seven days), while Singapore's rule is seven days, but two days with a doctor's note. The point is that traveling with a newborn means you'll need to read a lot of fine print on rules and regulations when it comes to the age of travel and a variety of other key things I'll cover below.

Minimizing exposure to others is the most important thing to consider when flying with a newborn. As a new parent, your top goal is to make sure your child doesn't get a fever within the first three months, which can lead to complications. Newborns haven't yet developed a powerful enough immune system to handle basic defenses, so this is why you may have friends who don't want many visitors until the baby is three months old. At that point, most babies' immune systems are sufficient.

While I offer different advice later about boarding with toddlers, preboarding with newborns is a good idea, as you don't want to be fighting for overhead space to store those diapers and wipes. Most airlines allow families with babies or young children to board first, even before passengers who hold top-tier elite status.

When it comes to the safest place for small children or babies to sit on a plane related to health and germ avoidance, sitting as close to the front is always best. Since boarding and deplaning is when passengers are crowding and breathing on each other, sitting in the front minimizes exposure to other passengers when deplaning. If two people are traveling with the baby, one can preboard to get overhead space and get set up, while the other can board last to minimize time on the plane and the crowded boarding process.

"When traveling with a baby, fly during less busy times so as to maximize your odds of finding an empty seat next to you," said Dr. Daneshmand. The least busy days to fly are often Tuesdays, Wednesdays, and Saturdays, and also during the workday as most business travelers usually try to get the first flights out and the evening flights home. I think the sweet spot would be late morning, as the chances of flight delays increase as the day goes on.

If your baby or child is occupying their own aircraft seat, they should sit in an approved child restraint system and use it in accordance with the manufacturer's instructions. Put them in the window seat, and you should sit in the middle seat as to best shield them from other passengers. You can also put on the air vent to "push away" any germs that flow near your baby—just be careful it's not blowing directly in their face. Putting them in the window seat can also minimize risks of things falling on them from overhead bins or injuries from bar carts or spilled hot drinks.

To help your baby's ears adjust to the pressure changes in the cabin, try to have them nurse or drink from a bottle (or use a pacifier), as the sucking will naturally help ears adjust. If your baby has had any ear infections or issues, Dr. Daneshmand recommends "checking with your pediatrician regarding the safety of flying and use of acetaminophen or ibuprofen." If you're on a very long flight, using saline drops for your baby's nose can help keep their nasal passages moist and prevent colds and coughs that can occur from the dry air.

Seats, Seat Belts, and FAA-Accepted Child Restraint Systems

While commercial aviation is incredibly safe from a fatal-accident perspective, when traveling with children, you need to worry about extreme turbulence and in-cabin incidents, which are becoming more common and unexpected. Another rare but possible incident that could cause serious injury to a small child is an aborted takeoff, where brakes are applied to stop a takeoff quickly. For these reasons, I always put my son in the window seat, which gives him protection from the aisle and also keeps him far away from escaping and getting into trouble.

Flying on either a domestic or international airline with an infant under the age of two also comes with a dizzying assortment of seating rules. Most US airlines, such as Delta, United, American, and Southwest, allow a child under the age of two to either sit in an adult's lap or occupy a seat—complete with an FAA-accepted child restraint system—or be able to sit upright in their own seat without assistance.

Just know that if you purchase a seat for your baby, it'll often be at the full (or slightly reduced) price (and they can start earning frequent flyer miles, but more on that later). Having an infant in a car seat occupying their own seat is the safest and most convenient option, but the chances of extreme turbulence are low, and your drive to the airport is likely more dangerous than your flight, so don't let anyone shame you when making the decision between getting your baby their own seat or having them fly on your lap.

When it comes to babies sitting in car seats on the plane, Child Passenger Safety Technicians can help answer your questions. Child Passenger Safety Technicians are certified professionals trained to educate parents and caregivers on the proper use and installation of car seats, booster seats, and seat belts for children.

I spoke to Lia Tuso, a Child Passenger Safety Technician who specializes in aviation, for more clarity on how to safely fly with babies, toddlers, and young children.

"The safest way for a child under 40 pounds to fly is in an FAA-accepted child restraint system or car seat." Presently, the only FAA-approved harness is the CARES harness, manufactured by AmSafe ($83.99). Although there are cheaper knockoffs and alternatives, Tuso recommends getting the original on the AmSafe website (https://www.amsafe.com/product/kidsflysafe-com/). While the CARES harness may be used with children weighing 22 to 44 pounds, it is often not the first recommendation by

Child Passenger Safety Technicians. Notably, it doesn't fit children well until the higher end of the weight limit and it requires a child to maintain an upright position throughout the duration of the flight, which is naturally quite challenging for toddlers. "Using a child restraint system or car seat on the aircraft is the safest way to minimize the risk of injury should an accident, runway emergency, or severe turbulence occur," Tuso told me.

She also gave me some additional tips:

- Verify your car seat is permitted for use on planes. It should have a label that says something like "certified for use in motor vehicles and aircraft" in red lettering. Note, booster seats are never permitted for use on aircrafts.
- When traveling on a domestic airline, you are required to use your child restraint system or car seat per the manufacturer guidelines. Know that an infant rear-facing-only car seat must only be used in the rear-facing position. If you are traveling with an infant using this type of car seat, it is especially important to check your international airline policies prior to travel, as some airlines prohibit car seats that are solely rear-facing entirely.
- The aircraft seat belt is intended for children who weigh more than 40 pounds. Once your child exceeds 40 pounds you no longer need to use a child restraint system or car seat on the aircraft. (The FAA is always evaluating this, so stay alert for possible changes in the future). "Even after your child has reached this weight minimum, you may still consider using your car seat on board the aircraft, as this is the safest way to transport it," says Tuso.
- The most common front-facing travel car seat for children ages two and older is the WayB Pico ($345–$390), which is easy to transport and to install in both airplanes and cars.
- Review your car seat user manual before you travel, and practice your installation at home. Your aircraft installation may vary from your vehicle installation.
- If you must check your car seat, be sure to use a protective bag or box. Always inspect your car seat thoroughly for damage upon receipt at

baggage claim. Contact your car seat manufacturer with questions regarding any damage to determine if a replacement seat is needed.

- Visit the Federal Aviation Administration's "Flying with Children" web page for additional tips.

Remember, lap infants are free on domestic flights (and discounted on international flights) until they turn two, so many parents will want to take advantage of this for as long as possible. Just know that every baby is different, and some may prefer to sit in your lap so you can feed or calm them, while others find it easy to nap in their car seats. You'll find what works best for you, your baby, and your family—sometimes by trial and error.

Belly Loop Belts, Bassinets, Babywearing, and Child Comfort Beds

Some international airlines won't let you buy a seat for a baby under the age of two; instead, they offer the adult a child seat belt (known as belly belts or supplementary loop belts) that loops through the adult belt to use for a lap infant. "Both the FAA and Transport Canada prohibit the use of supplementary loop belts (belly belts) on their aircrafts. Because these belts attach to the adult and sit entirely over the infant's abdomen, the infant absorbs the forces as the adult's body bends forward over the child, leading to an increased risk for severe injury to the infant. In simple terms, the infant acts similarly to an airbag," Tuso says. "To provide the best protection and reduce the risks posed by unexpected turbulence, both the FAA and Transport Canada recommend using an approved child restraint system for infants and children." Other airlines state that your baby will need to be able to sit upright to occupy a seat. Before traveling, make sure to understand the rules each airline has about traveling with infants, as they often vary.

"If your baby is sleeping on your lap during the flight, stay alert and check on the baby often so as to ensure that the baby can breathe easily and there is no obstruction or covering over the face," says Dr. Daneshmand. For children in car seats, Child Passenger Safety Technicians recommend removing your child from the car seat every two hours. If you're on a long-haul flight, a quick walk up and down the aisle while the seat belt sign is off is just enough of a stretch break.

Many airlines offer bassinets, which are baby beds that generally latch into the bulkhead wall—a lie-flat seat for your infant. Bassinets are usually only available on widebody flights, so call your airline to reserve a bulkhead seat as they are often unmarked on seat maps and you can only select them by calling. Bassinets are not child restraint systems and can't be used during takeoff, taxi, landing, and turbulence for safety purposes.

Babywearing during takeoff, taxi, and landing isn't permitted. While it is up to the flight attendant to enforce this policy, it's important to understand the reasoning behind this FAA regulation. First off, baby carriers and baby wraps are made of materials that do not pass the required standards of flammability and strength. Next, testing concludes that the adult moves forward crushing the child and increasing the risk for injury to both the infant and the adult during rapid deceleration. Tuso adds, "We know that babywearing doesn't have an acceptable potential for safe transport of infants on aircrafts, as confirmed by the International Civil Aviation Organization."

In recent years, inflatable beds and other child comfort sleeping devices have become more popular. Caregivers should know that none of these products are safe to use when the seat belt sign is on, but especially during takeoff, taxi, and landing. "In order for the aircraft seat belt to operate as intended, it needs to be worn correctly," says Tuso. "Children are especially at risk when they're sleeping in a horizontal position with the seat belt across their chest or below their armpits." While these devices may be helpful for some peaceful shut eye during a long-haul flight, many airlines don't permit their use.

The best advice for dealing with logistics like age and seating rules when flying with an infant is to read the fine print and policies in advance once you have your chosen airline in mind. Most airlines have clear child restraint system and car seat policies on their website. You'll know exactly what is and isn't allowed, which means you can pack and prepare accordingly.

Car Seats

When it comes to infant travel, a combination car seat and stroller is a convenient option. Not many are FAA-approved at the time of writing, but I recommend the Evenflo Shyft Dualride ($599.99+) and my personal favorite, the Doona ($550+). The latter was an ideal option for my son as a newborn—some of his easiest traveling days were when he was tucked into his Doona snoozing away on flights.

However, Dean is in the higher percentile for growth and outgrew his infant carrier sooner than most infants. These types of combo travel solutions can be really helpful, but it's important to know that they aren't a forever seat. Children typically outgrow infant carriers around 12 months, at which time you will need to find a rear-facing convertible car seat. A popular rear-facing convertible car seat for travel is the Cosco Scenera Next ($60+), as it weighs six pounds. Always review weight and size limits before purchasing car seats.

The WayB Pico's lightweight and portable car seats are popular travel options for forward-facing children over two years old. Know that what works for one family may not be a safe option for your child, and I encourage you to speak with a Child Passenger Safety Technician if you have car seat–related questions.

Keep in mind that renting a car seat is not recommended due to the safety risks involved. "Often rental car companies will provide a car seat that is not a safe option for your child's age, weight, and height. Additionally, rental car companies might clean the seats with harsh chemicals or against the manufacturer's instructions," explains Tuso.

Finally, there's no way to know the crash history of the car seat. If you must rent a car seat, renting from a baby gear company like BabyQuip or Babies Getaway may be a safer option. They will also have strollers, travel cribs, and other child items you may need.

Plus, if you want to take an Uber you'll probably have to have a car seat, as many rideshare services will decline to pick up passengers with a baby in the parent's lap, and in most cities you're required by law to use a car seat in a rideshare.

Finally, I always recommend practicing installation at home before traveling. It can be stressful trying to get your car seat properly installed in a rental or rideshare vehicle, but it's worth taking the time to do it. And of course, always use your child's restraint system in accordance with manufacturer instructions.

Strollers

The rules about bringing strollers and car seats on board, checking them at the counter, or gate-checking them can be confusing and overwhelming, as they vary from airline to airline.

Most airlines allow adults to check one car seat and one stroller free of charge, either at the gate or the check-in counter. However, check the rules if you're flying with a non-US airline, just in case. Whether or not your child is sitting in their car seat on the plane or needs to sit in the stroller to ride through the airport can help you determine the best place to check them or if you'll be checking them at all.

My top tip is to get a stroller you can take on board so you'll never have to deal with standing at the oversize baggage claim (where strollers and car seats come out) with your cranky baby for nearly two hours after a nine-hour flight from Europe to wait for your umbrella stroller to come out. Even if you want to bring a larger stroller, you can gate-check it instead, and often they'll be able to give it to you at the gate on arrival, but not always. Remember, though, all gate-checked strollers still need to be able to fit through the TSA machine, so large double strollers, for example, will have to be checked at check-in.

If you're wondering if your stroller can fit in the overhead bin, it should fold up to less than the following dimensions: length of 22 inches (56 cm), width of 18 inches (45 cm), and depth of 10 inches (25 cm).

The most widely accepted travel stroller is the YOYO Stokke ($449+), as it's smaller than these dimensions when folded. However, more brands are also making travel strollers that are now acceptable to carry on with most airlines, so check and review sizing and airline rules before purchasing.

Since I'm so tall, I struggled to find a travel stroller that extended enough for me to comfortably handle it. Tall parents, take note: One of my favorites is the Ergobaby Metro+ Deluxe ($399+), which features a handle that extends to make it easier to use. I've had to imply it's a YOYO to certain gate agents, but I've never been denied boarding with it, and it has fit in the overhead bin of all planes, even smaller regional jets, when folded. I once had to put it in a red trash bag to fly with it in the overhead bin on Japan Airlines, so you may be subject to some strange rules, but at least you can bring it along with you.

Traveling with Milk and Formula

You don't actually need to be traveling with an infant to bring breast milk on a plane with you, according to TSA regulations. You can pack it in your checked bags or carry it on with you. It's not subject to the 3.4 ounces/100 milliliters in a quart-size bag rule, but you do need to tell the TSA agent at the beginning of the screening process that you have breast milk. Know that these items may be subject to additional screening processes, and you may have to open them.

This rule also applies to infant formula, as well as baby-related water, toddler drinks, and baby/toddler food (like pouches or jars) that are larger than 3.4 ounces.

The European Union also has similar rules. You can bring more than the allotted 3.4 ounces/100 milliliters limit, but only enough to reasonably last you throughout the trip. While I've never attempted to bring particularly large quantities along with me, I've always had the items screened separately but never opened in security.

Just remember to tell the security agent you're traveling with these liquids so you won't be stopped after the fact, which can slow down your experience getting through security. As policies may vary by country and/or airline, it's best to check both before traveling to ensure you understand exactly what you can bring.

If this all just seems like too much, you can also ship breast milk using services like Milk Stork or even FedEx. Milk Stork organizes the logistics and comes with the supplies you need to keep milk frozen or refrigerated. If you choose to go the FedEx route, make sure to use sturdy Ziploc bags and source dry ice, gloves for handling it, and a cooler.

I also suggest never fully depending on an airline for things like meals, snacks, or formula. While you could probably live without a crummy airline economy meal if they run out of pasta, not having formula for your baby or the right snacks for your cranky toddler makes for a very difficult flight for everyone involved.

0–24 Months: Paid Tickets, Award Tickets, and Loyalty Programs

Each airline has its own rules and pricing for booking plane tickets for infants and children—both lap infants and separate seats for under and over age two.

Currently, all airlines allow babies under two to fly for free as lap infants on domestic flights. For international flights, expect to pay around 10% of what the full-fare adult ticket is for that flight. Often this can be exorbitant, and you may have success negotiating with the airline or asking them to price it to the cheapest available fare, not the full fare. It never hurts to ask. Some airlines may charge a flat fee, such as Ryanair, which charges €/£25 per trip.

In general, I always recommend booking an infant at the time you book your ticket, when possible, rather than adding them to the reservation later because the longer you wait, the higher the fares will be on your flight, meaning the airline's fee to add your lap infant will be higher—it's a percentage.

Plus, doing this in advance can ensure your infant is properly ticketed and you won't have issues on the day of your trip.

Always double-check your reservations, especially when you use miles on partner airlines. It can often present more issues with infants-in-lap, so make sure everything is ticketed appropriately and you're able to check in.

When you upgrade with a lap infant, be prepared to pay more taxes and fees. Once, I'd booked business class to Tokyo round trip, and Dean cost $600 to add onto the $6,000 ticket. When I used miles to upgrade to first class, I had to pay a whopping $2,300 for Dean since they base the 10% on the going first-class fare, which at the time was $23,000.

Not all airlines will charge exorbitantly for lap infants. For international travel, United Airlines has a maximum charge of $300. American has a glitch when booking with miles where an infant will be the same price as an adult, but if you book the adult tickets and call to have a lap infant added, it will be free (domestic) or 10% of the adult fare internationally.

Some airlines make lap-infant upgrading much more affordable using miles. Emirates allows upgrades using miles—even on award tickets—and when I upgraded Dean and myself from business to first class on a ticket from New York to Milan, it was 39,000 miles for me and 3,900 miles for Dean and no additional cash (which would have been expensive as Emirates First Class on that route is $8,000+ one way).

While some airlines make it expensive to travel with a baby (Qatar won't even let you book a baby in business or first class online—you need to call and add them on after you book yourself), some loyalty programs make it very easy and affordable to add an infant. By far, the best is Aeroplan, which is Air Canada's loyalty program and a Star Alliance partner. Infant lap tickets cost just 2,500 miles or $25 CAD for international trips each way (domestic routes and flights between Canada and the US are free for infants).

Virgin Atlantic is another optimal program for ticketing lap infants using miles, charging between 1,000 and 5,000 miles per segment, depending on the class of service.

If you choose to buy your child under two a separate seat (if you're traveling alone with two children under the age of two or just want to buy your infant their own seat), the cost may be reduced from an adult fare ticket, so it may not always be the best use of your points. Infants that occupy their own seats are typically charged as a child fare, which, in some cases, can be 25% less than an adult fare. Remember, airlines have specific policies regarding children under two occupying their own aircraft seat. For example, some require the use of a child restraint system or car seat, while others prohibit rear-facing-only car seats. Review your airline's child restraint system policy prior to booking a seat for your child under two years old.

If your baby is under two when you leave on your trip but two or older when you return, typically, most airlines will make you pay the full child fare or use miles to book a full-priced award for your child. Other airlines will make you pay the one-way child fare on the return. The exception is British Airways—so plan that London trip around your baby's second birthday. Although your child will need to have their own seat once they turn two, the airline will maintain the price of the infant fare.

I recommend signing up your infant for frequent flyer programs just after they're born. Dean started earning miles almost immediately after his birth since I bought him his own seat when possible when he was an infant because he slept soundly in his Doona, and it felt like the safest option. If you forget to sign up for a program, keep your boarding pass. You can usually go back and retroactively credit miles after you fly in most programs. Plus, having a frequent flyer account allows you to preload TSA PreCheck onto all of your reservations automatically.

However, in some programs, kids will need to turn two before getting their own account, and others, such as British Airways, won't let babies or children have their own accounts, but they can be part of household accounts.

Some programs require filling out paperwork, but others, such as Delta, make it easier. Parents only have to click a couple buttons to create a Sky-Miles account for their kids. You may have to keep up with mileage expiration dates with certain programs, but American Airlines AAdvantage miles don't have expiration dates on accounts where members are under 21.

How to Get a Passport for a Baby

If you plan to travel internationally, your baby will need a passport. It's best to get on this right away after they're born, so if any international travel opportunities arise, you and your family will be set and ready. I started getting organized for Dean's passport before he was even born, looking into the process and noting the documents I would need.

Get a start by immediately requesting a long-form birth certificate after your baby is born. I requested 10 birth certificate copies when Dean was born so I'd have plenty of extras. This is even more essential for LGBTQ+ parents, as you always want to have a birth certificate with you when traveling. This is also important for single parents or when traveling internationally.

The US State Department website contains all the important information you'll need, including the paperwork to fill out, the exact fees, and how to make an appointment. Do note that both parents should be present when applying for a baby's passport, but there are forms you can fill out if one parent can't be there.

The hardest part of the process was the photo, which I brought on myself by thinking it would be easy to do at the post office since they had photo capabilities. However, I quickly realized the folly of my ways because babies must have their eyes open, and it has to be *just* the baby in the photo, not even your hand propping them up.

New babies have zero neck support and sleep all day, so even catching them with their eyes open is like spotting a leopard on safari: rare. So, trying this in a post office in my new-father-sleep-deprivation state was pure chaos as the 20-year-old camera had a long delay, making it nearly impossible to snap him when his eyes opened briefly.

Instead, just lay your baby on a white sheet at home, take a picture on your phone, and then get it printed at a local convenience store that prints passport photos.

Once you have a photo that meets all the requirements, there are a number of online photo editors and apps that can help you crop it to the correct size.

What to Bring When Traveling with Infants

Most parents think bringing more, rather than less, is the way to go when traveling with an infant, but it's all about packing smarter. Remember, you still have to carry all your bags as well as your infant (and possibly a stroller and a car seat), so being conscious about not overpacking is important, especially if you're traveling alone with your infant.

One of the best tips is to bring one diaper per hour of the flight and airport time (including layovers). Although this seems excessive, if you're met with delays or cancellations, this could be a game changer.

Ziploc bags are lifesavers. Bring them to hold food and formula, to store fresh clothes, or to hold soiled items. Wipes are another item you don't want to run out of on board. Bringing a change of clothes in your carry-on, not only for the baby but for yourself, is also essential, especially on long or international flights. No one wants to sit on a plane covered in spit-up (or worse). Wear clothes you don't mind getting rid of—at worst, you can literally throw your clothes (or the baby's) away if you're met with an insane blowout.

For newbie parents: Blowouts are massive explosions of bodily fluids that can be so large you can't even fathom that they came out of such a tiny baby. These often occur at the most inopportune times, such as during boarding or as soon as you need to fasten your seat belts for takeoff.

When it comes to changing your baby's diaper on board, find a bathroom—most, though small, have changing tables. If you can't locate a changing table, ask a flight attendant for guidance. **Don't change your baby on your tray table or seat.**

However, if you do have a situation where there's a blowout emergency and bathrooms are full or locked, ask the flight attendants for help. You may even be able to use the galley floor for a diaper change if all else fails, just make sure you have something to lay your baby on (like a portable diaper changer or blanket) as you don't want to dirty the floor that others will walk on. Remember, many flight attendants are parents, too, and they've experienced countless flights with babies and children on board. I've even had FAs watch Dean when I've been traveling alone and had to use the bathroom.

Finally, make sure to find a family bathroom at the airport before your flight for a final diaper change. Of course, babies never plan their blowouts, but having a fresh diaper right before boarding may minimize the chances of situations occurring during takeoff, which can be stressful if you can't get up and move around or are seated in a bulkhead without access to key items in the overhead bin.

This is also when having a credit card that offers lounge access can really come in handy. Many of the newer or recently renovated lounges have family bathrooms, feeding rooms, and other spaces apt for families.

Know that you can organize your route at your home airport to include lounge visits, family bathroom adventures, and even play areas for kids. Most airports have maps online that you can view to get a lay of the land and set up a path that will allow you to get your baby ready for the flight in a family bathroom or lounge or give your toddler a chance to blow off some steam in a play area before boarding.

Where to Sit on the Plane

Most bassinets are located in bulkhead rows, so if you plan to use one, you'll want to sit there. But if you aren't going to use the bassinet, bulkhead seats aren't the best (some airlines also may not allow you to sit there with children or babies on certain aircraft). Additionally, most bulkhead seats have nonremovable armrests, which may make car seat installation challenging.

Yes, you'll have more legroom, which could be useful when flying with older babies that are learning to stand (my son loved to stand between the bulkhead wall and seat, hang on to my knees, and play when he was just learning to stand and walk), but because you can't store your items at your feet during takeoff and landing, it's really annoying if you leave your bottle or another essential item in the overhead bin and your baby starts to scream during takeoff.

Not all babies will take to bassinets (Dean never did), and you can't use them during takeoff, landing, or turbulence, so you may have to risk waking up your baby to take them out if turbulence hits. This is a situation when having your baby sit on their own in a car seat might be preferred, as they'll often sleep through any rough air.

You may want to be careful having babies or small children sitting in aisle seats, where carts may bump their limbs or hot beverages are being passed around and could spill on them.

Remember, babies can't sit in exit rows, so just plan accordingly. Infants and children traveling with a child restraint system or car seat are commonly required to sit in the window seat, as to not block emergency exit access. Child restraint systems and car seats are prohibited in the aisle seats and emergency exit rows, and some airlines also prohibit them forward or aft of an exit row.

If you're exceptionally tall, it may be worth having the bulkhead, you just have to organize your belongings and make sure you have what you need during takeoff and landing. Babies also can't occupy certain seats as lap infants if they don't have additional oxygen masks, so you may be limited when choosing where you sit. I once got kicked out of an exit row, even though my nanny and Dean were seated in the row behind me. Staff knew I would be holding him at some point during the flight, and it simply wasn't allowed.

Finally, the US Department of Transportation's Airline Customer

Service Dashboard (available online) has a breakdown of which airlines guarantee adjacent seats for children 13 and under to sit next to an accompanying adult at no additional cost for all fare types. Sadly, only four US airlines guarantee family seating: Alaska, American, JetBlue, and Frontier, so I recommend choosing seats as soon as you book your flights as it will create more stress on your day of travel if you're begging to be seated next to each other on a sold-out flight.

Should Babies Travel in First Class?

You probably know where I stand on this issue, as Dean has flown in first and business class all over the world. While he's usually a very well-behaved traveler, any child is going to have their moments.

The way I view it is that in most business- and first-class cabins, you get noise-canceling headphones, and domestically most travelers in the front of the plane have them, so it's easy to block out unwanted noise.

Commercial air travel is public transportation, so if you want to control who flies on the airplane you're on, you should charter your own. If you can't do that, I'm not interested in your thoughts on where me or my child belong on the plane.

But to make sure I'm not out of line, I asked Richard Branson, cofounder of the Virgin Group, which includes airlines like Virgin Atlantic, if it was cool to bring a baby in first or business class or if it's better to fly in economy. He's a grandad himself and told me, "Babies are delightful, even if they keep you awake on a flight. The sounds of kids should be welcome."

I couldn't agree more with his sentiments. I've flown many times with my infant in first class, and he behaved better than many adult passengers. Although there's always the possibility of meltdowns, I find it actually becomes much harder to keep a child calm while flying as they become toddlers with infinite mood swings and opinions versus an infant who just wants to snooze. In most cases, tiny babies sleep for a majority of the flight, anyway.

However, for children close to age two and in certain travel situations (like if you want a bassinet, as only some airlines offer them in business class), economy or premium layouts may actually work better for families than business-class pods, so make sure to understand the aircraft layout before booking travel.

Some cabins prohibit the use of a child restraint system or car seat. Namely, Delta's flatbed seats in the Airbus A330-200 and A330-300, United Polaris business on Boeing 767, 777, and 787, American's first class in the Airbus 321T, and business on Boeing 777-200, 777-300, 787-800, and 787-900.

In most cases, if you and your partner or another adult you're traveling with are sitting in separate cabins, if the baby comes into business class, they need to have a business-class ticket. I was once on a flight where a dad was in first class and a mom was in business class. The flight attendants asked if I minded if the baby visited first class to see his father. I didn't, but in most cases, if one person is in economy and the other is in business, the baby will need to be listed on the business-class ticket to sit there. You can always try asking FAs if your baby can visit a higher cabin class, but there are no guarantees.

Tips and Tricks for Traveling with Infants

These are my five top travel mantras for families:

- **Don't stress.** Your baby feeds off your energy, so set the tone. Traveling with infants can be nerve-racking, especially if you're already an anxious flyer, so do what you can to not let nerves get the best of you. Your babies absorb all of it, so having a good attitude can help them adapt more easily to the process of airports, flights, and traveling in general.
- **Plan.** Organizing and preparing can decrease your stress level and ensure you don't forget anything important.
- **Set up a family travel structure.** Have a checklist of necessities that you can use for every trip, making future trips easier as you get the hang of things. Packing lists and delegating prep to family members can create processes you can repeat again and again for each trip. As your family changes and grows, these lists and preparation tactics can also evolve.

- **Always pack extras.** A parent's worst nightmare: Naptime without a pacifier or a delayed flight without wipes or diapers. You will inevitably lose that pacifier or forget things, so making sure to have enough of the really important items (yes, this includes snacks) is key.
- **Know that it's okay to fly with children.** Even though the attitude around kids can be negative in the US, most of the world is welcoming and friendly to family travelers. Many European countries have security and immigration lines just for families and are much more accepting of children than they are in the US.

A crying baby is *not* a reflection of your parenting. Just do your best to calm them in flight and try not to panic. I don't recommend packing "sorry" gifts. Babies have a right to fly just like anyone else, and these types of gifts set an unnecessary precedent that we need gift packages to tolerate small humans.

Yes, it would be pretty cool to receive a set of Bose noise-canceling headphones from a fellow passenger—perhaps a frazzled parent of twins. That's exactly what Amal and George Clooney did on a recent flight to "prep" passengers for possible tears and bad behavior from their twins. But that's taking things too far. You shouldn't have to apologize or give gifts for having a kid. Remember, we were once all babies, too.

Babies will cry, though, so what should you do? I found that walking Dean down the aisle, rocking him in the crook of my arm, and shushing worked wonders and would calm him back into a state of sleep.

Flying with babies earlier gets them used to it, and the humming of engines actually serves as ambient noise. Babies often cry when they're hungry, tired, or just not feeling great, so be prepared with milk, formula, snacks, and gas relief treatment.

Don't be afraid to walk babies and small children down the aisle (you can also ask FAs if you can stand or walk in the galley). Try to remain as calm as possible, especially when holding your baby. They can feel your energy and heartbeat, so staying calm will help them stay calm.

Even to the smallest babies that don't understand, explaining exactly what's about to happen each time you fly can help them know what to expect as they get older and begin to understand. For example, "First, we'll board the big airplane. Next, we'll find our seats and store our luggage in the overhead bin, and then, we'll sit down and put our seat belts on."

What to Do When Babies Start Walking

Don't expect flight attendants to be childcare workers; that's not their job. Although Etihad launched a Flying Nannies program in 2013, it's no longer in existence. If you fly with your children, it's your responsibility to look after them.

Screen time is controversial, and each parent should make the best choice for their children when flying. The American Academy of Pediatrics discourages using screens for kids under the age of two, with limited screen time between the ages of 18 months and two years when watched with a caregiver. "Pediatricians have serious concerns regarding the use of media entertainment for children under two years of age, so educate yourself regarding their use and potential effects on your children," said Dr. Daneshmand.

If you're okay with giving your child screen time in limited quantities, this can be an easy way to keep your children occupied during a flight, offering parents a much-needed break. Travel can be stressful, and getting a few minutes of quiet time when your child is calm can work wonders for your mental health, which, in turn, can make you a calmer and better parent. If you prefer not to show your kids TV shows or movies, there are many mess-free coloring apps and educational games that toddlers can play on a tablet.

The best way to get toddlers or kids to behave on planes is to "get your kids excited about flying," says Tuso. This might include reading books about planes, telling stories about flying, meeting the pilot, or just making flying feel exciting for them.

And if your child won't stop kicking the seat in front of them? Tuso suggests using the phrase, "Not your space." It's best to use this phrase at home before attempting to travel, and kids can also say it to set their own boundaries both while flying and in general. It's a nice way to help your kid learn how to recognize their space and the space of others. Finally, if you're traveling with another adult, let that adult (or yourself) board first with all the gear: strollers, carry-on bags, car seats. The other adult can stay at the gate and let your toddler run around a bit longer. Then, have the toddler(s) and the second adult board last. This way, kids don't have to "sit still" any longer than the actual flight time or feel the stress that's sometimes emitted during a hectic boarding process.

Depending on if your baby or toddler sleeps well on planes, you might want to plan flights around sleep times.

This can also work well for naps. Tire your toddler out preflight, then they'll fall asleep during takeoff if it's their usual naptime. However, if your baby (this is sometimes the case with older babies or toddlers) doesn't sleep well on planes, you may want to do the opposite. Just be ready to entertain them on the flight if you know they won't sleep.

How to Win at Traveling with Kids and Unaccompanied Minors

Yes, it gets easier. As kids get older, they'll start to become pro travelers, especially if you started them off early.

Tips and Tricks for Traveling with Kids Over Two

Things like travel-size magnetic board games, card games, books, stickers, crayons, and snacks—don't forget to bring more than enough snacks—make it easy to keep children entertained when traveling. Offering your child the window seat can provide endless entertainment, especially during takeoff and landing. I like to bring suction toys and window clings that toddlers and kids can stick and unstick to windows and tray tables.

Kids often love to bring their own backpacks, and it helps bolster their independence to carry their own bags. Finally, I recommend that kids bring nonslip socks with grips on the bottom. Children and toddlers love to take their shoes off on planes but can keep their feet clean and safe with these types of socks.

I also recommend taking wet wipes, no matter what age your children are. They can double as tissues or napkins in an emergency, help you wipe up spills, clean up kids' faces and hands, wipe down tray tables or seats, and more.

And of course, you can always ask a flight attendant if your child can get a tour of the cockpit.

Traveling with Children Who Have Special Needs

If you're traveling with a child with special needs, you can contact TSA Cares ahead of time to get the DPNA code (Disabled Passenger with Intellectual or Developmental Disability Needing Assistance) added to your boarding pass. This means you'll get priority security, priority boarding, and in some cases, special seating arrangements when traveling with a child who has medical or behavioral needs. You can do this online or by calling 855-787-2227 (note: this number may only be able to arrange priority screenings; use the online form at the TSA Cares website for other assistance) if your flight is within 72 hours. If you're traveling with a child who has medical or behavioral needs, there are specially trained Child Passenger Safety Technicians who are able to assist. Visit the SafeKids.org website to search for a Safe Transport for All Children (STAC) trained technician.

Elite Status for Children

Children can earn elite status, just as they can hold frequent flyer accounts. However, it may not be possible on all airlines, and if there are spending thresholds that need to be met, this may be waived for minors too young to get credit cards.

If you're able to gift elite status to someone as a benefit of your own elite status, you could gift it to your child. But, this may not be the best use of a status gift, as your child will most likely already be traveling with you and can piggyback off your elite benefits, like priority boarding, seat selection, and so on, when booked on the same reservation, but they will earn more miles for any paid flights if they have elite status.

Unaccompanied Minors

Sending your child on a plane alone may seem daunting, but it can be an exciting and confidence-boosting experience for them (and it doesn't have to be overly stressful for you). This service is usually available for kids ages five and older, and you'll have to pay an unaccompanied minor fee, but this varies by airline.

You may remember hearing about how Spirit Airlines sent an unaccompanied minor to the wrong airport in Florida in 2023. While that story alone is enough to make any parent shiver in horror, there are ways to mitigate potential safety risks.

Most airlines allow parents to use a "gate pass," a pass that allows the parent through security with their child to ensure their kid gets on the right plane, avoiding any possible issues and ensuring the child feels safe and calm. After all, the best way to confirm your child gets on the right flight is by making sure they board the plane yourself. Ask the airline ahead of time how to get a gate pass so you can accompany the minor to the gate, and you'll be 100% sure they get on the right flight.

You can also minimize worry and hassle by booking nonstop flights when possible. Most airlines won't allow an unaccompanied minor under the age of eight to have a connecting flight or layover, so be ready to book a nonstop flight. If your child is older than that, make sure to allow sufficient time between flights to avoid missing flights. While each airline has its own policies for unaccompanied minors on connecting flights, in most cases, a staff member should accompany the minor to their next gate. If the flight is canceled or changed for any reason, the airline will rebook or change the flight for the minor. Many airlines won't allow a child to take the last flight of the day.

Make sure to leave your minor with a copy of their flight itinerary, as well as contact numbers for you and whoever is meeting them at their final destination. You should also plan to give your child a way to contact you, like a phone with a charger (or even an Apple Watch or AirTag so you can track them if needed), leave plenty of time at the airport so you won't be rushed, and brief your child ahead of time on what's about to happen. Giving them some extra cash in case they get thirsty or hungry is a good plan, too.

Choose a seat for them as close to the crew as possible (many airlines have reserved spaces where unaccompanied minors sit together within eyesight of the crew), and make sure to explain to your child that they can ask a flight attendant for anything they may need.

TSA PreCheck, Global Entry, and CLEAR

These services can help you speed through security and customs, which can be even more helpful when traveling with your family. Children under 12 are allowed to go through TSA PreCheck with enrolled parents or guardians, and teens 13–17 can go with enrolled adults if they're on the same travel reservation. The TSA PreCheck should appear on the teen's boarding pass if they're on the same travel reservation.

Unaccompanied minors who frequently travel alone will need to have their own TSA PreCheck if they want to get through security faster. However, even if you hold TSA PreCheck, you won't be able to accompany your child using a gate pass through this lane. If you plan to accompany them to the gate, it may not be worth it to get it. Those under the age of 18 can go through the CLEAR lanes with enrolled family members without having to enroll themselves.

If you do travel abroad frequently, I suggest enrolling the entire family in the Global Entry program to make arriving back in the US a breeze. Both babies and children will have to get their own Global Entry membership if they want to accompany an enrolled adult through these lines when going through customs. Anyone under 18 needs parental consent to enroll and will have an "interview," which is really just when they take a picture of the baby or child, though you'll no longer have to pay a fee for anyone under the age of 18.

If you're struggling to get an interview appointment, try using AppointmentScanner.com. For a small fee, the service will notify you via text when interview spots open at Global Entry centers.

Since so many credit cards offer Global Entry credits, if you hold a few, you can manage to enroll the whole family for free, especially now that there's no charge for kids.

Chapter 11

How to Win at Travel When Travel Goes Wrong

When travel goes sideways, don't get mad—take action.

In a rapidly changing travel world, I can assure you of few constants. You *will* face delays, cancellations, and problems with flights, accommodations, and beyond when traveling. We've all seen the viral videos of travelers in hysterics over canceled flights (my personal favorite is the distraught couple yelling about missing their dogs, Shelby and Dolly; watch for a giggle), screaming at gate agents and flight attendants, or worse, even attempting to harm someone over a travel delay.

I understand getting frustrated over not being able to get home or missing that epic cruise you've been waiting for due to an airline mess up, but breaking and causing a scene will get you nowhere with airline staff and you could potentially get kicked off a flight or face legal issues.

Some travel mishaps are unavoidable, but many you can see coming and figure out your plan of attack before it happens. This way, you'll have much higher odds of achieving your goal of getting home or wherever you need to go.

How to Win at Flight Disruptions

When travel disruptions happen, people automatically go into complaining mode, which I don't judge—it's a natural reaction. But I never give myself the luxury of wasting precious time bemoaning a situation over which I have no control. Instead, I spring into action to take care of myself and my traveling party because there is a likelihood that few seats remain, so every second that passes is time for another traveler to snag those seats from underneath me.

Understand the landscape so you know your rights (spoiler alert: not many in most countries, including the US) and, more important, what your viable options are in the case of delay or cancellation.

Understand Your Rights (or Lack Thereof)

There are two governing forces when you fly. The contract of carriage (or conditions of carriage) and the laws governing aviation in the country where the flight takes off and/or lands.

Contract of Carriage

The contract of carriage is the contract you enter into with the airline when you purchase a ticket. Before you can enter your billing information, you generally have to agree to it. Delta's general conditions of purchase verbiage states, "You agree to accept all Fare Rules, all Trip Extras Terms and Conditions, and all terms in the Contract of Carriage applicable to your ticket."

If you want to be a smart traveler, I *highly* recommend you read the contract of carriages of the airlines you fly the most. They are fairly easy to read, and they'll help you understand the rules of the airline so when you approach a reservations or gate agent for help, you can understand the rules that the employees have been trained on.

Most of the conflict I witness, when consumers are screaming at airline staff, is due to the consumer having absolutely no idea what they agreed to when they bought their flight. Arguing with a gate agent over how you'd like to be treated without reading the contract of carriage is like representing yourself at trial with no legal experience.

In a vast majority of cases, it's not going to end in your favor. It's critical to know when you're asking for something that is owed to you versus when you're asking for a favor. All too often, I see passengers berating gate agents while asking for a favor, and it makes me cringe. I know I wouldn't go out of my way to help someone who is abusive to me—would you?

In general, these contracts of carriage dictate the limits of liability the airline will take accountability for regarding missing and damaged luggage, timelines for filing claims against the airline, the rules for check-in times, refusal to provide travel, and the policies the airline has in place if your flight is disrupted.

Every airline's contract of carriage is different, but most are the same in that they stack the power in favor of the airline and allow the airlines to make changes unilaterally.

I'll pull the most relevant line from American Airline's contract of carriage for flight cancellations: "If we or our airline partner fails to operate your flight or your arrival is delayed more than 4 hours, our sole obligation is to refund the unused ticket value and any optional fees according to our involuntary refunds policy, subject to our policy for rebooking your delayed/canceled flight."

If you want to run to the DOT to file a complaint because you think that isn't fair, you won't find much help as the DOT states:

- You're entitled to a refund if the airline cancels your flight and you choose not to travel.
- You're entitled to a refund if the airline makes a significant schedule change or delay and you choose not to travel.
- You're entitled to a refund if you've been moved to a lower class of service.
- You're entitled to a refund of fees (things like baggage, seat upgrades, Wi-Fi, etc.) if you were unable to use the service due to a cancellation, delay, schedule change, etc.

If you want protection that covers costs related to delays and cancellations, it is absolutely critical that you buy your travel with a credit card that offers trip delay and cancellation coverage and/or purchase travel insurance. While some airlines may offer you miles or a voucher for the inconvenience of a long delay or cancellation, that is out of the goodness of their heart, and not because they have to. Annoying, I know, but I don't make the rules.

Legal Protections

The second and more important governing force is the rules provided by the country you're flying out of (and sometimes into), which generally supersede that airline's policy.

In 2024, the Department of Transportation finally released guidance that mandates airlines operating to/from or within the US to issue automatic refunds if a flight is delayed three or more hours domestically or six or more hours internationally if the consumer chooses not to accept the changed flight.

While this stops far short of the EU and Canadian protections that provide compensation for when things happen, it is a huge improvement because many US airlines would force consumers to fill out onerous forms and wait months before getting a refund for canceled flights. This rule also mandates that airlines automatically refund for all ancillary fees, like checked bags, seating assignments, and Wi-Fi if the consumer doesn't end up taking the flight. You should familiarize yourself with the DOT guidance, and if an airline doesn't abide by the rules you can file a complaint form, and airlines will have to respond in a reasonable amount of time.

For example, US airlines must abide by EU regulations on compensation when departing the EU. Interestingly enough, EU carriers must comply with EU regulations even when departing the US, so if you ever have the option to choose a European carrier when going to Europe, just know that your flight leaving the US will be covered by generous EU261 compensation if something should go wrong. All things being equal, I will fly EU airlines to Europe for that reason—if the flight is canceled, I know I am legally owed up to 600 euros. Plus, I'll be rebooked on an alternative option (in addition to any compensation owed from my credit card).

See how knowing the rules and who to go to for compensation makes all the difference? Most US flyers are so used to being treated poorly that they don't know when they have legal rights to compensation when flying abroad and won't hold US airlines accountable for mishaps. When flying domestically in the US, there are sadly few consumer protections for when things go wrong. Meanwhile, Canada and the EU focus more on passenger rights (namely, with EU261), which means passengers can get some compensation for things like delays or cancellations.

Winning at "Flight Bumps," or Voluntary Denied Boarding

Airlines will routinely oversell flights because, inevitably, passengers won't show up or will miss their connections, so to make as much money as possible, they'll sell more tickets than there are seats.

If everyone shows up, then they have to offer compensation to passengers who are willing to take another flight. Sometimes, this works to your advantage when you want to stay longer anyway, and increasingly airlines will reach out in advance when a flight is oversold and try to get volunteers over the phone so the airport staff don't have to waste time begging people to switch.

There's no set compensation when airlines take volunteers—it's a game of trying to pay as little as possible, and airlines will make you put in an amount you'd take to be switched to another flight. For most domestic flights, I see compensation ranging from $200 to $600 to take a later flight, but if no one is biting at the gate, agents at many airlines are authorized to offer upward of $10,000 in vouchers to get passengers to voluntarily switch, because if the airline has to involuntarily bump a passenger, it will cost them and they'll also have to report it to the DOT.

Most airlines want to avoid the appearance of denying passengers a product that they paid for, so you can always try to negotiate here. And always request to be put in first class on the next flight they'll be putting you on.

US Regulations on Involuntary Denied Boarding

On April 9, 2017, United Airlines Express Flight 3411 started off normally. The plane boarded and was ready to take off until United realized that it needed to get four employees to Louisville to operate a different flight. This procedure, called deadheading, is common, as a number of different scenarios could necessitate an airline needing to get crew from its hub to a smaller outpost, such as sick crewmembers or the crew "timing out," meaning they've worked too many legal hours and can't work more.

Airlines will deadhead crews on standby (reserve crews) so that passengers can get to their final destination. The airline offered $400 to get volunteers to take another flight, but no one bit, then they offered $800. Again, silence.

So they randomly selected four passengers to be asked to leave the plane. Three out of the four of the passengers agreed. The last passenger, Dr. David Dao, a pulmonologist from Kentucky, declined, as he had to treat patients the next day.

Airline employees called the Chicago Department of Aviation's security, a quasi-police force at O'Hare Airport that's mostly there to ensure smooth operations but doesn't have the authority to arrest. The officers used extreme force to drag him off the plane, smashing his head into an armrest and rendering him unconscious.

The entire incident was recorded and went viral immediately. The outcry over the treatment was fast and furious, even drawing a sharp rebuke from then-president Donald Trump. Overnight Dr. Dao became the poster child for passengers who are treated poorly by airlines, and eventually, he received a substantial but confidential settlement from United Airlines.

While it was the security officers who used excessive force and bear most of the responsibility for the incident, multiple passengers on the plane blamed the United supervisor who came on the plane with a belligerent attitude and immediately resorted to calling security instead of trying to defuse the situation and negotiate with passengers.

The Dr. Dao incident pushed all airlines to avoid involuntary denied boardings by incentivizing customers to take more generous voluntary bumps. It also resulted in airlines shifting their policies. In 2016, the involuntary denied boarding ratio for US airlines was .65 per 10,000 passengers. In 2023, that number dropped to .35 per 10,000 passengers (about half as many).

While rare, it still does happen, so it's best to know your rights. You're owed compensation if:

- You have a confirmed reservation
- You checked in to your flight on time
- You arrived at the departure gate on time
- The airline can't get you to your destination within one hour of your flight's original arrival time

Depending on your itinerary (domestic or international) and the amount of time your arrival is delayed, you may qualify for up to $1,550. Make sure to familiarize yourself with the details on the "Bumping and Oversales" section of the DOT website.

How to File a Claim with the DOT

If you're not satisfied with the way an airline handled your baggage, refund, flight delay, or anything related to your travel, submit a Department of Transportation complaint using this online form: https://secure.dot.gov /air-travel-complaint.

What to Know About EU261

This EU regulation holds that consumers are entitled to the following if their flight was canceled or it arrived in the destination more than three hours after its scheduled arrival time; amounts are based on distance:

- 250 euros (about $271) per passenger on flights that are 1,500 km or less
- 400 euros (about $434) per passenger on flights more than 1,500 km within the EU (or flights between 1,500 and 3,500 km)
- 600 euros (about $650) per passenger on flights more than 3,500 km

The rule is valid on flights flying within the EU (from one EU destination to another) and flights departing from the EU (regardless of destination). If it's a flight to the EU, you have to be flying an EU carrier to get EU261 protection.

Make sure to save all the paperwork and evidence of your delay, including your boarding pass (always have a screenshot of all boarding passes and save paper ones), confirmation, and anything else relevant. When you get home from your trip, you can claim using instructions on the airline's website.

Canada's Air Passenger Protection Regulations

Canadian airlines operating flights to, from, or within Canada are required to offer compensation for delays over three hours. This provision is in addition to a refund (or rebooking) of flights as well as offering treatment such as accommodation for overnight delays or food, water, and Wi-Fi for delays over two hours.

There are different requirements for large and small airlines, but a large airline like Air Canada is required to offer the following for arrival delays over three hours:

- $294 ($400 CAD) for arrival delays between three and six hours
- $515 ($700 CAD) for arrival delays between six and nine hours
- $736 ($1,000 CAD) for arrival delays of nine hours or longer

Check the Canadian Transport Agency website for more details and how to claim.

How to Get Compensated for Issues Beyond Delays and Cancellations

Understanding what reasonable compensation is can make all the difference. If your seat doesn't recline or your in-flight entertainment screen is broken, asking to be reseated is fair. So is asking for some miles as compensation for these types of issues. You might get one or the other, or even both, depending on your fare class. Getting a full refund of your ticket is not going to happen, so asking will likely end in a no.

Meanwhile, knowing your rights and asking for what you are legally entitled to is important because the airlines expect you not to know your rights and may try to get away with more.

Fix the Problem, Then Deal with Compensation Later

Your main issue at hand is figuring out a new answer to your problem. Finding a new hotel, getting rerouted due to a snowstorm, getting a new flight after getting bumped—these things take precedence.

Just make sure to save any and all documentation to ensure that you'll have whatever you need when it's time to make claims for compensation.

Be Kind

Being kind will get you so much further than being a jerk. Stay calm and treat people with respect, and your issue will probably be fixed a whole lot faster.

Ask Like a Pro

Sometimes knowing the right way to ask is all it takes. Shape your own destiny by contacting airlines and hotels in the right way, understanding how to search for rerouting options, knowing your rights, and asking for what you need to feed gate agents or front desk staff the right information. The more you know, the better chance you have of getting what you need and want.

Make Your Claims (Especially with Your Credit Card Insurance)

Once you've made it home, claim compensation. Hopefully, you've saved any paperwork or proof of delays, cancellations, lost luggage, or anything else you might need. Don't forget to file a claim with your credit card because your credit card is usually much more generous with compensation than airlines and hotels, assuming you've booked with the right one (more on that below).

Do These Things a Few Days Before Flying

Starting to organize your trip beforehand can help circumvent possible issues, especially if bad weather rolls in.

Always Check the Weather 48 Hours Before Your Flight

Look up the weather forecast 48 hours before a flight from your departure city and from where your flight is coming from. Many airline apps, plus apps like FlightRadar24, will tell you where your flight is coming from.

If you know your plane is coming from Buffalo and a huge winter storm is coming to the Northeast, be proactive and monitor the situation. Airlines will often issue weather waivers—these allow you to change your flight for free to avoid mass cancellations at the last minute. Being proactive means you'll have the first go at getting a different flight.

Set Flight Alerts

Do this using the app of the airline you're flying, as well as using an additional app like FlightAware. You can monitor the status of your flight, where it's coming from, the flight plan, and other information that can prove useful if you need to be proactive about changing or moving a flight.

What to Do When Your Flight Is Delayed: A Step-by-Step Guide

It's the day of your flight departure, and you get an alert from the airline app saying your flight is delayed. What do you do? The following process is one I use to get answers and figure out how I can get where I want to go.

Gather Your Options

Dig into your choices—what other options do you have to get you where you need to go on your current carrier? Check your airline app to see if the airline is offering you other options. What about other airlines? You may be able to take a later flight that will get you in earlier than your original delayed flight.

Book Backups and Ask for "Protection"

Many frequent flyer programs allow you to cancel award tickets for free until departure, so booking an award seat that you later cancel is always a solid backup plan if the delay increases or it turns into a cancellation.

If you're not sure you want to take the later flight, you can ask the airline agent to "protect you" on the later flight. Airlines will generally do so for their elite customers, which means you'll still be confirmed on your original flight, but they'll hold a seat on a later flight for you in case that flight gets canceled or significantly delayed.

This also helps with connections. If you're in the air and worried you may not make a connection, instead of landing and running to a gate and facing disappointment when it's too late, I suggest messaging the airline via chatbot or DMing on X to ask them to protect you on the next flight. You can still make a run for your connection, but if you don't make it, you won't be freaking out, as you have a confirmed seat on the next flight.

Oftentimes there are few seats remaining, so knowing this information means you can get ahead, especially if everyone else on your flight is also scrambling to make a connection or dealing with the fallout of a delay or cancellation. This way, you can relax in the lounge with a cocktail, having already fixed your problem before it officially happened.

Not all airlines will do this, but it never hurts to ask. Plus, asking to be protected makes you sound like a pro traveler and someone that they want to keep happy as a customer.

Lounge ━━▶ Lines

If you're at the gate and your flight keeps getting delayed, don't wait in the long line to ask the harried agent what's happening—most of the time, they don't know anyway. They're so used to people screaming at them that they aren't the best agents to speak to about rebooking.

I recommend going to a lounge (if possible). Those agents are usually experienced and willing to help you—and maybe even bend the rules when necessary.

If you don't have lounge access, you can wait in line at the general customer rebooking desk, but I'd also get on the phone and try rebooking yourself on the app or messaging customer service. When there are limited seats available on flights to your destination, time is of the essence. Don't just stand in line because by the time you reach an agent, all confirmable seats might be gone, and they'll likely just put you on standby.

Keep Calm and Be Respectful

If you do need to be rebooked by a gate agent, don't yell at them. We've all seen it—those shouting, "I can't believe my flight is canceled, I hate this airline, I'm never flying [said airline] ever again. You better get me there or I'll tell all 1,000 of my Facebook followers never to fly this airline ever again."

• • • •

You'll have better success if you try something like "Hello, how are you today? Thanks for helping me—I really need to get to Los Angeles today. I know all of the remaining nonstop flights are sold out, and I can take standby; however, I see there's a nonstop flight to LAX on your partner airline—can you please book me on that option at this time? I've confirmed there are available seats."

Despite your politeness, the gate agent may say something like "Sorry, I can only rebook you on this airline." This is where knowing your rights comes in handy.

The DOT's cancellation dashboard, which you can access online, shows you which airlines rebook on partner airlines (as well as other handy information on your rights). Note that while Spirit, Southwest, Frontier, and Allegiant don't rebook passengers on partner airlines, other US-based airlines do.

If you're flying an airline like Delta and hoping to get rebooked on a partner airline, tell the agent something like this:

"As per the Department of Transportation, Delta does rebook disrupted passengers on partner airlines, so I would greatly appreciate it if you could rebook me on flight X at Y time. I have confirmed there is available inventory. Thank you so much."

If there's no partner inventory, ask to fly to a different airport. This can be especially helpful if you're flying to a destination like New York, where if LaGuardia is not an option you might be able to get to JFK or Newark instead. Say something like this:

"Can you put me on X flight to X airport at X time? Also, I see there's a first-class seat available. Is there any chance you can book me in that to make up for the inconvenience? Thank you!"

It never hurts to ask—gate agents have a lot of power. They won't research all the best options for you but are often willing to help if you show up friendly and prepared. If that particular agent isn't willing, take what they can give you but then try other options, like via phone, web, or chatbot. Depending on your elite status and the airline's partners, they can even rebook you on other airlines, though that is getting increasingly harder to do these days.

If the airline can't rebook you and the flight is extremely delayed (or canceled), don't accept sleeping in the airport or taking standby. This goes back, yet again, to knowing your rights. In the US, airlines owe a full cash refund of your flight, so never take a voucher unless it's substantially more than the cash compensation and you understand and accept the details (like expiration and limitations).

If the airline won't get you to where you need to go, rebook yourself and then submit for compensation from the airline, your credit card issuer, and travel insurance (if you bought it).

How to Use Travel Credit Card Insurance to Your Advantage

Travel card insurance varies by credit card issuer. Certain premium Chase Sapphire travel credit cards have some of the best travel credit card insurance policies out there, but other credit issuers have some solid options, too.

Here's what to look out for:

- **Trip cancellation and interruption insurance:** This insurance may reimburse you for travel (airfare, tours, and hotel) you need to cancel due to an injury or severe weather conditions.
- **Trip delay reimbursement:** You may be eligible for reimbursement for meals and hotels if your trip is significantly delayed.

Make sure to read the fine print on who is covered (in some cases, family members or travel companions may be covered), the coverage amount, and any disclaimers. In almost all cases, you have to have paid for the trip (such as airfare) using the card that offers these types of protections.

Medical insurance works like a supplement to your existing health insurance, which may not cover medical costs that you incur abroad. Evacuation insurance covers the costs associated with an evacuation following a weather event or other disruption.

How to Avoid Lost and Delayed Baggage

US airlines lose up to 2 million suitcases a year. While checking a bag is never foolproof, here are some things you can do to keep your belongings protected.

Best Practices for Checking Luggage

Here's what to do when checking a bag:

- **Always use a bag tracker.** I prefer AirTags, but any kind will do. This way, if the airline loses your bag, you can pinpoint where it is and help the airline find it. Hide the tracker in the interior pocket of your luggage in a zipper compartment so it doesn't fall out.

- **Take pictures of your luggage (especially on the belt) and your bag tags.** You can show these to the staff if your bags go missing.
- **Confirm the destination on the printed baggage tag is correct, especially if you have a complicated itinerary or multiple connections and/or airline partners.** I ask the gate agent to show me the tag before they put it on just to double-check (and make sure they attach a priority handling tag if you're entitled to that benefit or ask them to add a fragile tag if it contains sensitive items).
- **Have unique luggage.** If your bag is basic and black like everyone else's, it's harder to find. Unique, bright, or bold luggage is easily identifiable and won't get mixed up with other people's bags. If you do have a basic bag, add a ribbon or sticker, which can help identify it.
- **Always have a baggage tag.** Add a tag on the outside of your luggage, and also add your information to the inside of the bag, if possible, in case the tag on the outside breaks off. Make sure to use +1 if you have a US phone number as it's the US country code.
- **Never check expensive, irreplaceable items or medication.** Pack all medicine, electronics, or valuables in your carry-on.

What to Do If the Airline Loses Your Luggage (or It's Delayed)

So you've waited and waited, and it's clear your bag isn't on the belt.

- **Check the location of your bag tracker.** If it hasn't been updated in a while, you can force a connection to the AirTag by clicking the "Play Sound" button on the AirTag. That sends a signal to call the AirTag, and it will often update the location after you do that.
- **If it's not on the belt, double-check the oversize luggage belt.** Sometimes, luggage will mistakenly get put there, or airport personnel might pull luggage off the belt for elite members and/or those in first class, so do a full sweep of the baggage claim to make sure your bag wasn't taken off or put on the oversize luggage belt.

- **Go to the baggage office and file a claim.** You must file a claim within 24 hours of the bag going missing, so do it right away so the airline has official notification of your claim.
- **Review the relevant rules for missing baggage depending on your flight.**
  - For domestic flights, the DOT "allows airlines to limit their liability for a lost, damaged, or delayed bag. Airlines are free to pay more than the limit but are not required to do so."
  - The maximum liability amount allowed by the regulation is $3,800 per passenger.
  - Airlines are required to compensate passengers for reasonable, verifiable, and actual incidental expenses that they may incur while their bags are delayed, subject to the maximum liability limits.
  - Airlines can't set an arbitrary daily amount for interim expenses. For example, an airline can't have a policy that they'll reimburse a passenger up to only $60 for each day that a passenger's bag is delayed.
  - Review the airline's contract of carriage so you know the airline's policy in case they try to shortchange you, but always let them offer first in case they're feeling generous (rare) and offer more than the standard compensation.
- **Keep receipts of all items you buy.** The same goes for other expenses related to the inconvenience of the missing luggage, such as transportation to and from the shops.
- **Review your credit card policy on delayed and lost luggage to see what's covered.**
- **Save all receipts and documentation to submit claims later.** Make sure to read the fine print on how long you have to submit claims.

Earn Miles and Points for Baggage Disruptions

Checking bags that are delayed may lead to earning additional miles, among other compensation. Both Delta and Alaska Airlines offer delayed baggage mileage bonuses where, if your bags don't come out in 20 minutes or less, you can claim additional miles. Find more details on this in the earnings chapter. Delta offers 2,500 miles, and Alaska offers 2,500 miles or a $25 discount code. Frequent flyers can take advantage of this, as bags often don't come out within 20 minutes.

Janelle Rupkalvis, travel expert and content creator (@janelleonajet), earned 47,500 Delta SkyMiles in 2023 thanks to claiming each time her bags didn't come out on time. This takes some organization and time to fill out the forms, but getting enough SkyMiles for a free first-class domestic flight makes it all worth it. Janelle sets her 20-minute timer the minute the Delta aircraft door opens. "By the time I deplane and make my way to baggage claim, I only have to wait a few minutes for my bags. I spend a minute or two filling out the claim form online, and within seconds, 2,500 SkyMiles are in my account."

Alaska's policy isn't quite as user-friendly, as you'll have to stop by the baggage office to speak to a customer service representative and claim within two hours of your flight's arrival. Still, if you're a frequent Alaska flyer who checks bags with the time to make the claim, it may be worth it.

The Montreal Convention

This 1999 treaty protects passengers, luggage, and goods. The Montreal Convention applies to any international carriage between contracting states. However, there are some caveats: The treaty is only valid on international flights or flights within the EU. So a flight from Spain to France would be covered, as would a flight from New York to Germany, but not a flight from Chicago to Los Angeles. US domestic travel is governed by the DOT.

The part of the treaty that is most useful to travelers is the part that governs your compensation from the airline for baggage issues. You can claim up to $1,700 if your bag is damaged, delayed, or lost.

However, if you know your bag is worth more than $1,700, certain airlines may allow you to pay an "excess value" charge when checking it to up the total value of compensation. Or, you might want to consider additional insurance for your bag, or having a credit card that insures your lost or delayed baggage.

Submit your claims for damaged bags within seven days and delayed bags within 21 days, and if your bag is "lost" for more than 21 days, it's considered fully lost, and you have two years to file a claim with the airline.

What to Know About Lost and Delayed Baggage Insurance

Baggage insurance is supplemental to coverage provided by your airline or via your homeowners or renters insurance policy. Baggage coverage may reimburse you for the actual or replacement cost of your possessions if your bags are delayed or lost.

For example, Chase Sapphire credit cards offer baggage delay insurance, which reimburses you for essential purchases for baggage delays more than six hours up to $100 per day for five days. The lost luggage reimbursement offers reimbursement for up to $3,000 per passenger, between the actual cash value (less depreciation) and any reimbursement the airline gave you. Note that there's a lot of fine print to sift through, including caps on things like jewelry, cameras, and watches.

In most cases, similar to trip cancellation, interruption, or delay insurance, you'll have to have paid for the trip using the card. This is why it's important to review your card's travel protections before booking your tickets. Booking your airfare with the right travel credit card can mean getting compensation should things go haywire.

Damaged Wheelchairs, Mobility Devices, and Accessibility Issues

A lot about traveling as a passenger with a disability is about asking what services are available, making sure airlines and hotels know you have a disability so they can ensure the right accommodations, and knowing your rights before traveling.

· · · ·

Cory Lee (@curbfreecorylee), who, since age four, has traveled to more than 48 countries with his wheelchair, told me more about dealing with issues when traveling as a person with a disability.

Oftentimes, there are systems and services for assistance in place, but they're not widely advertised. For example, Lee told me that Disney has a DAS (Disability Access Service) pass available, which you can register for online ahead of time.

While the travel industry has a long way to go when it comes to accommodating travelers, Lee does say things have improved in recent years. "There have been many improvements over the past 10 years. When my mom and I went to the beach, she used to have to physically pick me up out of my wheelchair and carry me to the sand—arduous and difficult. Now at [many] beaches there are sand access mats so I can stay in my wheelchair and roll."

Sometimes, it comes down to picking the right brands. Certain companies are better than others when it comes to accessibility. For example, when it comes to hotels, Lee is a points player who's loyal to Hilton because the company "guarantees accessible rooms through its app." However, "I would love to see some type of universal accessibility design at all Hilton properties," he mentioned, like "roll-in showers without steps and beds without block frames or with lifting capabilities."

In general, airlines can work on becoming more accessible, too, starting with "better training for ground staff," said Lee, who's even been injured during the boarding process. If you're worried about boarding or other needs, Lee suggests putting your information online during booking but also calling the airline to reiterate your needs that same day and again the day before your flight—this is especially important for anyone using a wheelchair. Lee also minimizes the opportunity for damage to his wheelchair by taking off certain parts, like the headrest and joystick and taking them on board with him.

Picking a seat ahead of time is the right plan—Lee suggests an aisle seat. "Wheelchair users can request bulkhead seating," Lee advises, "but you may not be able to lift the armrest on certain aircraft," so take that into consideration when deciding what seat works best for your situation.

And plane lavatories aren't just uncomfortably small for most passengers. Some passengers with disabilities can't even use them. Lee mentioned a flight he recently took to Brazil where he monitored his food and water intake 48 hours preflight because he knew he wouldn't be able to use the lavatory on the aircraft.

"Know your rights," Lee insists. Review the Air Carrier Access Act to understand what you're entitled to, as many staff members aren't familiar with the rules. For example, if you're flying to or from a US airport, according to the Air Carrier Access Act, airlines are "required to get your wheelchair as close to the gate as possible." You may need to remind staff numerous times to ensure this happens.

And when it comes to damage to wheelchairs, you can file a complaint at the airport, and another with the DOT online. "The airline is required to pay for damages or replace the wheelchair, if needed," Lee said.

He also suggests "taking as many photos and videos as possible before you get on board and after." And the most important thing? File any claims while you're still at the airport, even if it takes time. "As soon as you roll out of the airport door, you're not protected," he stressed.

And if you see a person with a disability (or just anyone) struggling? Offer to help. Lee suggests offering to put their bags in the overhead bin, for example. "Don't be afraid to offer to help. If someone doesn't want help, respect that and don't persist. But asking once is amazing."

How to Handle Hotel Mishaps

What to Do If You Show Up and Your Hotel Is Sold Out

Similar to airlines, hotels will oversell rooms because people don't show up, whether that's due to canceled flights or a change of plans—it happens more often than you might think.

If you plan to arrive at a hotel late in the evening (I would say after 8 p.m.), note it on your reservation and also call the day of to remind the front desk; otherwise, there's a chance they'll think you are a no-show and give your room to someone else. Note that not all hotels have 24/7 check-in, especially smaller hotels and bed-and-breakfasts, so always double-check the check-in hours, especially if your flight is delayed.

While showing up to a hotel and not having a room can be a huge hassle, understanding the rules will help you navigate the situation, get re-accommodated, and likely come out ahead, as hotels will not only pay for your new hotel but refund your original stay.

There's no sense in freaking out once a hotel has confirmed you won't have a room. Instead, do your best to advocate for yourself to get put up in a similar or better hotel.

When a hotel moves you to another hotel, it's called being "walked," and every hotel has different policies for this situation based on your elite status and how you booked your reservation—ironically enough, some include free phone calls.

- **Marriott Elite members:** Ultimate Reservation Guarantee— re-accommodations plus anywhere from $50 to $200 and 45,000 to 140,000 points.
- **Hilton:** The guest must be relocated to another Hilton-branded hotel, if possible. The hotel must pay the full cost of the first night's stay, including any expenses incurred, such as transportation and phone calls to family members and business associates. However, rules don't apply if a property is 10% overbooked.
- **Hyatt:** If booked directly with Hyatt, you'll get a free night at a comparable hotel, free transportation to and from that hotel, and a free phone call to let your family know where you can be reached.

Tip: Hotels will treat you better when you book directly with them and are a member of their loyalty program. In fact, these members are generally the last to get walked.

I spoke with Shawn Newman, a hotel front office manager who has worked for Marriott, Hyatt, and Hilton, to ask him about how hotels assign rooms booked on OTAs.

"An OTA room type is always a request unless it's a higher room type such as a suite, but traditional rooms are based on request. OTA reservations would also be the first priority for relocation if the hotel is overbooked."

What About Compensation?

When it comes to compensation, how do hotels decide what warrants getting money and what warrants getting points? What type of hotel failures or shortcomings deserve compensation? Does this vary depending on elite status?

Newman says, "For compensation, I had one GM state that a room must have three separate areas for an overall good stay or compensation should be provided. Thirty-three percent was a comfortable bed with clean linen, 33% was a hot shower, and 33% was HVAC, TV, and amenities in the room working and in good condition. If one of these failed, then compensation up to 33%, either in the way of points or cash off the bill, was in order. Points are always the preferred way as we want to maintain the amount of revenue brought into the hotel; however, if we have to adjust the room rate, it would be done after the rate has been run."

Keep this information in mind, and if something isn't working, tell a staff member. Be polite but assertive—you might as well ask for what you feel is fair. Obviously, asking for a complete refund because your TV channels aren't coming in may be a lot, but you could ask for a room change and some points. You just might get it, too.

When it comes to things like bedbugs or pests, you should definitely request more and document any evidence. "For bedbugs or any type of pest, we would reach out to our professional cleaning company to service the room to determine what kind of bug it could be. In 12 years, we only had one bedbug issue, and the entire stay was refunded back to the guest. We wouldn't provide any compensation for any bugs unless the room comes back positive; however, in the case of roaches, we would provide compensation, up to 50% off the rate, and a room move, if available," Newman told me.

How to Handle Vacation Rental Mishaps

Showing up to a hotel and not having a room is generally rare and can be avoided by clearly communicating with the hotel in advance (confirming reservations and arrival times) and booking directly.

However, vacation rentals can be much less reliable, and there are fewer protections. I encourage purchasing travel insurance when booking vacation rentals because it will cover most things that can go wrong, like last-minute host cancellations that require you to rebook at much higher prices, poor quality/uninhabitable reservations, sickness, items being stolen from the property, and so much more.

In these cases, at best, a rental website like Airbnb is going to refund you but not cover all other expenses. You may save a lot booking via Airbnb, so use some of those savings to protect your trip and give you peace of mind, because remember: In most cases, you're not dealing with professional vacation hosts who are educated in hospitality management and consumer service.

A host canceling right before a trip can cause great financial hardship and hassle since similar accommodation can be much more expensive—or even not available at all during special events.

Airbnb's policy on this is pretty straightforward and favors the host, as there is a small $50 penalty for last-minute cancellations (though this can be waived with proof of a qualifying reason). The renter is only owed a full refund, but that can take up to 15 days (in most cases) or even two billing cycles to get.

Or, you can get more immediate Airbnb credit, and sometimes you can ask for additional compensation for the inconvenience (I've heard of people getting 10% more), but I wouldn't count on it.

When booking vacation rentals, opt for properties with reliable hosts who have many 5-star reviews and communicate often with them, especially in the days leading up to the trip, to make sure everything is in line.

If your rental does get canceled at the last minute, try to get a resolution from Airbnb and then file a claim with your credit card or travel insurance for any additional costs you endured from the cancellation. It never hurts to ask.

How to Handle Car Rental Mishaps
Pay with a Credit Card That Has Protections
Start by booking your rental car with a credit card that has primary auto coverage, as it adds an extra layer of protection should anything go wrong. For that coverage to kick in, you need to pay the full cost of the rental with your eligible credit card (or redeem your credit card points through the portal).

Key terms to know:

- **CDW (collision damage waiver):** This covers costs related to an accident.
- **LDW (loss damage waiver):** This covers collisions and theft of the vehicle (so LDW is better than CDW).
- **Primary coverage:** This means your credit card coverage will be the first policy to cover any incidents, so you won't have to worry about your personal auto insurance rates being impacted by a claim.
- **Secondary coverage:** This means the credit card will cover anything your personal auto insurance doesn't cover.

Liability coverage isn't usually in credit card rental coverage but is covered by personal auto policies, so read your policy and make sure your liability coverage extends to rental cars (and make sure the countries you travel to are covered, as there are often exclusions like Jamaica and Ireland).

. . . .

If you don't have personal auto insurance or your personal policy won't cover your rental, I would highly recommend buying liability coverage. It isn't cheap, sometimes $25 a day, but if you were to cause bodily harm, your liability could be in the hundreds of thousands of dollars—or more.

Notable exclusions: Australia, Ireland, Israel, Italy, Jamaica, New Zealand, and any country on the Office of Foreign Assets Control–sanctioned country list, and many specialty vehicles like passenger vans, trucks, and vehicles over 10,000 pounds are often not covered (or there's a maximum coverage of $75,000), so if you rent luxury or specialty vehicles, triple-check your coverage to make sure you're covered.

How to Prevent and Handle Vehicle Damage

I'm usually in a rush when traveling, but I always take extra time when I'm renting a car to make sure everything is in order. As a best practice, you should always take pictures and videos of your rental car when you receive it and note any dents/scratches before you leave the parking lot (also check the gas gauge and make sure it matches what your rental record states).

Tip: Don't forget to take pictures of the roof! Often, they'll claim damage here, and many people forget to check the roof and leave themselves exposed if there are no photos to prove it was in good condition when the vehicle was returned.

Save these images/videos in a folder in case you need to use them later. They'll often be the only way out of paying expensive damage fees that may be assessed well after you return the car. If you hold certain credit cards, having elite status with rental car programs can also prove you're a loyal and preferred customer, which can reduce the chances of this happening.

When returning your car, take pictures and videos, and also ask the rental agent to sign a statement that you returned the car in good shape. Sometimes this isn't possible at busy airport agencies, but do so when possible. If you speak to an agent who takes your keys, get their information and verbally confirm with them (ideally on voice note) that the car looks good and there's no damage.

If you do get charged for damage and you have primary coverage through your credit card, I would let them handle it. If you have secondary coverage, I would try to avoid any claims on your personal insurance so your rates don't go up. Ask them for a detailed breakdown of the damage with time stamps and proof. Then, you can submit a claim disputing their charges if it doesn't match up.

If they don't drop the claim, file a complaint with the relevant local authorities, like the state attorney general's office, with all documentation. I like to contact senior executives at the company, which you can usually find on LinkedIn. I often find they want to quell any consumer issues, especially if you work at a prominent company or have a large social media following. Always be nice but straight to the point with details so they can forward it to their staff to take care of it.

Check Your Passport (and Not Just for Expiration)

Check your passport (and all of your family members', including children) for the following:

- Expiration date *and* validity
- State of wear and tear
- How many blank pages you have

Start by putting reminders in your calendar nine months prior to expiration for renewal. You always want to have six months of validity whenever traveling internationally, and many countries outright require this (even though some countries like Mexico only require it to be valid for the length of your trip. When possible, you want to give yourself padding). Remember that US passports for children are only valid for five years, not 10. Finally, do your due diligence to check entrance and vaccine rules for the country you're planning to visit well in advance.

Years ago, on a trip to Bali, my boyfriend assured me his passport was fine and he would have just over six months of validity for our upcoming trip, but when we arrived, he was rejected, as he had miscounted by a few days. Customs made us wait in an immigration detention area with rats running around the room. The agents made it seem as if they wanted bribes, but in the end, they made him get on the flight back to where we came from, which luckily was close—Kuala Lumpur.

Others were not so lucky. We were also detained with an American couple hysterically crying and begging not to be sent back to Doha, as they would miss their daughter's wedding. There was no mercy shown, and everyone learned a valuable lesson that day: It's your responsibility to make sure you satisfy the entry requirements of the country you're traveling to.

While airlines make every effort to ensure passports and visas are valid, humans are not flawless creatures, and mistakes happen. When they do, the airline generally gets a large fine for allowing you to travel without the proper documents and you will likely have to spend time and money paying to reroute yourself and then rush to get a replacement passport.

Some countries such as South Africa have requirements to have two entire blank pages for them to stamp on arrival. If you are running low on blank pages, it might be time to renew, as the State Department stopped issuing extra pages for passports and will require you to renew. When given the option, always opt for a passport with as many pages as possible.

I keep my passport in a leather passport protector in a special zipper pocket of my carry-on that is stored at my seat (never leave your passport or valuables in the overhead bin, especially if you plan to sleep on the flight) until I need to use it. There are many passport holders that you can strap around your body to avoid pickpocketing. Bali denies entry for travelers with worn passports, so make sure to keep yours in good condition.

How to Handle Theft and Loss Abroad

Being pickpocketed or robbed can be stressful, especially when traveling.

Although it's not avoidable, if you're traveling to places where this is common (some European cities, like Barcelona), you can take a few additional precautions. Leave important documents like your passport and a small wallet with extra cash and credit cards in your hotel room's safe. Never put your purse or backpack on the back of a chair in a restaurant, and always keep a close eye on your belongings, especially at the beach, on public transport, or in crowded attractions.

If your ID, cash, phone, and credit cards do get lost or stolen, here's what to do:

- File a police report so you have documentation.
- Freeze all credit cards so they can't be used. Many credit cards offer assistance in these situations.
- Try to track your phone using Find My iPhone. Don't go chasing thieves, but there's a chance the wallet was tossed after a thief took out cash, fell out in the taxi, or is being held in a shop or somewhere in lost and found. Disable the phone in Find My iPhone so it can't (easily) be used or sold.

- Change your iCloud password ASAP in case they are able to get into your phone for two-factor authentication.
- Freeze your credit reports on the three major bureaus so no one can apply for lines of credit—you never know what information they have on you.
- Change social media passwords and force logouts from all devices.
- Call your credit card hotline, which can help in situations like pickpocketing, lost passports, medical emergencies, or even landing in jail abroad.

The American Express Global Assist Hotline (1-800-333-AMEX) is available for cardholders of numerous Amex cards and can help if a passport/wallet is stolen and you need to make arrangements for replacements and a cash wire to hold you over. They'll coordinate with hotels directly to pay your bill and even coordinate legal help and medical evacuations. Note that your trip must have originated from your US billing address within the past 90 days, and you must be traveling more than 100 miles from this address.

If you lose your passport abroad, you'll need to go to the nearest embassy or consular office, where they'll work with you to get an emergency replacement that will allow you to get home. This must be done in person, and when possible, you should have a secure digital folder with copies of your social security card, passport, and birth certificate. In situations where you lose all of your identification abroad, having these can help expedite getting an emergency passport.

In the extreme case that you're arrested abroad, ask prison authorities to notify the US embassy or consulate or attempt to reach out to them yourself. These bureaus should be able to find you an English-speaking attorney, provide an overview of the criminal justice process in that country, and assist you in reaching friends and family who can help or send funds.

Chapter 12

How to Beat Jet Lag and Stay Healthy When Traveling

Travel can benefit your mental health. Studies have shown that travel can reduce stress, improve your mood, and give you a happier outlook on life.

However, if you don't know how to manage travel or you overdo things, it can wreak havoc on your body in the process. I've spoken with top athletes, scientists, and doctors to get their best tips and tricks on how to be a healthy traveler and battle jet lag. This chapter will help you understand more about the physical demands of travel on the body and mind and give you the tools to manage it.

Focus on Travel Health Before You Travel

My best tip for staying healthy while traveling is to have your health in order before you travel. Prevention and understanding your own biological rhythms—knowing how and when you need sleep, what you should eat to keep your body energized, and so on, can help.

You don't want to deal with any surprises when traveling. If you look at health and jet lag as one general category, it's easy to do specific things before you even start your trip to keep your body and mind in top shape. These habits can help keep you healthy when you're on the go.

I spoke with Jake Deutsch, MD, for advice on how to approach health when traveling, including how to look at jet lag, what should be in your emergency RX kits, how to handle getting sick abroad, and so much more.

"Prevention and preparation are the modern ways to handle travel health and medicine," Dr. Deutsch advised. "Thinking about your immune system is really important." Whether that means asking your doctor for a preemptive antibiotic to store in your travel medicine bag in case of an emergency infection or banking up additional hours of sleep, preparation is key. And we'll start by talking about jet lag.

The Jet Lag Drag

Taylor Swift, when asked if she had jet lag, responded, "Jet lag is a choice," when she quickly returned from her Asia tour to see her boyfriend Travis Kelce play in the Super Bowl. I know exactly what she means, because when you're excited to be somewhere (or see someone you love) that rush can easily override the temporary effects of jet lag. Funny enough, I had seen her perform in Tokyo that week and I was enduring a rough bout of jet lag upon my return back to New York City (I think Japan to New York is one of the worst routes for jet lag).

While Taylor's comment captures that emotional boost we sometimes feel, jet lag itself is actually caused by a mismatch between your underlying 24-hour circadian clock and the timing of behavior in the new time zone, such as sleeping and eating times. Jet lag is not a choice but an unavoidable biological fact of transmeridian travel we can't overcome by motivation, a positive mindset, or just "pushing through it."

Science proves that switching time zones does indeed mess with your body, and not even a billionaire with their own jet and medical team can fully escape jet lag, at least not without a science-based solution that times their behavior to reset the circadian clock to the new time zone as quickly as possible. There are many proven techniques I'll highlight in this chapter that can help your body adjust much quicker, whether you're flying in style or in economy like most.

I spoke to Mickey Beyer-Clausen, the CEO of Timeshifter, a leader in circadian technology and the creator of the world's most downloaded and highest-rated jet lag app, to explain how we can decrease the effects of jet lag and rest better when traveling, all of which can benefit our health. The app was created with Dr. Steven W. Lockley, a Harvard neuroscientist, and creates personalized jet lag plans to help you adapt your circadian rhythms to new times zones quickly and fight jet lag when traveling (it's even recommended by the CDC).

He confirms what I've always suspected to be true: that everyone gets jet lag (even pop stars). "Everyone has jet lag, and you can measure it. You might not feel all the symptoms, but common ones include fatigue, insomnia, and problems with concentration," Beyer-Clausen said. "All of our systems have circadian clocks and rhythms, but the most important one is in the brain. People often define jet lag as a sleep disruption, but it affects everything the circadian clock controls, including immune function, metabolism, and digestive systems."

Jet lag is one of the worst ways that travel affects your body. If you've ever traveled to another time zone, especially one that's multiple hours off from your own, you've probably experienced jet lag.

Why You Get Jet Lag

Jet lag happens when the part of your brain that regulates circadian rhythms (the internal clock that tells us when to eat, wake up, and go to sleep) is out of sync with the time zone you're in. It means your mind and body are often at odds with each other. Your brain is telling you to be awake when you're supposed to be asleep and vice versa.

We all know that sleep is critical to health, so if you aren't sleeping, it can quickly impact your trip (and your mental and physical health). This is why managing jet lag is key—don't try to be a superhero.

Symptoms of Jet Lag

Light cases, like heading from California to New York (crossing just a few time zones), can mess you up slightly, making you feel foggy at a work meeting or ready for bed a few hours earlier or later than usual. But, even this relatively modest challenge can be important, especially if you need to be at your best for a key business meeting or ready to run the New York Marathon. More extreme cases, such as traveling to Europe or Asia from the US, can completely disrupt your body's circadian rhythms, keeping you up all night, exhausted all day, and really decreasing the quality of your trip, whether for business or pleasure. There is nothing worse during that special vacation if you are trying to spend quality time with a partner who is on a different time schedule and feeling jet-lagged.

According to the Mayo Clinic, symptoms of jet lag aren't just limited to fatigue or sleep issues—they can also cause diarrhea, constipation, mood changes, inability to focus, or a general feeling of malaise.

My jet lag is significantly worse when flying east. In particular, flying from New York to London destroys me because I never have enough time to get real sleep on the plane (when it can often clock at just six hours from takeoff to touchdown). I can handle fatigue during the day, but the worst is at night when I wake up at 2 or 3 in the morning. With every minute that goes by, I know the following day is going to get harder and harder—especially as a parent and when I have work commitments. I also have brutal jet lag coming back from Asia.

The general rule on circadian adaptation states that it takes one day to shift the circadian clock by one hour unless you follow a science-based jet lag plan. I experienced this firsthand on a recent trip to Tokyo, which was a 13-hour time zone adjustment, and I had disrupted sleep (random wakeups throughout the night and trouble falling back asleep) for a solid 10 days. I finally adjusted when I was about to head home.

Maybe jet lag doesn't affect you as badly as it does me. Perhaps you get it even worse, or it feels more intense on certain routes. If you're wondering why some people tend to feel the symptoms of jet lag more intensely, it's because everyone's body has a different internal circadian clock that affects how easily we can travel east or west. "This is why jet lag must be dealt with individually. Circadian clocks have different speeds in each of us, which determines whether we are early birds or night owls," said Beyer-Clausen. "Most people have an internal circadian clock that runs longer than 24 hours, which is the equivalent of naturally 'traveling' a bit west each day. These individuals, often referred to as night owls or evening types, tend to find it easier to travel west rather than east. On the other hand, about a quarter of people have an internal clock that is shorter than 24 hours. These early birds, or morning types, typically prefer traveling east over west. The difficulty of adjusting to new time zones largely depends on each person's unique internal clock."

Dr. Deutsch suffers from jet lag like the rest of us but suggests thinking about sleep deprivation and jet lag as a large part of overall health when traveling to mitigate its effects. "I'm always thinking about what happens to our long-term health when you have a state where you're defi-cient in sleep, so having strategies to minimize the effects of jet lag are key for health optimization."

Combating Jet Lag: How to Avoid It, Manage It, and Survive It

You may not be able to completely avoid feeling a little off from jet lag, espe-cially on long trips, but there are ways to combat it, as well as to recalibrate your body once you've already got it. According to Beyer-Clausen, there are no generic rules to help manage jet lag. Each person's clock is different, and many other factors affect the severity of jet lag, including the number of time zones crossed and the flight times. For example, the jet lag advice is very different if you are taking a morning flight from New York to London com-pared to an overnight flight. Beyer-Clausen also emphasized that "the correct timing of light exposure and light avoidance is the key to addressing the un-derlying cause of jet lag," a concept we'll dig into deeper later in this chapter.

For specific advice on a particular trip, you will need to use an app like Timeshifter that can give you personalized advice based on your chrono-type, sleep pattern, and trip information.

If you don't use a science-based app, then you simply need to get to the new destination with enough time to adapt naturally, keeping in mind that it will take one day for every hour of time difference for your body to fully adjust (or possibly longer, if you do the wrong things at the wrong times).

Grigor Dimitrov, professional tennis player, tries to give himself four days to acclimate before he has to play. "The first day or two with jet lag, it's hard to practice and train at my full potential, so I try to get at least four days if I'm switching time zones. We also have to adjust to the conditions and speed of the court, the balls, and the altitude if playing somewhere like Madrid," he told me.

If you do have an important event, get there a few days early so your body can better adjust and will be in top form in time. While most of us aren't play-ing professional tennis matches, if you have an important business meeting, a destination wedding, or another event you want to be 100% for, arrive at least a few days early. However, as my trip to Tokyo taught me, sometimes even that may not be enough if the time zone difference is significant.

Here are some things to do that help you best combat the effects of jet lag.

1. Get daylight and darkness at the right times to regulate your circadian rhythms.

The light-dark cycle is the only natural time cue that can reset the circadian clock in the brain. The timing of light exposure, and light avoidance, is critical as light can shift the clock in opposite directions (either earlier or later) based on its timing. In general, evening light shifts the clock later (needed when traveling west) and morning light shifts the clock earlier (needed when traveling east), but the timing of "evening" and "morning" is not straightforward once you get to the new destination.

Take an example of flying from New York to London: If you take a 7 a.m. morning flight from New York, and land at 7 p.m. London time, you need to stay awake and see light until bedtime. If you take the overnight flight leaving New York at 7 p.m. and land in London at 7 a.m., you need to avoid light in London (for example, by wearing sunglasses) until 10 a.m. London time as light before then (equivalent to the middle of the night in New York) will shift your clock in the wrong direction, to California, making your jet lag worse.

The generic advice of "just get on the new light-dark cycle as quickly as possible" is therefore often wrong and will make your jet lag worse. Once adapted, that advice is fine, but for the several days after landing, light (and dark) exposure should be carefully timed.

In addition to shifting the circadian clock, light is a stimulant, so it's good advice to avoid light in the hour or two before bed, even when at home. The light from screens is particularly disruptive as they emit the short wavelength blue light that maximally alerts the brain. If you can't sleep at night in your new destination, try to keep bright lights to a minimum so your body is in darkness. If you absolutely must watch a screen in a bedroom, Beyer-Clausen suggests watching "a screen like a TV that's far away from your bed on a wall and to dim it down. Don't use a tablet that's right in front of you. This is a big, bright surface that's too close, taking away a lot of the darkness right around you. You could wear sunglasses to dim the light entering the eyes even more."

Even when not traveling, the alerting effects of light can be highly disruptive to sleep, and continue for several hours after the lights are turned off. For example, watching your iPad at full brightness before bed can suppress natural melatonin production, according to Beyer-Clausen. If you're able to tone down your light environment before bed, by dimming the light as much as possible or stopping the use of electronic devices, this is what will make the most difference.

2. Use melatonin and caffeine as supplementary tools.

Light and dark exposure at the right times is the only way to quickly reset your circadian clock to new time zones. Using synthetic melatonin supplements can also reset the clock, but "not without the right timing and darkness," said Beyer-Clausen. "Light is much more powerful than a melatonin supplement. If you want to benefit from melatonin, light (and avoidance of light) exposure is key, as is taking the right type and dose of melatonin at the right time." He recommends fast-release, low-dose (0.5–3 milligrams) melatonin-only preparation (not combined with other sleep aids or vitamins), which will help reset the clock (versus slow-release, which is often what is sold at drugstores) for sleep. Melatonin can also help with sleep if taken before sleep at a time when your body is not naturally producing melatonin, but it needs to be timed in conjunction with its circadian effects to avoid confusing the system.

"It is not always intuitive when to use, or not use, melatonin, and it's not right for every sleep opportunity. Using an app like Timeshifter will help you time it properly," Beyer-Clausen advised. In most countries, melatonin is a prescription medication and so you may need to see your doctor to get access to it. As with any drug, there are also side effects such as headache and nausea in a small proportion of people. Never take melatonin for the first time on the plane in case of any unknown allergic responses. Instead, "ground test" it at home at bedtime a few days before you leave. Also, melatonin should not be used in children, pregnant or lactating women, migraine sufferers, and people with primary psychiatric disorders. I'm not a doctor, so consult your doctor first before using this substance.

Caffeine does not reset the circadian clock so it will not cure jet lag. However, caffeine can help with some of the sleepiness experienced with jet lag, and help you stay awake at the right time to get exposure to light, if used in the correct way. The trick to using caffeine is "little and often." 20–30 milligrams of caffeine every hour on average is plenty to maintain alertness. This is the equivalent to a cup of tea or weak coffee, or a standard soda (not an energy drink), every one to two hours. While there are differences between individuals in their sensitivity to caffeine, even if you think you sleep well after drinking caffeine, your brain activity patterns during sleep will still be affected.

3. Try to sleep on the plane, but do it smartly.

"Sleep doesn't regulate your circadian clock. It's the other way around. Your circadian clock regulates sleep and alertness. If you're sleeping at a time when you should be prioritizing light, you will be making jet lag worse. Sleep itself won't help you with jet lag. It's actually the closing of your eyes and getting a dark signal that regulates your rhythms," said Beyer-Clausen.

Sleeping the entire flight may help you with sleep deprivation, but it won't necessarily help you with jet lag, and neither will popping that sleeping pill to knock you out for the flight. Sleep smart, and don't panic if you can't fall asleep on a plane. Just getting darkness can help regulate your rhythms. If you're unsure when to sleep, when to get darkness, or how to do it, the Timeshifter app can give you personalized advice based on your chronotype, sleep pattern, and trip information.

"Even if you can't sleep and want to watch a movie when you should be avoiding light, put on your sunglasses and dim down your entertainment screen," he advises. This means you can create a light-dark cycle without actually sleeping, helping you to better adjust to the new time zone before you even arrive.

As I mentioned, sleep deprivation isn't the same thing as jet lag, but both can greatly affect your travel health. Make sure you are not sleep-deprived before starting your trip. Prioritize sleep in the days before the trip, and try and get a little more than you usually do, especially if you are "preadapting" your circadian rhythms before the flight. "If traveling east, you should go to bed and wake up an hour or two earlier than normal for one to two days before you leave, or later than normal before a trip west," said Beyer-Clausen. "We should always be stealing those moments of getting additional sleep," said Dr. Deutsch.

4. Select flights to set you up for success.

While many aircraft manufacturers would like you to believe their planes are better for jet lag, there isn't a specific aircraft scientifically proven to minimize it. "No form of plane oxygen can lessen the effects of jet lag," according to Beyer-Clausen, because, as we've learned, jet lag is related to light—not the air we breathe.

The airlines *could* use lighting to help but often utilize their aircraft's LED lights in the wrong ways, which makes jet lag worse. Airlines use plane lighting to their own advantage—turning on bright lights to serve meals at the time that's most convenient for them, not when it may be best for your circadian rhythms to adjust. There's really no way a commercial airline could use lighting to properly jive with every passenger's personal circadian rhythms and adaptation, though they could help some people by improving it.

However, from a passenger standpoint, as you begin to travel, you may discover routes that better fit your circadian rhythms. Some people suffer less from jet lag during a late-night flight that gets into Europe in the early afternoon, while others might prefer to leave from the US around 4 p.m. and get in at the crack of dawn the next day.

My best tip for control is to choose your preferred timing and route that works for your circadian rhythms, but don't think too much about how the actual plane type can help your jet lag because it can't (though I personally prefer flying on quieter aircraft like the A380, A350, and 787, and more and more studies are coming out about the negative effect of loud noise on our overall well-being).

5. Pack thoughtful gear and get creative with solutions.

We already talked about how airlines sometimes turn the lights on at times when it's better for you to be in the dark. This is when having your own gear is important. If you want to be in darkness but all the cabin lighting is on, that's the moment to pull out those noise-canceling headphones, ear plugs, your neck pillow, and an eye mask.

Likewise, you can watch media on your phone or use the seatback entertainment screen at full brightness, and use the overhead lights, even if the cabin is dark (sorry for your seatmates!). The galley area and bathrooms are also places to get light exposure when needed, even if intermittently. Fifteen minutes of bright light will give 75% of the benefits of an hour of light and so even short pulses can help if taken at the right time, according to Beyer-Clausen.

You can also help create dark environments in hotels or rentals by bringing travel blackout shades or using a sleep mask at your destination.

6. Use Timeshifter

Since jet lag is largely caused by the misalignment of circadian rhythms, the app Timeshifter aims to help you manage that. Each time you travel, you enter information about your trip in the app, like the time of your flight, the time zones you're crossing, and more. You also fill out some personal information, such as your normal sleep timing and chronotype (whether you are a morning or evening person), that can help the app understand more about your own circadian rhythms.

Then, Timeshifter maps out when you should be exposed to light and darkness (if you recall, light exposure is one of the largest regulators of your circadian rhythms), as well as other things that can assist in adaptation, like how and when to use caffeine, melatonin, and take naps.

According to Beyer-Clausen, "Timeshifter offers preadaptation. Even before you leave, you can start adjusting to the new time zone." I find that the app does help me when traveling, but I recognize it's not always possible to follow the instructions exactly. The good news is that you don't need to follow Timeshifter's advice 100% to enjoy the benefits. Even just following the advice to the best of your ability can help you adapt much faster than normal, especially the suggestions about when to get light and darkness. The app tells you when to get bright light, get some light, avoid light, and sleep.

I also like that the app partners with top travel brands like Inter-Continental Hotels and Resorts, United Airlines, Lufthansa, Swiss, and Austrian Airlines to offer subscriptions at discounted prices and sometimes even free subscriptions for elite members. It's also recommended by the CDC for international travel.

Jet Lag in Kids

Jet lag affects kids the same way it affects adults. The difference is that children usually need more sleep.

Although your children may have a different circadian rhythm than you, a good rule of thumb is simply to have them follow your adaptation schedule, but ensure they get the *additional* sleep they need. For example, if you sleep eight hours per night and they sleep 10, usually going to bed two hours before you, follow that schedule when traveling to the best of everyone's ability.

Some children are better than others at adapting to new sleeping environments, but creating a comfortable environment can help them get to sleep when they need to and stay asleep. Here are some tips:

1. If your child is sensitive to light, consider using a Slumberpod ($180), which is a portable sleeping tent for babies that provides a near-dark environment.
2. Choose flight times that best align with their natural sleep schedules. Dean normally sleeps from 7:30 p.m. to 7 a.m. so I found that taking 9:30 p.m. flights to Europe would tire him out and he would sleep from takeoff to touchdown. My worst flight with him was between New York (JFK) and Tokyo, because I chose the noon departure versus the midnight to fly the A350-1000 on Japan Airlines. Dean was apparently as excited as I was, because he was up for 10 hours of the 13-hour flight.
3. Never wake a sleeping baby is a common tip for newborns, but not for traveling kids. If your child's afternoon nap is usually two hours,

try to keep it that way when traveling. If you let them take a huge nap during the day, you're asking for trouble trying to get back on a normal schedule.

4. Limit light during middle-of-the-night wakeups. Light regulates jet lag, so if the family is up in the middle of the night, try to keep the room as dark as possible. You can play with games or toys, but if it's too early to start the day and you want them to try and sleep more, keep the room dimly lit and hope that they'll eventually tire out and go back to sleep so you can wake up on a normal schedule.

5. Try to keep up with bedtime routines. Even if the kids aren't tired when they need to be, try to do the pre-bedtime routine you do at home and stop screen time at least an hour before bed to hopefully get them sleeping on the schedule of the location. Don't use the iPad for games or watching videos when they should be in darkness, as the light emitted from electronic screens is very disruptive.

Can Holistic Medicine Cure Jet Lag?

Some people say grounding can cure jet lag—stepping out onto grass or soil with bare feet or having contact with a natural body of water. Apparently, this realigns your energy with the earth. As jet lag can only be alleviated by resetting the circadian clock, this approach is unlikely to work and I couldn't find any scientific evidence to prove that it does, but I know many people who swear by it. I always feel better when connecting with nature, however, and it is not going to cause any harm (unless you go outside and see sunlight at a time when you should be exposed to dim light or darkness), so why not give it a go?

Travel Health: How to Stay Healthy and Feel Good When Traveling

Aside from jet lag, travel can be exhausting—both business and leisure travel. Things like sleeping in unfamiliar environments and changes to your diet and routine can affect you mentally and physically. Flight delays and cancellations can be stressful, and air travel can also put undue stress on your body, especially during flights when you're sitting for long periods of time and breathing drier plane air. You may not be in a destination long enough to fully adapt to a new time zone. Or maybe you're traveling on the same time zone, but a delayed or long travel day has got you feeling exhausted. Sometimes, you need to focus on feeling as well as you can in order to take advantage of your time away, be functional in those work meetings, or enjoy your family trip.

So, here are some ways to stay healthy and boost your energy when traveling.

Stay Hydrated and Skip Alcohol When Flying

This will help your body stay strong amid time differences, schedule changes, new foods, and more that travel often brings on. Alcohol hits you so much harder in the air. It also dehydrates you and makes your recovery harder. Enjoy a better cocktail on the ground at your destination, and sip water on the plane instead.

Exercise

Exercise can help mitigate the exhausting effects of travel on your body. Not only can a jog in a local neighborhood get your endorphins flowing, but it's a great way to get the lay of the land, especially if it's really early in the morning and there are few people on the streets. You can ask your hotel for a running map of the neighborhood (in destinations where this makes sense).

Remember, professional athletes aren't exempt from the lethargic effects that travel and jet lag can cause. Grigor Dimitrov swears by exercise as a way to feel better when traveling.

"The key for me is trying to work out when I arrive in a new city. I feel that the gym helps give me energy for the rest of the day," he shared.

I also chatted with Joey Gonzalez, global CEO of Barry's who travels extensively, for some additional tips on fighting jet lag with exercise.

If you have 15 minutes in a hotel gym, "try some light or HIIT cardio exercises on the treadmill to help overcome the effects of jet lag. You can alternate a walk, jog, and run speed every 30 seconds for 15 minutes," he said.

Sometimes, the gym just isn't an option, but you can still do some light exercise in your hotel room. "If you're in a hotel room without any equipment, try alternating a cardio move like jumping jacks with a static strength move such as plank position," Gonzalez advised. And while you can't bring heavy weights with you, you could consider tossing a resistance band in your suitcase. Gonzalez often travels with bands, "as they're compact and can provide a broad range of strength training exercises."

He also said you can start intercepting the effects of travel while still on the plane. "Preventative measures include staying hydrated, avoiding excessive alcohol and caffeine, and performing mobility exercises like calf raises and stretching during the flight."

Choosing hotels with well-equipped gyms is a must for some (as well as the ability to make some unique room service orders). "I always make sure the hotel I am staying at has a good gym. This is one of the reasons I am reluctant to stay at Airbnbs, as they often don't have the same level of facilities that the best hotels do. I also do ice baths after each of my matches in my hotel room, which helps a lot with recovery. My number one order from room service is eight buckets of ice," said Dimitrov.

And it doesn't have to be a hotel gym. Picking accommodation near gyms, parks, or fitness activities means you might be able to squeeze in a run, yoga class, or fitness class. Depending on your vacation style, this might be a unique way to get to know the culture and/or the area. Taking a fitness class in Italy, aerial yoga in Hong Kong, or jogging through Madrid's Retiro Park may help you alleviate your jet lag, boost endorphins, and give you an opportunity to feel like part of the local scene.

Gonzalez has one other tip that may also work for you: fasting. "My best hack is a 16-hour fast, which is a very effective way to reset your body, as food availability can wield powerful influence over our sleep cycles. Just make sure to time it so that the completion of the fast takes place at breakfast time in your new destination," he suggested.

Keep Your Immune System Up

It's important to do this not only during travel but before and after. Taking probiotics is one way to give your immune system a boost. "A probiotic is always among my recommended supplements because it helps balance our gut microbiome. Our digestive tract has the largest portion of lymphatics, which is essentially modulating our immune system. Probiotics help prepare your digestive tract for bacteria that you're not used to being exposed to, particularly in less developed countries," said Dr. Deutsch.

Use a Mask If/When You Deem Necessary

Rather than self-diagnose others ("I saw a woman in row four coughing!"), consider wearing a mask yourself if you're concerned about getting sick on a plane or when traveling. I realize this is a hot-button topic, especially post-pandemic, but it's an easy way to keep other people's respiratory droplets at bay and give you some control over your environment.

Dr. Deutsch says an N95 mask is fine. "It's just another layer of caution," he said.

This can also help you avoid breathing in pollution in countries that face contamination. I've been offered masks by hotels during particularly bad moments of air pollution in countries such as Thailand and India, so having one handy is always a good idea, even if you don't use it.

Be Careful When Drinking Water Abroad

Always research your destination to see if the drinking water is safe and always confirm with hotels or vacation rentals if the water is filtered. In locations with poor quality water (or if your water is ever not clear or has an abnormal smell or taste), be overly cautious and not only drink bottled water, but use it even for brushing your teeth. Don't get water in your mouth when showering, as even small amounts of contaminated water can wreak havoc on your body. When possible, use a thermos and refill it with filtered water or, at worst, drink bottled water. Also be careful with getting drinks made with ice from local water taps as it can still get you sick. It's better to be safe than sorry.

Stay Up-to-Date on Vaccines

You should always check on what vaccines you need when traveling abroad, both required (by certain countries) or recommended.

"Having those travel vaccines is incredibly important. I recommend going to the CDC's website first, then speak with your doctor or a travel medicine specialist to get the vaccines or treatment you need, like a yellow fever vaccine or malaria pills," Dr. Deutsch said. "Making sure that you have hepatitis A and B vaccines is key if you're a traveler." Hepatitis A can be transmitted from drinking contaminated water or eating contaminated food, so this is a particularly important vaccine to consider when traveling to countries with a high prevalence of hepatitis.

Hydrate

Traveling can be challenging because schedules change frequently, so it can be easy to forget about drinking water. "I recommend keeping up with at least two or three liters of water a day, especially since you get dehydrated when you fly, which can lead to constipation and reduced sleep quality," said Dr. Deutsch.

Proper Skincare

Keeping your skin hydrated is just as important as hydrating with water, especially on long flights. "Skincare products are important to me. My skin takes a lot of abuse being out in the sun every day and with all the travel. I try to make sure that I always travel with those things in my carry-on so I can use them throughout the flight," mentioned Dimitrov.

And while plane windows tend to block out most UV rays, it couldn't hurt to put on a broad spectrum sunblock (especially for children) during long daytime flights if you're in the window seat.

Know Your Body

If you know long flights upset your stomach, that you don't function well on little sleep, or your body doesn't react well at 38,000 feet when taking Xanax, do what you need to do to keep yourself safe, healthy, and in a controlled state.

Take Meds Along with You—But Understand the Rules

According to Dr. Deutsch, you should always have the following in your base-level travel medicine kit:

- A basic antibiotic (ask your doctor for a preventative prescription), especially when going to remote locations
- Eye drops

- Antidiarrheal chew tablets (they're easier to get through security)
- Antacids
- Typical OTC medication for fever for cold, cough, and allergies (don't forget Benadryl)
- A sleep aid (always test at home before using on a plane)
- Antinausea medication, especially for cruising or if you need to take flights on small planes
- Electrolyte packets
- Neosporin and Band-Aids
- Bug repellent
- N95 masks

Before traveling to exotic destinations, make an appointment with a travel doctor to see what other prescription medications you should consider (like antimalarials).

Make sure to pack these items in your carry-on, assuming they don't violate the liquids rule. While you should never assume you'll be able to get medication when abroad, it can actually be much easier to get certain medications when traveling, and pharmacists can be very helpful.

For example, if you have cold symptoms in France or Spain, pop into a pharmacy and tell a pharmacist your symptoms. They'll do their best to help and will often try to speak English, too. You can also get things like flu and COVID tests at pharmacies in many countries for just a couple of dollars.

While I don't necessarily recommend self-diagnosing, you can also get antibiotics OTC in many countries, such as Thailand, at an affordable price. I once picked up a Z-pack there when I knew I needed it. It's nice to know that in case of an emergency, that might be available to you. If you lose your medication while traveling but have your prescription, you can show it at a local pharmacy and explain the situation—hopefully, they can replace your lost meds.

However, you need to be very aware of taking things like CBD, diazepam, Xanax, and Valium into certain countries. For example, the UAE has very strict rules about what medicine you can bring in, how much you can take, and whether you have a medical prescription for it. Medication that has stimulants is illegal in Japan—this includes Adderall.

One man was detained in a Dubai jail for five weeks for taking enough antianxiety medication into the UAE to last him for a six-month stay. He also was denied access to his medication, which caused him extreme mental duress. Avoid this by understanding the rules and always having a prescription with you.

DVT Is Real—Here's What You Need to Know

Deep vein thrombosis (DVT) is basically a fancy term for blood clots. Although anyone can get a blood clot when flying, certain people may be more susceptible to this due to prior medical conditions.

"When we move and contract the muscles of our legs, this helps pump blood back to the heart," explained Dr. Deutsch. "When we're sitting still for too long, it can cause a pooling of the blood, which can clot. It won't happen to most people, but anyone with risks (like you're a smoker or take birth control) or an underlying condition is more susceptible."

DVT can happen and not cause noticeable symptoms, but usually those who have it will notice things like pain or cramping, usually in one leg. Swelling, redness/purpling, soreness, or the feeling of warmth in a certain spot on your leg might also be a sign you have a clot. In severe cases, you might notice shortness of breath or chest pain.

Although DVT is really dangerous, you can prevent it from occurring by getting up and moving around every couple hours when flying. "Movement is the most important thing," according to Dr. Deutsch. The American Heart Association suggests wearing compression socks to reduce the risk of DVT, especially on flights longer than four hours.

Ideally, move your legs and ankles around while seated, tightening and releasing leg muscles or lifting your heels up and down. When it comes to ultra-long-haul flights, Dr. Deutsch suggests doing "deep knee bends or getting up and doing a couple laps around the cabin as prevention." It's also important to talk to your doctor ahead of travel to make sure you have a plan in place if you do have risk factors.

If you suspect you might have a blood clot (sometimes, symptoms can show up weeks after flying), seek medical care immediately. Not to be a fearmonger, but many young, healthy people have gotten DVT, so don't think it can't happen to you. Try to move around on flights, and if you have any symptoms, see a doctor immediately to get treatment before the clot dislodges.

How to Manage Traveler's Diarrhea

Before traveling, it's important to understand food safety norms in your destination. According to the CDC, "the highest-risk destinations are in Asia (except for Japan and South Korea) as well as the Middle East, Africa, Mexico, and Central and South America."

It's simple to figure out if you can drink the local water or not with some light research on your destination. If you have any doubts, drink bottled water and stay away from raw vegetables, ice, fruit, anything that's been sitting out in the sun for a while at a food market, and any food that might cause reactions if not refrigerated or handled properly, like sushi or shellfish. Frequent handwashing is always a good plan, too.

If you do end up with a stomach bug or food poisoning, this is when having the right medicine can help. While sometimes, if you're in the comfort of a hotel room, letting your body work through whatever is bothering it can work, if you have to get on a plane or train, an OTC medicine like loperamide can be a lifesaver. This type of medicine should always be in your travel medicine bag, regardless of destination. After all, even if you are in a "safe" destination, when you travel, your eating habits are often different from usual, so it's best to have these meds as a backup.

Rehydration is also important, so drink lots of water. Dr. Deutsch also suggests turning to electrolyte packets (he likes the ones from Coast), which can "replenish [more than just] the minerals you lose." If you find you're still suffering after a few days, it's time to see a doctor. You may need antibiotics or another type of medicine.

Handling a Medical Emergency Abroad

No one wants to get sick or have any kind of medical emergency abroad, but it can happen. Let's discuss your options.

For Less Serious Situations, Use a Telehealth App

For nonemergency medical situations, you may want to use a telehealth app to speak to a US-based doctor to get a prediagnosis before going to a local clinic where language might be a barrier, or they have standards that may not meet what you're used to. Knowing what it could be and arming yourself with information is key.

A telehealth app may also be useful if you're traveling within the United States. In some cases, your insurance may cover this (or you'll have to pay a low fee), but it may be a great way to get a quick prescription (think a Z-pack or allergy meds) while in another state when you can't see your regular doctor in person.

Some of these apps may be free with your insurance (such as Doctor On Demand), so check on this and make sure to download and register for apps before traveling so your profile and information are all set up if you run into a situation where you need to use it. The last thing you want is to be sick and trying to download an app when you have a slow internet connection or bad signal. If you don't have insurance, you may want to try GoodRx Care.

Leverage Hotel Staff

Once, my friend got an acute UTI in the Maldives. It was the middle of the night, and she was hesitant to contact resort staff, but it turned out the resort had an on-site doctor who was able to give her the medication she needed for instant relief. It's always better to address any smaller health issues ASAP when traveling before they turn into full-blown emergencies.

Always ask at the hotel if there's a doctor on-site or nearby, especially when abroad, because they might just have one or be able to point you in the right direction.

Dr. Deutsch also advises asking the hotel if you have a specific medical need. "Many hotels will put a refrigerator in your room, which can help keep certain medications cool," he said.

Full-Blown Emergencies

If you have a serious emergency that requires a medical evacuation, check the travel insurance and credit coverage information in chapter 11. Many credit cards will cover these costs if you used them to pay for all or a portion of your trip, so paying with the right credit card can save you thousands of dollars, even if you didn't buy travel or supplementary health insurance.

Speaking of travel insurance, I suggest having it when traveling abroad. In most cases, if you do have a travel insurance policy, they'll be able to quickly find you a local doctor or hospital to treat you when you need it.

Chapter 13

How to Manage Fear of Flying

Fear of flying may never disappear. You just have to learn how to master it.
—WHOOPI GOLDBERG

Mastering it might just mean flying in first class (on points).

Can you imagine being so afraid of flying that you hire a bus to drive you cross-country with two full-time drivers so you can make the trip in 30 hours flat? Being so nervous to step foot on a plane that you hire an anesthesiologist and a private jet to put you under so you can be transported across an ocean?

While I can't imagine going to these lengths, I know many people who battle with varying degrees of fear of flying. Aviophobia, aerophobia . . . it goes by many names, but fear of flying is way more common than you may think. Forty percent of people have some kind of fear around flying.

Flying, especially on commercial jets, is safe. So much so that it can be difficult to even calculate the odds of dying on a passenger flight because *they're so low.* In the US in 2023, more than 100,000 people died from drug overdoses,[1] more than 43,000 from gun violence,[2] nearly 41,000 from car crashes,[3] and *zero* from commercial airline crashes. Out of 37.7 million commercial flights in 2023 globally, there was only a single fatal propeller jet crash in Nepal.

There is no other mode of transportation as safe as flying. And it makes sense—the entire global aviation network is highly regulated and monitored.

---

* The content in this chapter is for informational purposes only. It does not substitute professional medical advice.

Anyone cleared to fly a commercial plane has passed rigorous training and supervised practical experience, and even when they get in the cockpit, they will spend years being the number two before even taking full control of the aircraft. They're drug tested, and even then, there are computer systems and redundancies that can help them recover even if mistakes are made. How does that compare to what you see on any highway on a Friday night?

According to research, more than 25 million people in the US are scared of (or at least anxious about) flying, with a reported third of those with a fear so severe it stops them from flying.

Part of fear of flying comes from lack of control, especially when you're uncomfortably crammed into a tiny seat, the doors snap shut, and your life is in the hands of someone up front that you can't even see.

Capt. Sully Sullenberger, former US ambassador to ICAO, the International Civil Aviation Organization (and the pilot who landed US Airways Flight 1549 in the Hudson River in 2009 after a bird strike), explained why fear of flying affects so many people—and a lot of it has to do with control. "Riding in a car is a common, everyday occurrence. We understand how cars work, we often know the driver, and we can just pull over and stop. Being in an airplane isn't an everyday thing, we may not understand the physics of flight, we probably don't know the pilots, and we can't just pull over."

Other factors can come in the form of claustrophobia, fear of heights, panic about germs, fear of crashing, motion sickness, or just plain fear.

After safely landing the aircraft in the river, Captain Sullenberger didn't have any increased anxiety around flying. "I returned to flying as soon as I could. Getting back in the cockpit was like coming home, like putting on a favorite pair of jeans." Just think—if he can do it, so can you.

You're Not Alone in Your Fear of Flying

It may help you to know that some of the people I know who fly the most don't love air travel or have a fear of flying. I have friends who have visited dozens of countries and flown countless flights that absolutely despise flying. Fear of flying also isn't a "sensible" or "organized" fear. It may come and go, or you may only have it sometimes.

Understanding you're not the only one with fear, nerves, or panic can help—just knowing you're not alone. Having always been interested in how people develop and handle a fear of flying, I had a chat with Whoopi Goldberg. The actor, comedian, author, radio host, television personality, and EGOT winner (one of 21 people ever to have won Emmy, Grammy, Oscar, and Tony awards!) has a fear of flying that she's dealt with over the years.

In 1978, Whoopi was spending time with family and friends, enjoying a carefree and happy afternoon barbecue, unaware that tragedy was about to strike. That is, until she looked up, feeling helpless, as two planes headed toward one another. She witnessed these two planes collide, with debris and wreckage falling all over her own neighborhood.

She watched in horror as Pacific Southwest Airlines Flight 182 collided with a private Cessna 172 aircraft in her San Diego neighborhood, one of the deadliest plane crashes ever to occur in California.

Her fear of flying didn't start right after the crash. "I was fine for a very long time, and then I had a nightmare. And the nightmare was so vivid and so scary, it freaked me out so badly. I just thought, I'm never doing this again. I'm never getting on a plane again. When you see stuff like that, you think, it didn't happen to me. I'm here. So that was terrible, and move on. But my brain said, I'm gonna shield you from all of this for a while, but I'm gonna wake you up with it at some point, and you're gonna have to deal with it. And I just literally stopped going anywhere. I bought a bus," she told me.

Whoopi's fear of flying was so extreme that she used a bus to travel domestically, hiring two drivers so that she'd be able to get cross-country in just two days. She tried before to get on planes and had panic attacks so intense she couldn't manage to board or turned around on the jetway and left. Her bus travel plan worked for a while until she had to fly to Europe to see *Sister Act* onstage. The only way she could fathom taking the trip was if she didn't even realize she was flying. So that's what she did.

"We got a private jet and got permission to have an anesthesiologist on the plane. I wanted to wake up there," Whoopi explained. So, Whoopi was put under for the flight, waking up only after the plane had safely landed in London.

If you can't hire a private jet and an anesthesiologist, don't worry. You may not need one. There are other ways to combat your fear of flying, some of which worked for Whoopi as time went on.

These days, she's flying again. Whoopi's been able to overcome her fear of flying—perhaps not fully, but enough to get on a plane without being under anesthesia, even flying commercial aircraft between destinations like New York and Italy, where she recently purchased a vacation home. If she can do it, you can, too.

Keep Your Mind Busy and Calm

Whoopi found that distraction, like listening to Audible stories or music with her noise-canceling headphones, and a carefully curated prescription for antianxiety medication from her doctor helped keep her busy but calm.

She suggests doing whatever it takes to stay calm. "With so many scenarios in your head, you need to allow yourself to just chill because once you chill, you're not focused on everything that can go wrong."

Understand How Planes Work to Keep You Safe

Understanding how planes work (the aviation industry now has sophisticated communication systems and other safeguards to minimize the chances of flight collisions) has made a difference. "Talking to pilots was a big help," Whoopi said. She also touted the benefits of Virgin Atlantic's fear of flying courses (you can do these online or in person).

"Airplanes are expertly designed, built, and operated, with lots of redundancy and many levels with huge margins of safety. Crews are well trained and experienced in how the entire system works without you even knowing it to keep everyone safe," explained Captain Sullenberger.

If hearing from a pilot helps your fear, consider using the Dial a Pilot service, which will connect you with an actual pilot for a 30-minute call for $65.

Dial a Pilot offers calls with pilots that you can use before you fly or as you need them. These pilots can reassure you about statistics, turbulence, and other triggers you may have when flying. Of course, you can always read up on what turbulence is online, but having it explained to you personally by an expert who deals with these phenomena daily creates a connection that can help minimize nerves and anxiety around flying.

But What About Turbulence?

Turbulence is the sudden change in air flow that causes a plane to move, often up and down but sometimes left and right or even in a slight roll. Things like jet streams can cause turbulence to occur.

The wake from nearby planes can also cause turbulence. The winds can bend and flap without damaging the plane's structure. Severe turbulence is rare, and while turbulence can always happen, just know your pilots aren't worried and, according to a pilot, "are always trying to avoid bad weather or change altitudes to offer you a smoother flight."

Pilots are always doing their best to move the plane out of turbulence. "Turbulence is just air moving. It's a temporary inconvenience. And you can protect yourself in a very simple way . . . [by] keeping your seat belt fastened. Airplanes are designed and built to handle turbulence with a big safety margin. Pilots avoid turbulence or manage it when they can't avoid it by changing altitude and/or by reducing speed," said Captain Sullenberger.

Most important, turbulence doesn't take down modern commercial aircraft. It's similar to driving and hitting a pothole—sometimes you can see one, but sometimes not. In rare circumstances, it could require maintenance, but most of the time it won't.

And perhaps my favorite tip: The larger the plane, the less turbulence you feel. Fearful flyers should take a page out of my book and fly on my favorite aircraft, the behemoth that is the Airbus A380. The A380 even helped my dear friend Lays Laraya cure her fear of flying.

If you're worried about turbulence on an upcoming flight, you can always check your flight on Turbli.com to see what your route looks like and ease your mind, or at least be prepared for what's to come.

Face Your Fears

Lays developed a fear of flying after being in a crash on a plane piloted by her own father. Her dad, a doctor whose father was a commercial pilot, had the itch to fly airplanes, even if it wasn't his full-time career. He got certified in his spare time and purchased a Piper Comanche plane for the family to travel around Brazil. In 1997, they were setting off on a family vacation on the plane, Lays's first (and last) time flying with her father, when things went horribly wrong.

Lays remembers her father and mother quarreling over the amount of luggage, but finally he relented because they were only four on a six-seater plane, so a little extra luggage shouldn't be an issue. The family of four loaded up and began their takeoff roll down the small dirt runway in Brazil.

The plane began to lift, but she recalls her father saying, "Hang on, we're going to crash."

"It happened in the swamp-like Mato Grosso state in Brazil that's like Florida. So when the plane hit the ground, it caught some trees. So that absorbed a little bit of the impact. But also it stopped on a small pond, which may have put out any sparks. My dad, fearing an explosion, kicked open the door and got us out. But the plane didn't explode and our lives were spared, and somehow, we only had minor injuries."

Although Lays feared flying after the crash, her father and brother kept flying regularly. She never got back in that plane, but she did fly commercially, out of necessity, as she had a lifelong goal of working at Disney in Orlando in their executive tourism program.

She first started to treat her fear by taking sleeping pills so she would be fully asleep before takeoff. "What was important for me was not to witness takeoff. Sometimes, if the sleeping pill didn't work, I would get very anxious during takeoff. I would ask someone from the cabin crew to hold my hand."

Besides trying to stay informed on how planes and turbulence work, Lays deems empathy as something that's helpful to fearful passengers. Now, she is sometimes the one to hold a fellow passenger's hand if they're nervous or have reached out to her for reassurance. She hoped to overcome her fear by continuing to fly. "You just have to do it. The more you do something you're afraid of, the easier it gets."

She thinks that the fear of flying has a rational part and an irrational part. The rational part can often be helped by knowledge, like understanding more about the training pilots have or what causes turbulence and how planes are built to overcome it. But the irrational part, the anxiety and terror that persists even when you understand that flying is safe, is tougher to get over. This also syncs up with what Whoopi told me—that the rational part of her fear was quelled by pilots explaining how planes worked, and the irrational part was tougher to deal with, but in both cases, the power of touch and empathy—a passenger reaching out to hold your hand—helped.

Living abroad sparked the travel bug in Lays. "Now, travel was tolerable. What really turned things around for me was my first flight on the Emirates A380 in 2013. It was a day flight, and it was the first takeoff I ever enjoyed. Takeoff on this plane is slower, it feels longer, and it was such a big plane I felt like nothing could take it down. I felt safe."

Lays's fascination with the A380, the adrenaline that exploring the world brought her, and, of course—one that I can understand—the challenges and joys of chasing points and elite tiers all contributed to her overcoming her fear of flying. She's been tracking her stats since that very first Emirates flight—she's flown 494 flights and over one million miles throughout 46 countries, and she's not stopping anytime soon.

My Take: Fly Better and Quell Anxiety

My advice is not only to take Lays's advice and do something you're fearful of but to travel in comfort and style so that when someone asks you the most memorable part of your vacation, you might actually say the flight. I'm not a doctor, but I'm prescribing anyone with a fear of flying to fly in business or first class (which will be doable if you follow the tips throughout this book). Flying in your own suite will definitely help with claustrophobia and the food, drink, and entertainment will definitely help distract you from your underlying anxiety.

How to Handle Fear of Flying

These are some of the more common ways to combat your fears.

Step One: Consider the Odds, Educate Yourself, and Talk Yourself Down

According to the International Air Transport Association (IATA), there were five fatal accidents among 32.2 million flights in 2022. You're much safer flying than driving or even crossing the street. Understanding this may make it easier to step onto that plane. This can help the rational side of fear.

Step Two: Identify and Manage Your Triggers

Figure out what it is that scares you or sets you off. Are you fine until turbulence hits? Does feeling claustrophobic send you into a panic? Does hearing babies cry set you off? Whatever exacerbates your fear of flying, figure out what that is and try to make moves to combat it.

If turbulence is what panics you, consider a window seat so you can look into the horizon. Or, speak to a flight attendant who might be able to reassure you when turbulence hits. You may want to start with domestic flights that don't fly over mountain ranges or the Atlantic to avoid more turbulent routes. Soothing music, meditation, distraction, or taking small sips of water may help. If you get motion sickness from turbulence, come prepared with motion sickness pills, bands, or oils.

If you're feeling claustrophobic, always pick an aisle seat or use those miles for an upgrade to a seat with additional space. Close your eyes and try deep breathing.

If certain things set you off—passenger chatter or babies crying, control your environment as best you can. Bring noise-canceling headphones, which can help you block out surrounding sounds, and distractions such as your own media and music.

Step Three: Cognitive Behavioral Therapy (CBT)

This type of therapy can help adapt thinking and behavioral patterns. It's an especially helpful treatment for fear of flying because it focuses on facing fears as opposed to avoiding them. CBT focuses on helping people develop skills they can use to cope with the fear of flying in the hope that when they are flying, they will have the tools they need to handle the emotional responses that arise.[4] These tools can be things such as taking ownership of your choices, accepting discomfort, meditating, and focusing on the arrival, not the journey. Feeling and noting discomfort but flying anyway is a major sign of progress that people may achieve with CBT.

According to studies by researchers at Georgia State University and Emory University School of Medicine, CBT has been shown to be an effective method for treating a fear of flying. If you'd like to try it, consult a mental health professional.

Step Four: Hypnosis and Emotional Freedom Technique (EFT)

Hypnosis, which is usually done with a therapist, alters your state of awareness by ensuring you're in a very relaxed state. Once you're in this deeply relaxed place, mental health professionals can help you get to the root of and eradicate your fear of flying.

There are also self-hypnosis podcasts or meditations you can download to try this yourself. Whether or not this works depends on the person, but it might be worth a try, especially if your fear is stopping you from actually getting on a plane.

One of my friends, Lori Zaino (a travel expert who helped me write this book), has a fear of turbulence, despite having flown to more than 60 countries. She's well aware that flying is safe and flies often, even though she doesn't love it. Still, when turbulence hits, her body and mind go to dark places, and it seems to have gotten worse as the years progress. Now that she has a child, she wants to be a calm and nurturing presence for her son when they travel, instead of clamming up and panicking in bumpy skies. She decided to try hypnosis with a licensed therapist via Zoom to combat her deep, unsettling anxiety around turbulence. The session started with EFT or tapping. She repeated, "When the plane is shaking, I feel safe, secure, calm, and relaxed," while tapping several different pressure points on her face, with the instruction to repeat the process daily each morning. Then, the therapist led her into a deep, meditative, heightened state of relaxation, where she repeated similar statements in her mind about staying calm and safe during turbulence.

Did it work? "Maybe," she said. "It's definitely given me a closer look at why turbulence affects me and be more conscious of how I should react when it happens. It hasn't cured my fear. When turbulence hits, I still feel physically nauseous and start to sweat. My mind starts to panic. But now, I'm able to talk both my mind and body down a bit better, and my preflight anxiety is quelled, thanks to listening to a recording of the hypnosis daily starting a few days before the flight and practicing the tapping technique each morning."

These therapies work mainly with a mind-body connection. While there's no exact proof they can work, it's always worth trying. "For me, even just a small reduction in flight or preflight anxiety, or flying being 10% easier, is a win," Lori said.

Step Five: Ask your Travel Companions, Fellow Passengers, or Flight Attendants for Help

I once had a turbulent flight to South Africa. One of the flight attendants noticed my travel companion's discomfort and bent down to chat with her for a bit to distract her, asking her about her trip plans. She later told me it helped her greatly. Flight attendants can also reassure you that you have nothing to worry about and they may also have information that the pilot hasn't shared.

If you're flying with someone who has a fear of flying, ask them how you can help. If you see they're scared, comfort or distract them. Whoopi recalls "playing UNO for six hours on a flight" with her travel companion, which distracted her from her fears.

She also told me how she noticed a fellow passenger was scared during a turbulent flight. "I reached over and grabbed her hand." Lays also encourages showing empathy to fellow passengers you see experiencing anxiety.

If you see a fellow seatmate who has an iron grip on their armrests or is visibly panicked, check on them. I don't always advocate physical touch without permission, but if it feels like the right thing to do, you could take their hand or at least ask if they're okay or how you can help.

Step Six: Alcohol and Drugs: Avoid or Indulge?

A 1997 study by Stanford showed that while alprazolam (or Xanax, as you may know it) did reduce self-reported anxiety symptoms in some anxious flyers, it also raised heart rates and didn't prevent panic attacks in others. The study concluded that "alprazolam increases physiological activation under acute stress conditions and hinders therapeutic effects of exposure in flying phobia."[5]

But certain flyers swear by the right medication (when prescribed by a doctor)—including Whoopi, who, after trial and error, with her physician, has found the right combination of medication to calm her and help her sleep when flying.

It's important to consult your doctor before taking medication on a plane. Don't try Xanax for the first time on a plane! While these remedies might help and could be a Band-Aid for your fears, they won't cure your phobia. You'll have to consider a different kind of method if you want to banish your fear versus treat it. As Lays mentioned, sleeping pills only helped her temporarily.

When I discussed the idea of self-prescribing sleeping or anxiety medication on a plane with Dr. Jake Deutsch, he strongly advised against it, "especially when flying. It's a setup for disaster," he said. Mixing sleeping or antianxiety pills and alcohol can lead to zombie-like states where you are physically awake, but have no recollection of the incident and this scenario is where many people do crazy things on planes. To avoid waking up in handcuffs or with a huge fine, don't mix prescriptions and alcohol on a plane and always try any medications at home before using them on a plane.

OTC motion sickness pills, bands, or oils can also help if turbulence causes nausea, vomiting, or other symptoms.

Step Seven: Separate Fear from Danger

I'm not saying fear of flying is irrational. But in some cases (like a friend of mine who had a full-on panic attack once because he thought the plane wings were in the wrong position), fears can be overblown or extreme.

Try to understand that while it's okay to be scared, your fear may not be entirely rational. Tell yourself that it's okay to feel your fear, but your fear may not be *valid*. This goes back to step one, of talking yourself down. It's acceptable to be scared of your plane crashing, but when you find yourself panicking, tell yourself the facts: The odds of crashing are *far* less than one in a million.

Step Eight: Keep Flying

If you're already doing it, keep doing it. If you're not, start by watching a video of a plane taking off, then book a short flight, then a longer one. Talk to your therapist, sign up for a fear of flying class, and do whatever it takes to get yourself into the air.

Step Nine: Take Comfort Items

Controlling your environment as much as possible can help. Take along whatever you need to feel comfortable. If that's a squeezy stress ball, snacks, your iPad stocked with movies, whatever. Wear loose clothing and layers so if you panic and overheat, you can take that sweatshirt off.

Step Ten: An Unconventional Method (as a Last Resort)

One of my best friends growing up, Haley, had a major fear of flying as a teenager, but her family loved going to Hawaii. So I jokingly "blessed her" in gibberish, which I told her would protect her on her travels. It was a theatrical moment meant to make her laugh more than anything, but it worked. Her anxiety went down, and she focused on the "blessing" and said it was the best flight she had ever taken.

Unfortunately for me, this meant that because it worked, I had to do it for years to come—every single time she flew!

As time went on, I convinced her I could do text blessings, and one day, I got a text from her after a trip saying that she tried flying without bothering me for once. She no longer needed my blessings. Maybe we got to an age where we outgrew the silliness, or maybe she just realized she had nothing to fear but fear itself.

Chapter 14

Travel Etiquette: A Manifesto of Considerate Travel Behavior

*Etiquette is about kindness, respect, consideration, and thinking of other
people first. Use that as a guide in any travel situation.*
—MYKA MEIER, ETIQUETTE EXPERT

When it comes to travel etiquette, I think about passengers behaving badly on airplanes. Thanks to social media (accounts like @passengershaming), ridiculous and rude behavior is often documented—it's true that travel can sometimes bring out the worst in some people.

The number of passenger disruptions in the US skyrocketed nearly 500% in 2021 (while travel had dropped tremendously), according to FAA.gov/unruly (you know there might be a problem when the FAA has a landing page for unruly passenger information!). While the number has come down, we're still at an elevated level. It's everyone's responsibility to bring a sense of decorum back to air travel. We can all do our part to be more aware of our surroundings and try to limit the behavior that disturbs our fellow passengers.

I realize tensions can be high in increasingly stressful travel situations—a rise in tiny economy seats and understaffed airports can cause even the calmest and most collected travelers to be on edge—but having empathy and respect for fellow travelers and other cultures is key. This chapter will cover helpful tips to be a better traveler to other travelers, employees, locals, and the environment.

In December 2020, I visited Volcanoes National Park, Rwanda. This was my second visit to Rwanda. It was core COVID travel. We had to wait in our hotel rooms until our arrival COVID tests cleared us. The Rwandan government was even more protective of one of the country's top tourism assets: the mountain gorillas. At the time of writing, there are only about 1,000 mountain gorillas left in the wild spread out between Rwanda, Democratic Republic of the Congo, and Uganda.

There are 12 gorilla families living in the confines of Volcanoes National Park in Rwanda, and each day, one group of trekkers sets off to visit each family with a maximum group size of eight. So, on any given day, there are only a maximum of 96 visitors allowed to trek to see the gorillas. It's not cheap, either, with permits costing $1,500 per person in addition to the costs to get to Rwanda.

On the morning of the 2020 trek, I assembled predawn to meet my fellow group members (including local guides) and learn which family we'd be tracking. Rwanda has done an incredible job at balancing tourism with sustainability, and they've been able to create economic opportunity for former poachers, where it is now more lucrative to be a tour guide and tracker than it is to kill gorillas for meat or for their body parts (there's still a black market in Europe and North America for gorilla trophies).

I noticed one of the members of our group was wearing wildly inappropriate clothing for the difficult trek up a mountainside—a tank top, white resort pants, and flip-flops.

Having done this trek, I knew this combination of gear would be insufficient and downright dangerous, but I figured she must have been planning to change before the trek since you connect with your group at the meeting point and then head off with your group to leave from the launch point closest to the family you're assigned to that day. The national park rangers have trackers all across the mountain who keep tabs on each family, but they're constantly on the move. You never know if you'll be trekking for 90 minutes or four-plus hours to find your gorilla family.

Helga (that's what I'm calling her, a kind of "Karen" in German) didn't change, and she marched off in an outfit that would be more appropriate for a Hamptons clambake. I told myself to mind my business and that the professionals would handle the situation should it spiral. We trekked for about 90 minutes through stunning eucalyptus fields and forests and started making our way up the steep mountain. Helga began slipping and sliding, and everyone in the group took turns helping her. We heard excited shouts from our trackers ahead, and our guides huddled us: We were close to the family, and soon enough, our one-hour experience would begin. They reiterated the core rules:

1. Listen to all of their rules.
2. Respect the animals and always keep a distance of at least 15 feet.
3. Remain in a group.
4. No flash photography, and put phones away when the guides tell you to.
5. No loud noises or sudden movements.
6. A facemask must be worn at all times over both nose and mouth to avoid transmission of any diseases, but especially COVID, which could have catastrophic effects if it spread through the population.
7. Don't look the silverback in the eyes when he approaches, look at the ground and kneel in deference. He's the boss!

Simple enough, right?

Silverbacks are massive in size and could kill a human, though they are naturally shy and will only ever engage if they feel threatened. No tourists have ever been attacked by gorillas in the wild.

Things started to go wrong in our group when Helga wouldn't put her phone away when the guides requested everyone do so. She had an air of superiority and exuded, "I've traveled all over the world—I'm a modern-day Dian Fossey." While novice travelers can often make faux pas, the most egregious to me is the frequent traveler who feels superior to everyone and as if the rules don't apply to them.

I can forgive ignorance, but disrespect and arrogance boil my blood. It was hard for me to enjoy the tour as I started to notice Helga leaving the group to try to get closer and closer pictures of the animals, violating the 15-foot rule. Then she was out of breath and pulled her mask down below her chin as she was close to a group of young gorillas. That's when I snapped and told her she was putting an entire species at risk to snap a photo for her 50 Facebook friends.

With backup from the guides, she relented and put her mask on for a minute before pulling it back down. But then the main attraction, the towering silverback, the alpha male of the family, stomped in, and Helga couldn't contain herself. As our guides yelled, "Get down, heads down!" with our adrenaline flowing, being in the presence of a beast that could throw us around like rag dolls, I could see out of the corner of my eye that Helga was still standing and looking at the silverback.

The guides continued to urge her to look down, but she couldn't help herself. She was in a trance, and then she went for it. She flipped her phone around and got herself a maskless selfie with a silverback. Just feet away . . . before she dropped to the ground and let him pass.

Her selfish actions not only put herself and the group at risk but also the entire community living around Volcanoes National Park, people who are dependent on tourism dollars to feed their families. As we left the park, she slipped and slid all the way down the mountain, and I couldn't even look at her I was so furious.

While Helga lives in my head as the worst tourist I've ever encountered, there's no shortage of runners-up, so I thought I'd help bring some civility to travel by tackling the issue of travel etiquette from a nonjudgmental place because I do believe most people want to be good travelers, but no one teaches them how. I'm not the best etiquette expert, so I've leaned on some real experts in the field, including Myka Meier, etiquette expert (@mykameier), and Richard Branson, cofounder of the Virgin Group.

The Core Principle of Travel Etiquette: Be Aware and Be Nice
Be nice to everyone, but especially frontline travel employees. Don't scream at anyone; it's counterproductive. I know how frustrating it is when an employee is unhelpful, but follow my tips in the mistakes chapter to educate yourself on options and tools. We tend to snap when we don't have control, but the agent may not have all the info you need or be able to solve your problem.

If you find yourself getting upset, walk away, take deep breaths, and think of other options to get what you want (there are almost always other ways). *People who understand the system don't behave this way*, so educate yourself and be more strategic.

Likewise, if an employee has been exceptionally helpful, don't hesitate to give compliments by name or write glowing reviews.

. . . .

Be the bigger person—thank them for their time and earn some karma points, which will come back to you later; trust me. If someone is being unreasonable (to another person or employee), don't be afraid to be upstanding and say something. Of course, if someone is unhinged, call security.

I'll break this down into a couple of sections like flying and general travel, as each has its own set of etiquette ideals. But no matter the section, there are absolute no-nos and there are gray areas. On a long-haul flight, you shouldn't be putting your bare feet up on someone else's armrest or cutting your toenails. But if you're flying from one Hawaiian island to another in a pair of flip-flops, well, that's a gray area. It's probably fine to sport sandals if you don't expose your bare feet to other passengers in any weird ways.

So, how do you know what the rules are when it comes to gray areas? Use common sense and respect. Sometimes, we abandon these morals when we're upset, stressed, or smushed in a plane seat at 35,000 feet, but those aren't excuses for bad behavior.

You shouldn't do things that expose other people to your body or bodily fluids (e.g., sweat) or offend them, especially in a place where you're in tight quarters with someone else, like on an airplane. Richard Branson says, "I don't think you should do anything to upset other people," and I agree.

Air Travel Etiquette: How to Be a Respectful Flyer
Is it ever appropriate to take off your shoes and socks on an airplane?
What about wearing shorts or skimpy clothing?

There are some gray areas here, but I'll say it again: On a plane, we're sharing tight quarters. It's best to limit your body exposure to others as best as possible: feet, armpits, and more. Airline seats have gotten smaller over the years, and people have gotten bigger. A little respect goes a long way.

"It's about dressing comfortably, but dressing respectfully," Meier says. "You're sharing your space with people. It's about thinking of others first.

Plus, you never know who you might meet. Your seatmate could be your next boss, your next date, your next best friend. Travel is an opportunity to meet people you've never met before, so you want to make a good impression, even when casually traveling. You don't need to dress up, but make yourself respectable."

If you have to wear flip-flops or sandals, keep them on and limit the contact your feet have with others. I'm not a germaphobe, but planes can be dirty, so limiting exposure of your uncovered body parts is a solid plan. Plus, you don't want to sweat all over a plane and then leave it there for future passengers.

Meier concludes that wearing flip-flops on a plane depends greatly on the climate and destination. "I once flew from Miami to Grand Cayman, and most of the passengers were in flip-flops or sandals. If you wear flip-flops, never take them off [on the plane]. If you want to take your shoes off for sleeping, it's fine, but you should have a sock on. Your bare feet should never touch the plane or any communal [plane] space."

Should you recline your seat?

I've flown coach many, many times, especially before I got into miles and points. Despite my height, I feel that it's your right to recline your seat. Everyone flying in economy needs to understand that someone can and probably will recline their seat. If you're not willing to accept this, pay for a seat that has extra legroom.

For the person that's reclining: Just because you can, should you? I always look behind me before reclining. If there's another tall person behind me, I won't. Or, I'll ask them first. And you shouldn't recline during meal service.

Before getting angry that someone reclines their seat, kicking it or throwing a fit, just politely *ask*. This tip works well in recline situations and in life in general. Just ask nicely. Here's a basic script if you're not sure what to say:

"Hi. I understand why you want to recline your seat (it's tight in here!), but I'm really tall/have an injury/am feeling claustrophobic/am trying to use my laptop/would like to eat my meal. Would you mind putting your seat up, even just a little bit, or temporarily during mealtime? I'd really appreciate it."

They may or may not oblige, but either way, you aren't in the right to push someone's seat up, ever. Likewise, if you recline, do it slowly, or if you want to be polite, ask, or at least tell, the person behind you that you'll be reclining. Slamming your seat back could harm someone's laptop or knees.

If you're in a stressful recline situation, don't engage. Get a flight attendant involved. Don't yell, freak out, or harm someone. Just call the flight attendant, and they can help handle or defuse the situation, including moving a passenger, if that's a possibility.

And if you don't agree with my opinion? You may take Richard Branson, who agrees with me, more seriously. When asked if it's okay to recline an airplane seat, he said, "Reclining is certainly cool—miserable otherwise." If someone reclines their seat into you? Maybe you should just recline your seat, too. Slowly and politely, of course.

Should parents fly in first class and kids in economy? At what age is this okay?

If your kids are well behaved and at an age where they're relatively self-sufficient and don't need attention, you could consider this. But if your kids are needy, for safety reasons you shouldn't be away from them.

How would you feel if extreme turbulence hit and you weren't with them? While you may feel comfortable doing this with teens, I wouldn't recommend it with younger children. Personally, I would never leave my kid next to a stranger, though perhaps some teens could handle it. As a parent, people are creepy . . . I'll sit with my child.

How many times calling the call button is too much?

The point of the call button is to use it—just not excessively. If you're in a window seat and the two people next to you are sleeping and you need something, use it. If you're holding a sleeping baby and need something, use it. You should always use it in lieu of touching a flight attendant.

I recommend, however, at least when in economy, to be prepared. Come with your own water and even snacks. Generally, it's best to manage your own needs as best as possible during air travel. The rules for business and first class are different, especially because they often leave to sit in the galley, so you may feel the need to utilize the call button more if you're seated in a higher class and there's also a higher flight attendant to passenger ratio in business class. In economy I wouldn't use the call button during meal services unless it was an emergency.

Should I line up before boarding?

In a time when baggage fees keep climbing and people are incentivized to bring as much as they can on board as carry-on luggage, I understand the feeling of wanting to board as soon as you possibly can, so waiting in line to get on the plane is your prerogative.

Just be mindful of your zone and don't block access to the gate for those who need to board before you or speak with a gate agent. Be aware that anyone with a disability or families with small children are often invited to board first, followed by business-class passengers and those with elite status or priority boarding. If you're not in one of those categories, ensure you're not in the way.

What about clapping on airplanes?

If you're stressed about this question, don't be. Don't let silly things like clapping on airplanes affect you. Clapping when an airplane lands is cultural and totally normal in many parts of the world. Go ahead and clap, too! Be happy you landed safely. Don't be a grinch and waste energy on trivial matters like this one.

Who gets the armrest?

The armrest is for the middle seat passenger. They're getting the short end of the stick. Give them some grace (in the form of the armrest).

Who gets the window shades?

First and foremost, window shades belong to the flight attendants controlling the cabin. If a flight attendant mandates window shades be up or down, especially during takeoff or landing, oblige.

Beyond that, the window shade belongs to the window seat passenger. During day flights, expect that window shades will be open. If you want to sleep (even at night, when window shades are usually closed), you should bring eye masks, headphones, earplugs, or whatever you need to control your environment and get rest with the shades open. If direct sunlight is blinding, you may want to put it entirely or partially down.

During night flights, flight attendants may put the shades down. Remember, if you want to control the window shade, pick a window seat.

But don't get too annoyed with the window seat shade controller. They may just be trying to regulate their jet lag and shift their circadian rhythms using light. If I notice people around me trying to sleep, I'll often close my shade, because I've been there before.

How should you deal with crying babies on a plane?

I always recommend controlling only what you can control. This is especially relevant during things like air travel. Do this by coming prepared with noise-canceling headphones, which are a lifesaver in any environment where you can't control noise and other disturbances.

There may be a lot you don't know, so have some empathy. Don't assume a baby or toddler is crying because of bad parenting. Just imagine how stressed the family is. A little compassion goes a long way. If you're struggling to handle a crying baby, never approach the parents (unless you want to approach with kindness and ask how you can help). Instead, ask a flight attendant if you might be able to be reseated.

Is it ever okay to change a diaper on a tray table or airplane seat?

No. I understand that airplane bathrooms are tiny, and sometimes diaper blowouts can put you in a precarious situation, but please don't do this. People sit in those seats and eat off those tables. Respect the cabin in general and other passengers, especially the ones seated near you and future passengers who will sit in those same seats (likely before the plane gets a thorough cleaning), and take your baby or child to the bathroom. If you need immediate help, call a flight attendant using the call button.

What are the rules for eating stinky foods on a plane?
Just DON'T. According to Richard Branson, "There's no need to bring smelly food on the plane." You never know what smells might trigger someone. I once got food poisoning from parmesan cheese, and someone opened up a stinky Caesar salad on a propeller jet flight from LaGuardia to Ithaca in August. I almost puked.

Can I bring my own booze on the plane?
Don't bring mini bottles and spike your soda. Just pay for booze like everyone else (or enjoy it for free in first class or on many international flights) or abstain from alcohol during the flight. FAA regulations say travelers can't consume alcohol on board an aircraft unless served by a flight attendant, so while you can legally bring some of those mini bottles on board in your Ziploc baggie, you're not technically allowed to drink them.

How do you handle chatty seatmates on a plane?
According to Meier, it's good etiquette to "smile or say hello" when you first sit down. You should be able to tell "right away when someone responds if they're interested in communicating with you by their eye contact and body language. Did they look at you? Did they turn away and look out the window instead? Body language and eye contact can determine if somebody wants to interact on a plane."

If you don't want to interact, pick up a book or put in your earbuds. Meier's go-to polite response is to simply "put in your earbuds."

Traveling with Children and Pets
I'm all for traveling with children, but I also encourage managing your children. Obviously, we should all have a little grace toward children, who aren't as self-aware as adults should be, but adults traveling with children

should make sure children are following the general rules of travel—that includes keeping bare feet off seats, not kicking the seats in front of them, and using an indoor voice in places such as lounges and airplanes.

I'm also for traveling with pets. But remember that a place like an airplane is a shared space, and not everyone loves animals (some may be scared of or allergic to them). Keep your pet on a leash or in a carrier, and always pick up after them. If your dog bites something, it could create major issues, so only travel with pets you know are well trained and can handle being in busy and crowded environments.

General Travel: How to Be a Mindful Traveler Worldwide

Being a considerate traveler starts with being a considerate human being. Tagging a monument (or anything) is never okay. Behaving inappropriately when viewing wild animals isn't, either. Having general respect for nature and historical monuments is something I shouldn't have to point out, but I will. Follow these rules when traveling (and at home):

- Don't touch what you aren't supposed to—wildlife, cultural artifacts, etc.
- Don't feed animals.
- Follow "leave no trace" principles, which include properly disposing of your trash when in natural spaces, not taking home natural items like rocks or sand.

You should research where you're going to understand cultural norms, tipping culture, and so on.

In Japan, tattoos are offensive. Many Japanese onsens, or spas/thermal baths, won't allow people with tattoos to enter, or you may have to cover them. A friend of mine was once reprimanded in Thailand for sitting with her legs out in front of her on the floor in a temple. Pointing your legs at Buddha is disrespectful. Covering up when in many Middle Eastern countries is important and respectful. In some European countries, tipping is so rare that waitstaff will chase after you to return the money you left on the table. In some countries, even shaking hands is taboo.

But how can you figure out what to tip and other cultural norms you should be aware of? Social media might not be the best resource, nor is picking up an outdated guidebook. Meier suggests going to the tourism board's website for the country you'll be visiting. "They know the questions you want answered. There's usually a FAQ section, which addresses topics like tipping, safety, and other important information," she advised.

This is a great way to understand more about cultural appreciation versus cultural appropriation. A lot of this starts with self-awareness and education. For example, you should ask before taking photos of local people, and don't take photos of children without permission.

Sometimes, violating cultural norms isn't a huge deal. Meier suggests addressing it but not blowing it out of proportion. "If you make something a big deal, it becomes a big deal. Don't ignore it; address it with humility, respect, kindness, and authenticity. Apologize genuinely and ask how you could have done it better." Just do better next time.

However, in some places, it could affect your safety. My safety (and my son's) are my highest priority, especially since I'm an LGBTQ traveler. I will always respect the local culture. If you don't want to adhere to a particular society's cultural norms, don't go or expect consequences. Doing research ahead can help you avoid these cultural mishaps and prepare you for what to expect.

Jessica Nabongo, the first Black woman to visit every country in the world, reminded me that when you travel, you're entering different cultural contexts. Sometimes, checking our own impatience and biases is important to have a safe and enjoyable trip. She also suggests letting certain things go as not to ruin your vacation and see all of what a country has to offer.

Remember, you can't control the behavior of others, but you can control your own behavior and response. If being mindful and respectful seems too unreasonable, then you might want to just stay home. Let travel bring out the best, not the worst, in you.

Chapter 15

The Future of Travel and Loyalty

If the past 50 years have been any indication, tectonic shifts in technology, the economy, and legislation can greatly spur innovation and efficiency within the travel industry. The level of growth seen in recent years was once an impossible thought during the dark days of the COVID pandemic and shows the resiliency of consumer travel demand. Travel has rebounded faster than almost anyone expected, and potential breakthroughs in technologies like AI, supersonic travel, and sustainable jet fuel have the potential to significantly change the way we travel and its impact on the world.

Advancements in Aviation Technology

Our travel systems today are in desperate need of modernization, as witnessed by the frequent IT meltdowns that continuously affect the industry. The good news is many of these problems can be solved with technology such as AI, which is beginning to streamline travel starting with booking and hopefully continuing throughout the entire travel experience.

An area where I'm hopeful to see major change is budding aviation technologies, like supersonic travel and unmanned aerial vehicles. The prospect of supersonic travel making a comeback could dramatically decrease the time and possible carbon footprint of intercontinental travel. To understand just how close we are to reentering a supersonic era of travel, I sat down with Blake Scholl, CEO of Boom Supersonic, which is the first aviation startup to gain real traction toward developing commercial supersonic jets that promise to be safer and more sustainable than the Concorde.

Scholl started thinking about the possibilities of flying supersonic in his mid-twenties, but then quickly realized there was no credible effort to pick up where the Concorde left off and decided to start researching himself.

The Concorde ultimately failed due to profitability and safety concerns, with the last commercial flight taking place October 24, 2003. "It's unbelievable that the Concorde was created with drafting paper, wind tunnels, and converted military engines in 1969. Our goals are wildly different. The Concorde was a Cold War–era glory project, built to show that Western technology beat Soviet technology, not to build a sustainable business model," Scholl explained.

Just over two decades after the last Concorde flight, Boom made history in March 2024 when their test aircraft, XB-1, took flight in the Mojave Desert. While it was a major milestone on the journey to making supersonic travel a reality, much more still needs to happen as the test aircraft doesn't closely resemble what a passenger aircraft will actually look like. A Boom factory is now working on Overture, the world's fastest airliner. "Our goal is to be ready for passengers by the end of the decade. Then, we want to speed up the pace at which we deliver new airplanes," Scholl told me.

Overture plans to have 64 premium seats and fares like today's business class—meaning it's attainable for tens of millions of passengers—and potentially profitable for airlines on hundreds of routes. The cost of supersonic will likely come down over time—and eventually be attainable for the vast majority of travelers. Airlines like United, American, and Japan Airlines have already invested in Boom, knowing that if it works, it could bring massive profits, since premium, time-conscious travelers drive profit for major airlines and will likely continue to do so.

One of the biggest downsides of supersonic travel is the noise of the supersonic boom, which can rattle houses and thus makes airport communities protest supersonic service. Boom is aware of these challenges and is confident that airport communities will not experience any of the disturbances they faced with the Concorde. Overture flights can go faster over water where noise doesn't affect people and they still plan to be 20% faster than a Boeing or Airbus overland, but the routes that fly over water see the biggest speed-ups, like Seattle to Tokyo in as little as four and a half hours.

Overture aims to meet the latest plans to use sustainable aviation fuel (SAF), which is an emerging new category of liquid that's very much like jet fuel, but can be synthesized with green energy rather than being pumped out of the ground. Scholl believes that SAF is the way that long-haul aviation will be decarbonized. "Greatly reducing the time it takes to travel may sound trivial, but it can have dramatic impacts on society."

As an eternal optimist, I'm excited about the prospects of supersonic travel and how it could connect commerce and cultures like never before. However, there are many hurdles before a Boom supersonic jet starts carrying passengers, and there are many naysayers in the aviation industry who think Scholl's vision of a supersonic world is a pipe dream that is more vision than details. Time will tell, but if Boom is able to pull it off, supersonic travel could fundamentally shape the future of aviation and connect the world like never before.

Advancements in Sustainability

Sustainability is a key issue that the travel industry must continue to address, as many of the emissions improvements airlines had planned for the 2020s have been delayed due to major aircraft delivery delays by Airbus and Boeing. Delays for these new, more efficient planes mean flying jet-fuel-guzzling older planes for longer.

It will be many years before airlines have more efficient fleets. This means airlines need to invest in more sustainable aviation fuels, which many appear to be doing. SAF startup Twelve is working on technology that will create jet fuel by converting carbon dioxide with water and other sustainable fuels. Investors seem excited by their prospects, with Twelve raising over $200 million in Series C funding in 2024 (and $400 million more in financing).

This decade could also bring about groundbreaking change for urban mobility. In cities that keep getting more crowded and rarely any bigger, new technologies need to ease the chokehold of car traffic, which is loud and inefficient. No one is capitalizing more on consumers' loathing of traffic than Rob Wiesenthal, founder and CEO of Blade Air Mobility, which operates helicopters and seaplanes from busy urban centers all around the world, but with a main hub in New York City.

"You have to look at the evolution of cities. Take a look at the average speed in Manhattan, which has gone down over the past 10 years. Now think about the constant building and what's happened to the city. Buildings were relatively short, and the only way to accommodate everybody was to build up. So now you have infrastructure on the ground that was essentially designed well over 100 years ago—a subway system that does a pretty good job. But at this point, the only way to go is up," opined Rob.

UAVs, or unmanned aerial vehicles, could hold the key to easing the traffic on streets while reducing the emissions and noise of typical helicopters and seaplanes, which rattle neighborhoods wherever they operate. Essentially larger drones with the capability of transporting passengers, UAVs could fundamentally change traffic patterns around the world. When asked when we could imagine a *Jetsons*-like world with quiet unmanned aircraft whisking us around, Wiesenthal didn't have an exact answer, but felt confident that a version of UAVs would be operating in New York in this decade.

The UK government goes into greater detail about its timeline for UAVs in a March 2024 Future of Flight action plan that was published by the department of transportation, where it confidently predicted regular drone deliveries by 2027 and passenger and emergency UAV flights by 2030. Having ambulances that could whiz above traffic jams could save countless lives, and the UK government predicts upward of a £45 billion positive impact on the economy directly related to the efficiencies of UAVs over traditional vehicle transport.

Advancements in Accessibility

The travel industry still has a lot it could be doing for passengers with disabilities, who currently face unprecedented challenges navigating busier airports and more crowded planes.

"There's a notion that people with disabilities aren't part of the travel industry, so companies think they shouldn't cater to them," says Cory Lee, who's traveled to all seven continents with his wheelchair. However, according to a nationwide study, passengers with disabilities spend over $58 billion per year. Hotels need to be better, guaranteeing accessible rooms on hotel apps and offering showers and beds that can fit the needs of travelers with disabilities.

Before my discussion with Cory, I had no idea just how miserable something like a platform bed can be for travelers who use a lift to get in and out of bed. Simple design decisions can dramatically improve the quality of life for those with disabilities, and I encourage the entire industry to improve its policies for people with disabilities.

Airlines need to have better training for ground staff on how to prevent damage when loading wheelchairs in the cargo and how to carefully handle and transport passengers with disabilities themselves. And it goes without saying that aircraft should have seating and lavatories to accommodate these passengers, too.

Lee notes that he "can't access a bathroom on certain aircraft" and has fasted extensively before long-haul flights to avoid having to do so. Luckily, that should change soon, thanks to a new rule authorized by the Air Carrier Access Act (ACAA).

"Traveling can be stressful enough without worrying about being able to access a restroom; yet today, millions of wheelchair users are forced to choose between dehydrating themselves before boarding a plane or avoiding air travel altogether," said US Transportation Secretary Pete Buttigieg. "We are proud to announce this rule that will make airplane bathrooms larger and more accessible, ensuring travelers in wheelchairs are afforded the same access and dignity as the rest of the traveling public."

And travelers are anxiously awaiting new legislation. "New proposals for better, more accessible air travel would require annual training for staff on how to load the wheelchair into the plane and how to transfer wheelchair users into the plane," Lee said.

Delta has a new aircraft design that would allow wheelchair users to sit in their chairs, thus taking a huge stress out of the travel experience. These innovations would dramatically improve travel for millions of people with special mobility needs, yet they are still years away from reality, especially due to required government testing requirements. One organization, All Wheels Up, is helping fund those tests so wheelchair users can safely fly in-cabin. For the sake of so many travelers in wheelchairs, I hope airlines implement these new designs and in general train their employees to have more understanding and compassion for those in wheelchairs.

The Future of Travel and Loyalty

While I do think there is always room for improvement and advancement, I'm excited about the future of travel. Travel, as it stands now, is connecting the world like never before and is as safe as ever. Using loyalty programs and points, your options can only grow. Points and miles allow you to take that dream vacation you never thought was possible, donate to incredible causes, and stabilize your financial situation. Even if you aren't an avid traveler, using points for occasional travel means you can save that money and use it for other things.

Yes, the loyalty ecosystem is rapidly changing. But if there's one thing I've learned as being part of its evolution for nearly 30 years is that while change is inevitable, it also presents opportunity. Don't fear this change, embrace it. Use what you know to make the system work for you. Loyalty programs will benefit you if you evolve along with them.

How We All Can Become Better Travelers

While we can wait for the government or companies to make travel better, as travelers, we can all play our role. As I look toward the future with record numbers of travelers exploring the world, here are a few things that we can do to help us be better travelers.

1. Spread the Love (and Your Tourism Dollars).

Overtourism is real and will only get worse as more people want to travel, and the places to visit remain relatively finite. As travelers, it is our responsibility to research where we are going and do our best to make sure our tourism dollars reach those in the local community.

Venture outside major tourist hubs to travel deeper. Those popular cities and islands are great, but so much lies beyond the major sites and attractions. Plan time into your travels to see those special places that aren't as well known or famous, and be mindful when traveling to locations struggling with overtourism.

Support local businesses when you travel, too. Tourism can tax community resources, but the more money that goes into the local community, the better. So skip hotel breakfast and go find a café—chances are it'll be way better food at a much better price and you might even make a friend who can give you local tips on how to make your trip better.

2. Be Nice (It's Free).

This one is especially true for employees on the front lines. Stop assuming the worst in people and give them grace. When you get into an Uber, ask them how their day is going. When the flight attendants are doing their security demonstration, give them your attention and smile.

When things go well, write in to give kudos to those who helped make your travels enjoyable. Tip housekeepers when possible or write them a thank-you note. Be nice to fellow passengers and don't assume the worst, like someone who is asking to cut the security line is there simply because they're lazy and didn't plan. You never know the true story, so assume the best and be generous with your spirit. I can guarantee you at some point you will be that person and you'll need to rely on the grace of others to make that flight or fix another trying travel situation.

3. Pay It Forward.

Give as much as you can, as often as you can. And it doesn't have to be money, but your hand. Help a fellow passenger struggling with luggage in the overhead bin (especially my fellow tall travelers—put that height to use!). Use miles to help a friend get home to see their family after losing someone they love. The simple act of taking the time to make a difficult time easier is a gift. While it's impossible to value karma points because they have no award chart (not even a dynamic one!), I can assure you that the best trips you'll ever take are the ones where you go outside your comfort zone and somehow give back to those around you.

The best souvenirs I've ever gotten are the friendships and shared experiences, which leads me to one of my favorite travel memories, the best flight I've ever had.

My Final Story: My Best Flight Ever

People always ask me what has been my best flight. Although I've been lucky enough to fly nearly every major airline in first class, I don't have to think for a second to answer the question. It was an American Airlines flight from JFK to Orlando . . . in economy.

But this was no normal flight. It was a special flight through a partnership with American Airlines, Make-A-Wish, and *The Points Guy*, where we filled an entire plane with wish kids (children in the Make-A-Wish program) and their families.

Over the years, *The Points Guy* has helped raise millions of miles and hundreds of thousands of dollars in donations to Make-A-Wish, and nearly 70% of wish kids ask for a wish that involves travel. All of the wish kids on this flight had battled serious illnesses and spent more time in hospitals than any person should in their lifetime. Yet, their excitement and positivity toward the trip was palpable. I heard countless stories from family members that having this special trip to look forward to was a huge positive force that helped them through the darkest of times. In no uncertain terms, I realized that travel, or even the thought of travel, has the ability to heal.

As the flight departure time neared, each little VIP passenger was called over the PA system to board, as the adults cheered and whooped. Even random JFK passengers, who stopped to see what the fuss was about, started cheering along, too. The excitement was at a fever pitch, as many of these kids had never flown and the giddiness of the moment was a stark reminder to me to not be so jaded about travel, even when it doesn't go as planned. The idea that even being able to get on a plane is a privilege, one that many people battling health issues don't have the luxury of having, has always stuck with me. We taxied and finally took off to ecstatic cheers and squeals as we made our way down the eastern seaboard.

My job was to be the emcee of the flight, so I got to rile the kids up and play games, as well as introduce special guests, like children's author Lauren Settles, who did story time on the PA. The Genie from the Broadway show *Aladdin*, actor Michael James Scott, even did a rousing rendition of "Friend Like Me," and didn't miss a beat as we hit some pretty rough turbulence off the coast of Maryland.

On most flights, especially in economy, I am counting the minutes until we land, staring at the moving map and willing the plane to go faster. I never wanted this flight to end. I wanted to bottle up the hope and positivity of that cabin and share it with anyone having a tough time.

But sadly, the flight didn't last forever. I high-fived each excited passenger on their way out, fighting back tears of joy, because I knew I wouldn't be able to stop them once they started. As the last VIP passenger finally made their way down to the end of the jet bridge, I heard the terminal erupt in roars welcoming the special flight, and at that moment I knew what it really meant to travel.

As I walked out of the terminal that day, smiling through my tears, I realized that becoming a real traveler isn't about how many countries you've been to or how much value you can extract from your frequent flyer miles. The best journeys are not the ones we plan, but the ones that life plans for us. Opening yourself up to experience them—now that's winning at travel.

To donate your airline miles or credit card points to Make-A-Wish America or other incredible organizations, please visit howtowinattravel.com/donate.

Notes

Chapter 1: Welcome to the Platinum Age of Travel

1. "2023 Safest Year for Flying by Several Parameters," February 28, 2024, https://www.iata.org/en/pressroom/2024-releases/2024-02-28-01/.

2. Barnett, Arnold and Jan Reig Torra, Massachusetts Institute of Technology, "Airline safety: Still getting better?" *Journal of Air Transport Management,* August 2024, https://www.sciencedirect.com/science/article/abs/pii/S0969699724001066.

3. Ritchie, Hannah, "Airline hijackings were once common but are very rare today," OurWorldinData.org, July 1, 2017, https://ourworldindata.org/airline-hijackings-were-once-common-but-are-very-rare-today.

4. Average Domestic Airline Itinerary Fares, Bureau of Transportation Statistics, accessed September 27, 2024, www.transtats.bts.gov/averagefare.

Chapter 3: Turning Travel Goals Into Reality: How to Budget, Research, Plan, and Protect Your Dream Trip

1. Kumar, Amit and Matthew A. Killingsworth, Thomas Gilovich, "Spending on doing promotes more moment-to-moment happiness than spending on having," *Journal of Experimental Social Psychology,* May 2020, https://doi.org/10.1016/j.jesp.2020.103971.

2. Institute for Economics & Peace, Global Peace Index 2024: Measuring Peace in a Complex World, Sydney, June 2024, http://visionofhumanity.org/resources.

Thanks to Haley Sacks (@mrsdowjones) for sharing her financial advice. Thanks to Jessica Nabongo, Lays Laraya, and Shawn Newman for sharing their travel tips.

Chapter 4: How to Win at Booking Travel

1. "Airline Customer Service Dashboard," US Department of Transportation, accessed September 28, 2024, www.transportation.gov/airconsumer/airline-customer-service-dashboard.

Chapter 5: What Are Points and Miles?

Thanks to Bonnie Rabin for her information on protecting your points and miles investments.

Chapter 6: How to Win at Earning Rewards

Thanks to Eleni, a *TPG* reader, for sharing her points win.

Chapter 10: How to Win at Traveling with a Family

Thanks to Dr. Said T. Daneshmand for his tips on family travel; Lia Tuso for her advice on how to keep your children secure when flying; and Richard Branson on making flying comfortable for families.

When researching, I used information from the FAA's Flying with Children landing page (https://www.faa.gov/travelers/fly_children), as well as this circular from the FAA for information on approved child restraint systems on airplanes:

https://www.faa.gov/documentlibrary/media/advisory_circular/ac_120-87c.pdf, and this information from Cornell Law School: https://www.law.cornell.edu/cfr/text/14/91.107. Accessed September 28, 2024.

Chapter 11: How to Win at Travel When Travel Goes Wrong

Thanks to Janelle Rupkalvis for sharing her points and miles win; Cory Lee for sharing his personal story; and Shawn Newman for an insider's look at hotels.

Chapter 12: How to Beat Jet Lag and Stay Healthy When Traveling

Thanks to Dr. Jake Deutsch for sharing his tips on staying healthy when traveling; Mickey Beyer-Clausen, the CEO of Timeshifter, for introducing the science behind jet lag; Grigor Dimitrov for sharing his personal experience traveling as a professional athlete in order to excel across time zones; and Joey Gonzalez for his travel exercise tips.

Chapter 13: How to Manage Fear of Flying

1. National Vital Statistics System, Centers for Disease Control and Prevention, accessed September 27, 2024, https://www.cdc.gov/nchs/nvss/vsrr/drug-overdose-data.htm.
2. "Gun Violence: The Impact on Society," National Institute for Health Care Management (NIHCM) Foundation, https://nihcm.org/publications/gun-violence-the-impact-on-society, accessed October 11, 2024.
3. "Early Estimate of Motor Vehicle Traffic Fatalities in 2023," National Highway Traffic Safety Administration, April 2024, https://crashstats.nhtsa.dot.gov/Api/Public/ViewPublication/813561.
4. Kim, Simon, et al., "Use of skills learned in CBT for fear of flying: Managing flying anxiety after September 11th," *Journal of Anxiety Disorders,* 2008, https://www.sciencedirect.com/science/article/abs/pii/S0887618507000655?via%3Dihub.
5. Wilhelm, F. H. and W. T. Roth, Stanford University School of Medicine, "Acute and delayed effects of alprazolam on flight phobics during exposure," *Behaviour Research and Therapy*, September 1997, https://www.sciencedirect.com/science/article/pii/S0005796797000338?via%3Dihub.

Thanks to Whoopi Goldberg, Lays Laraya, Lori Zaino, and my friend Haley for sharing their flying vulnerabilities. I know others will resonate with these fears. Thanks to Capt. Sully Sullenberger and Dr. Jake Deutsch for sharing their expertise in the field.

Chapter 14: Travel Etiquette: A Manifesto of Considerate Travel Behavior

Thank you to Myka Meier, etiquette expert; Richard Branson; and Jessica Nabongo for sharing their travel experience and expertise.

Chapter 15: The Future of Travel and Loyalty

1. Future of Flight Action Plan, accessed September 28, 2024, https://www.gov.uk/government/publications/future-of-flight-action-plan.

Thanks to Blake Scholl, CEO of Boom Supersonic, and Rob Wiesenthal, founder and CEO of Blade Air Mobility, for sharing their travel predictions; and to Cory Lee for helping me understand how the industry can make travel more accessible.

Index

About the Author

Brian Kelly is the founder of *The Points Guy* (*TPG*), one of the most popular travel advice websites worldwide. A travel expert named *Forbes*'s #1 travel influencer and "The Man Who Turned Credit Card Points Into an Empire" by *The New York Times*, he shares money-saving and travel tips as a guest on *Good Morning America, CBS Mornings*, CNBC, and *LIVE with Kelly and Mark*.

Brian fundamentally believes in travel as a force for good, working with Make-A-Wish to grant travel wishes and the PeaceJam Foundation to bring Nobel Peace Prize winners to youth around the world. He's traveled extensively, but some of his favorite experiences include trekking with mountain gorillas in Rwanda and taking his son to fun places such as Tokyo Disney.

Although travel is his passion, there's no hotel in the world that beats spending time on his farm in Pennsylvania with his son, Dean; rescue dog, Marshall; and his horses, llamas, alpacas, and chickens. Follow him on Instagram @briankelly and TikTok @briankellytravel.